Contesting the Commons

Contesting
— THE —
Commons

Privatizing Pastoral
Lands in Kenya

CAROLYN K. LESOROGOL

The University of Michigan Press

— Ann Arbor —

2011   2010   2009   2008   4   3   2   1

A CIP catalog record for this book is available from the British Library.

Library of Congress Cataloging-in-Publication Data

Lesorogol, Carolyn K., 1965–
Contesting the commons : privatizing pastoral lands in Kenya /Carolyn K. Lesorogol.
p.   cm.
Includes bibliographical references and index.
ISBN-13: 978-0-472-07024-4 (cloth : alk. paper)
ISBN-10: 0-472-07024-X (cloth : alk. paper)
ISBN-13: 978-0-472-05024-6 (pbk. : alk. paper)
ISBN-10: 0-472-05024-9 (pbk. : alk. paper)
1. Commons—Kenya—Samburu District.
2. Land tenure—Social aspects—Kenya—Samburu District.
3. Privatization—Social aspects—Kenya—Samburu District.
4. Samburu District (Kenya)—Social conditions.
5. Samburu District (Kenya)—Economic conditions.
I. Title.

HD1289.K42S265   2008
333.3'167627—dc22   2007040369

Contents

Figures

Tables

Acknowledgments

I am grateful for the support and encouragement of many teachers, colleagues, friends, and family who have contributed in many ways to bringing this book to fruition. I have benefited tremendously from the intellectual environment at Washington University, both as a graduate student in anthropology and a faculty member in social work. Here, interdisciplinary study and a focus on institutions and social change are valued, and rigorous empirical research is encouraged and expected. The ideas explored here owe much to the work of Jean Ensminger, mentor and friend, whose pathbreaking research among Orma pastoralists represents a new direction in the study of pastoralism and economic anthropology. Douglass North's theory of institutions and economic development is fundamental to this study, and Jack Knight's intellectual input was pivotal to developing an explanation of the privatization process centered on bargaining power. John Bowen challenged me to think deeply about both theoretical and empirical questions, and I have gained tremendously from my interactions with him over the years. Pascal Boyer provided detailed comments on drafts and reminded me that not everyone knows the Samburu. I have enjoyed many discussions with Fiona Marshall about Kenya and pastoralism, both of which we have in common. Gautam Yadama and I share interests in the commons and real-world development issues, and I appreciate his input on this project. Thanks also to Edward Lawlor for his useful advice and continuing support. I would like to thank my colleagues in the George Warren Brown School of Social Work for providing a great atmosphere for productive research that engages critical social issues.

This study was generously funded by a dissertation improvement grant from the National Science Foundation, a Fulbright-Hays grant from the U.S.

Department of Education, a grant from the Center for New Institutional Social Sciences at Washington University, and a predissertation grant from the International Studies program at Washington University. I thank the Kenyan Ministry for Education Science and Technology for research permission and the Institute for Development Studies at the University of Nairobi for research affiliation.

Portions of chapters have appeared in earlier published works: chapter 5, "Transforming Institutions among Pastoralists: Inequality and Land Privatization," *American Anthropologist* 105, no. 3 (2003): 531–42; chapter 7, "Privatizing Pastoral Lands: Economic and Normative Outcomes in Kenya," *World Development* 33, no. 11 (2005): 1959–78; and chapter 8, "Experiments and Ethnography: Combining Methods for Better Understanding of Behavior and Change," *Current Anthropology* 46, no. 1 (2005): 129–36.

There are many people to thank in Kenya. My two research assistants, Prame Lesorogol and Jonathan Lekeriyo, did an incredible amount of work conducting household surveys, monitoring games, and helping with interviews. Their companionship was always enjoyable and their insights about many issues were useful. Others provided various types of research assistance on a part-time basis, and I would like to thank them: Anthony Letirok, Francis Lempushuna, Jeremiah Lekarikei, Simon Letambul, and Simon Lenolkulal. I truly appreciate the cooperation of all the Samburu families that were involved in any part of the research. Even in a difficult year when people were coping with a severe drought, I was invariably welcomed into people's homes, and my questions were patiently and respectfully answered. I particularly want to thank Saddam Lelesiit and Anna Kanai Lelesiit for providing housing in Siambu and the Lenolkulal family for their hospitality. I had many interesting discussions with Loraine and Michael Wexler and their family in Poro. I also thank the Dolifkas in Maralal for sharing their views about land with me. The staff at Ministry of Lands and Settlements in Maralal graciously allowed me to read files in their office and clarified the policies and procedures of land adjudication. I thank Mwenda Ntarangwi and his family for hospitality in Nairobi. Special thanks are due to Susan Epem and Sarais Lolngojine who helped care for my children while I was out doing research.

Family and friends have provided tremendous support throughout this process, and I would like to thank my parents, Stuart and Rosalind Kornfeld, my sister, Kathy Kornfeld, and my brother, Kerry Kornfeld. In Kenya, my in-laws Noosoroitare, Letampon, and Mpapa Lesorogol, Naisia Leseewa, Arno and Naina Lekuraa, Kondelia and Menye Mike Leirana, and the whole Lesorogol family have been good friends and companions. Bilinda Straight read and commented on early drafts, and I value her as a colleague and friend. I am thankful to Sarah Klein, Vanessa Hildebrand, and Erin Stiles. Finally, I thank my daughters, Sarah, Jennifer, and Emily, whose presence keeps me grounded in the real world, and my husband, Leretin, for everything.

CHAPTER 1

Introduction

We pulled up to the edge of the escarpment. From a distance, I could already see the large group of women assembled, decked out in their finery as if preparing for a wedding ceremony. On the very edge of the plateau, a rough structure was being erected that resembled a Samburu house, but one that had been cut in two. A warrior, also regaled in full ceremonial dress, was standing in the doorway to the house, perched on the rocky ledge. If he turned around to enter the house, he would have fallen over the escarpment, plunging hundreds of feet to the Rift Valley floor. It was then that I saw the film crew. They were hard to miss with their truck full of equipment, and their tent under which the director and his assistants were planning the shoot. It was a commercial for German coffee they were filming, and this site on the edge of Malasso in Samburu District, would be one of a half dozen shots to feature in the spot. They had traveled across the world to capture the image of the Samburu warrior overlooking the vastness of the Rift Valley. The women weren't even involved: they had just come out when they saw the truck, hoping for a chance to sing, and get paid a few shillings. (Author's field notes, 2001)

The film crew probably did not realize that they were working in one of the only parts of Samburu District where formerly communal land had, a decade earlier, been privatized. They also would not have appreciated that it was this change in the institution of property rights that enabled the owner to charge them for using his land, thus benefiting at the expense of the nearby community ecotourism site (equally scenic) that remains under communal control. Indeed, even if they had appreciated these nuances of the situation, they may well have chosen to pay the individual land owner rather than negotiate with the community, a process likely to be lengthier and more contentious. As for the community members, I did not hear any complaints about the decision of the film crew to deal with the individual land owner and not the community. Rather, other people—the young men in their warrior attire and the women hoping to sing—were eager to make their own individual transactions with the film crew.

Proponents of clearly specified and individualized property rights, including most economists, could cite this transaction as a positive example of the benefits accruing from efforts to privatize land, because poor people were able to realize the value of their land through a market transaction. Calls for privatization of land and clarification of property rights are often premised on the idea that communal ownership hinders development by limiting people's capability to use resources most efficiently. Critics of privatization, however, would likely voice concerns about inequitable benefits accruing from the transaction and the risk that culture itself is becoming commoditized along with land. Scholars of pastoral livestock systems would raise additional questions about the implications of privatizing pastoral land for livestock production and the sustainability of pastoral livelihoods.

However it might be evaluated, this event reflects the changing perceptions of property and autonomy resulting from the privatization of communal land. More broadly, it reflects the consequences of institutional change reallocating rights and benefits and reframing social activity and transactions. The central question, then, is how does institutional change occur and what are its effects? This book addresses this question by analyzing how forces both external and internal to Samburu society have prompted fundamental changes in the institutions that shape Samburu life. Moreover, I seek to understand how individual choices and actions, conditioned as they are by the normative frameworks and habits of culture, mediate and shape the contours of social change processes. It is the concrete actions of individuals and small groups that ultimately aggregate, sometimes in very unexpected and unintended ways, to move society along a trajectory of change. By understanding the microfoundations of social action rooted in individual behavior we will be better able to explain change processes and not just describe them as the necessary outcomes of the confrontation of exogenous forces with indigenous people like the Samburu.

These processes are examined in the context of privatization of communal land that occurred in the Siambu community in Samburu District, Kenya. The conflict over land tenure that engulfed Siambu during the 1980s provides an excellent example of the dynamics of institutional change. The shift from communal to private property was significant because it struck at the heart of pastoral livestock production, which requires access to large tracts of range land. It pitted a group of younger, educated men who sought private land ownership against the traditional elders of the area who defended the status quo. The Siambu case is a microcosm of the ways in which exposure to modernity and development influences the motivations and actions of particular social groups. Gaining entrance into the modern sector of Kenyan society provided strong motivation for change as well as new resources on which normally less powerful groups could draw in their bid to change the rules regarding land. Kenyan government policies favoring private ownership of land, coupled with the sympathetic orientation of government officers, lowered the costs to this group of challenging the prevailing system of communal ownership. In turn, this new concatenation of power challenged the elders to fortify their own base of support and move beyond it in order to safeguard their interests. The conflict between these groups enables us to analyze the dynamics of the change process by tracking how bargaining power was gained, utilized, and sometimes lost. The final resolution of the land issue, a compromise that allocated an equal parcel of land to each male head of household in the community, reveals what happens when bargaining power is virtually equal.

Much of the importance of institutions stems from their role in easing social interaction, including production and exchange relations. By specifying the "rules of the game" (Bailey 1969; North 1990) institutions lubricate the wheels of social life by reducing the costs of gathering information about what other social actors are likely to do. By providing credible clues about how others will behave, institutions lower the costs of all types of transactions, thus enabling society to produce and reproduce with a degree of efficiency impossible in their absence.

What then, is the effect of institutional change on transactions, production, and social relations? Since institutional emergence and change are the aggregate of myriad individual actions and is a site for contestation, the resulting institution is not necessarily any more efficient or beneficial than what preceded it (North 1990; Ensminger 1992; Knight 1992). Since improvements in efficiency cannot be assumed, the effects of institutional change are empirical questions. In the case of Siambu, it is possible to measure the effects of the shift from communal to private land on pastoral livestock production, household well-being, and also on individual behavior. Are people better off when they own their own land? Has the economy of pastoral livestock production been transformed into one in which cultivation of crops predominates? Beyond economic change, are there signs that individuals have been altered through the process of privatization? Do they, like the land owner mentioned earlier, behave in more self-interested ways than those who remain on communal land? Do they cooperate less as a result of the new tenure regime? Have elders lost authority as a consequence of losing control over land? These questions are addressed here using household-level economic data and innovative methods from experimental economics that enable us to make generalizations about behavior within and across social groups.

Before embarking on the analysis of the Siambu case in the next chapter, I outline the major theoretical concepts central to this examination of changing property rights, beginning with how institutions themselves are defined and conceptualized.

What Are Institutions and Why Are They Important?

Institutions are the formal and informal "rules of the game" (Bailey 1969; North 1990) that bind social actors together in a dense web of shared normative frameworks that include codified law as well as informal codes of conduct, norms, and conventions. Institutions prescribe the proper way to behave in a social group. Accordingly, those who violate the rules and norms embodied in institutions may suffer punishment and sanctions for their transgressions (Taylor 1982; Henrich et al. 2006). Indeed, societies also develop norms relating to the application of sanctions so that punishment behavior itself becomes normative.

Institutions are important because they ease and enable social relations among members of a group by providing credible information about how others will act in any given situation. Armed with this information, social actors are able to develop more or less accurate expectations about others' behavior and then to act based on these expectations. In this way, the costs of gathering information are greatly reduced with the result that social interaction of all kinds is facilitated. The existence of institutions, then, lowers the costs of transacting, which has direct implications for economic exchange in particular (North 1981, 1990; Bates 1981; Eggertsson 1997). Furthermore, actors are able to cultivate a degree of trust in other members of their community and to build stocks of social capital through relationships established on the basis of this trust (Coleman 1990; Putnam 1993).

While we tend to think of institutions as the large and elaborated bureaucracies characteristic of Western society—centralized government, universities, corporations—small-scale societies are also bound together by institutional cement, but of an informal variety. As Michael Taylor (1982) has shown, nonhierarchically organized societies maintain social order through the functioning of informal sets of shared beliefs and norms enforced by the group members themselves without recourse to the state. The Samburu represent such a society where ideas about proper behavior are inculcated from a young age, and violators are sanctioned in a variety of ways. Before the imposition of colonial rule in the late 1800s, order was maintained among the Samburu through informal enforcement mechanisms as well as councils of elder men who were empowered to adjudicate disputes and make other decisions affecting larger segments of society. Even today, though the Samburu fall under the aegis of the central government, the councils of elders still play a significant role in decision making and dispute resolution.

Institutional Emergence and Change

An important question for scholars studying institutions is how they emerge and change over time. Early anthropological discussions of institutions posited that institutions fulfill needs in society (Malinowski 1922; Evans-Pritchard 1950). While it is often the case that institutions are highly functional, since by their very nature they facilitate social interaction and transactions, it does not necessarily follow that they are entirely adaptive or efficient (Edgerton 1992). These theories were weak in that they relied on functionalist logic to explain the growth of institutions. The functions that institutions fulfill may well account for their continued reproduction, but they do not constitute an adequate explanation of their origins. To understand the reasons why particular institutions arise, we require both a theory and empirical evidence to support it.

A number of scholars have advanced theories of institutional emergence and change, often based on game-theoretic assumptions about individual strategic behavior (Ullmann-Margalit 1977; North 1990; Knight 1992; Voss 2001). An important element of this work is the recognition that the vast majority of institutions are undesigned. That is, they are the outcome of many individual actions and choices that occur over a long period of time that ultimately result in a consensus about an institution. While it is true that some institutions, such as formal law and government policy, are intentionally designed, these are few in comparison to the innumerable social norms, codes of conduct, and conventions that permeate social life. The fact that most institutions are undesigned has two important implications. First, it dispenses with the idea of an evolutionary trajectory through which institutions become more and more efficient, adaptive, or functional over time. This cannot be the case since institutions are the outcome of so many acts that combine in unpredictable and unintended ways. Second, it requires us to examine the microfoundations of institutional change. That is, we need to understand why people make choices and take actions as they do. While game theory provides models of strategic interaction, anthropological method offers the opportunity to observe actual behavior in situ, thus enabling us to empirically verify theoretical models. Combining theoretical insight with empirical evidence, we are better able to trace the course of institutional development. We may even be able to make reasonable predictions about the course of change, although it is important to remain cognizant of the fact that the volatility of social interaction means that outcomes always remain somewhat unpredictable.

As noted previously, many accounts of institutional change come from economics and employ game-theoretic assumptions and frameworks in their analysis. While this approach has been useful in focusing attention on the bases of individual behavior and its aggregation, it tends to devalue the differential power embodied in individual actors. By assuming that all actors are equally endowed with information, cognitive ability, and opportunity, these explanations leave out the critical dimension of power. Knight (1992) has attempted to bring power back into the analysis as a pivotal factor in understanding the dynamics of institutional emergence and change. He assumes that individuals act instrumentally to pursue social outcomes that they perceive will be of greatest benefit to themselves. Based on available information and their own goals (preferences) they choose to act in particular ways. They also behave strategically, considering the probable actions of others (largely based on the information provided by extant institutions). In addition, social actors are unequally endowed with power. To the extent that they can use their power to influence the choices of other actors, individuals will be able to shape outcomes to their own ends. In general, then, those actors with greater power will be better positioned to determine the outcomes of social interaction, and the resultant institutions will tend to benefit them more (Ensminger and Knight 1997).

One advantage of this theory is its parsimony. It does not seek to predict a particular outcome but rather focuses on the mechanisms that drive institutional change processes. For example, if we delineate the distributional consequences of an institution (i.e., how benefits are distributed across a population), we will be able to identify which parties are likely to raise a challenge to the institution (i.e., those who benefit least). From there, we may predict at which time a challenge is likely to be mounted (e.g., when costs are lower for action and/or when power endowments shift). Thus, the analyst seeking to understand a particular case of change should concentrate on dissecting the distribution of benefits from extant institutions, the variable power endowments of various actors, and how these are employed in the pursuit of specific ends. The theory suggests a method that will enable empirical demonstration of its utility.

An additional factor is that endowments of power are not fixed. Individuals and groups have access to a variety of resources that may constitute power, and this access changes over time. For example, in the Siambu case, young men generally have far less power than senior men who control livestock wealth, political authority, and access to marriageable women. However, with access to education, employment, and understanding of the state and bureaucracy in Kenya, these young men were able to build new sources of power, which they used in their struggle to gain land ownership. Likewise, the elders, once confronted with these new power relations, worked to counter them by increasing their own power. Such shifts in power, I argue, can be decisive in the outcomes of social conflicts. However, anticipating how power will be gained and lost is very difficult and poses a hurdle to developing a predictive theory of institutional change.

Models of Behavior

In order to analyze social change processes, we require a model of social action. We need answer the question, why do individuals behave as they do? Debate over the relationship of the individual to society is a long-standing one in the social sciences, one unlikely to be resolved soon. The two polar positions are the "oversocialized self" (Wrong 1994) and "homo economicus" (Acheson 1994). The oversocialized self is characteristic of the approach in anthropology and sociology and has roots in the classical social theories of Durkheim, Marx, and Weber (Harris 1999). In this conception, individuals are part of a "superorganic" entity such as society or culture. These entities are seen as being greater than the sum of their parts and, in fact, may wholly or very largely determine their parts. Thus, individuals are socialized through membership in these entities, and much, if not all, of their behavior is explained as the playing out of attitudes, norms, and beliefs that have been inculcated in them. The space for individual discretion, choice, and agency is highly circumscribed.

The other extreme view is that individuals are rational calculators who pursue their self-interest above all else. This view of the rational actor is characteristic of economics and much political science and has its roots in the work of Adam Smith and his followers. The rational actor has access to perfect information and is able to calculate costs and benefits constantly and accurately. He responds to incentives, and he approaches any social interaction as if it were a market transaction. His overriding preference is for economic gain. The scope for freedom of choice and agency is wide, although the preference for self-interested gain is assumed to be universal and fixed.

Both of these positions have been seriously modified over the last half century. In anthropology, the work of Fredrik Barth (1981, 1993) and F. G. Bailey (1969) established the importance of considering individual behavior and social interaction as the generative processes that create social forms, not the opposite. This emphasis is echoed in the work of practice theorists who also find (more or less) room for individual choice and behavior within the constraints of normative frames provided by society and culture (Ortner 1984; Fox 1985; Bourdieu 1990). While a high percentage of behavior appears to be relatively unconscious reproduction of social norms and cultural values, at other times individuals diverge from norms, challenge values, or behave in what appear to be more strategic ways. At such times, culture may itself change. Under what conditions do individuals challenge prevailing norms and values? At what points do they propose new innovations to existing institutions? What happens when they do so?

Rational choice theory has also come under intense scrutiny and been seriously modified in light of the recognition that individuals' capacity to calculate is hindered by incomplete information and limits on cognition (North 1990). Further, the assumption that narrow self-interest and material gain are universal preferences has given way to an inclusion of a broader range of goals. The field of experimental economics has developed new methods designed to systematically test the behavioral assumptions of rational choice theory (Camerer 2003). Through the use of experiments that are designed to isolate behavioral motivation, this field promises a more rigorous way to test our ideas about individual motivation. Perhaps not surprising, especially to anthropologists, many results in experimental economic games suggest that individuals do not behave as economic assumptions would predict. They are not entirely self-interested, selfish, or uncooperative. Indeed, some experimenters have posited that there are different types of individuals: those who tend to cooperate or reciprocate others' actions and those who tend to behave in a self-interested fashion (Ostrom, Walker, and Gardner 1993; Fehr and Gachter 2000, 2002). However, what remains to be explained is why some individuals are more cooperative or other-regarding than others.

I combine certain elements of these different perspectives on behavior and motivation.[1] On the one hand, I contend that even if much everyday behavior is highly conditioned by social norms and cultural values and beliefs, some behavior is considerably more goal oriented and strategic. In cases where potential individual gains or losses are significant, actors are more likely to behave strategically. They will pursue their goals and work toward outcomes that they believe are in their best interest, broadly defined. In this effort, they will bring to bear all the resources at their disposal in order to build up their bargaining power vis-à-vis other social actors.

On the other hand, individuals rarely detach themselves completely from the culture or cultures in which they live. Thus, in order to understand their particular motivations and actions, it is necessary to contextualize these within the cultural setting in which the behavior occurs. The great advantage of the ethnographic method is that it enables the analyst to gain insight into the local realities that underlie behavior. Furthermore, even when individuals behave in a more strategic way, the specific manifestations of this behavior are still recognizable from the perspective of their culture. For example, the responses of elders and warriors in Siambu to the prospect of individualizing land ownership differed. While each group opposed privatization, they responded in ways that were typical of their generation: the warriors' inclination was to oppose individual ownership by force, while the elders chose the route of discussion and informal sanctioning of those seeking private land.

Similarly, those seeking private land sought the support of Kenyan law and the administration, which was consistent with their experiences in formal education, employment, and military service. Even their behavior, considered deviant by their fellow Samburu, is understandable within the context of their individual life histories and exposure to alternative norms and values in the modern sector. My approach, then, is to understand the motivations and goals of individual actors, or small groups of actors, as well as the cultural context in which they pursue their goals. Finally, I also consider the consequences of their various actions in terms of the resulting institutions. The aggregation of many individual actions often leads to unintended results with corresponding implications for social relations as well as future behavior.

Common Property and Privatization

The conflict in Siambu centered on the form that land use and ownership should take. Those desiring privatization of land challenged a centuries-old practice of communal land management, and one of the puzzles to be answered here is why they rejected the tried and tested tradition in favor of something new and unknown. Part of the explanation lies in their exposure to alternative ideas about the values and uses of land, themselves based in theories of property rights. The economic theory of property rights suggests that individual ownership is often the most efficient form of property rights because it provides the clearest delineation of rights and responsibilities (Demsetz 1967; Cheung 1970). This belief in the superiority of private property implies the corollary belief that common ownership of property leads inevitably to inefficient outcomes such as overuse or underuse of resources. Proponents of the "tragedy of the commons" thesis (Hardin 1968) maintained that all users of a common resource had incentive to overexploit it since gains from doing so accrued to the individual while the costs were spread over all users. These ideas formed the basis for much of the policy related to pastoral lands in East Africa during the colonial period and continuing through the 1960s and 1970s, postindependence. As I will discuss in chapter 3, the perception of rangelands as tragedies in the making led to the design of policies of group land tenure conceived as ways to reduce the damaging effects of common ownership and incorporate pastoral livestock producers into the national market for beef.

Many anthropologists and ecologists have conducted detailed studies of pastoral livestock production systems (Dahl and Hjort 1976; Behnke, Scoones, and Kerven 1993; Scoones 1994; McCabe 1990; Young and Solbrig 1993), which challenge the view of pastoralists as creators of deserts. Instead, they argue that extensive pastoralism on communally owned land is a rational use of the semiarid environments in which they live and, given current levels of technology, might be the most efficient use of the land compared to alternatives like settled ranching (Behnke, Scoones, and Kerven 1993).

These studies coincided with a growing interest in the management of common pool resources (CPRs) by social scientists who sought to understand the institutional underpinnings of successful CPRs (McCay and Acheson 1987; Ostrom 1990; Bromley and Feeny 1992). Ostrom's (1990) influential study derived a set of design principles from empirical cases of successful common property systems. In essence, these design principles define the institutional parameters enabling groups of users to manage access and use of their shared resources. The design principles include rules about access and use, monitoring systems, graduated sanctions for those who break the rules, and forms of democratic governance over the resource. It is the presence of these types of rules and enforcement mechanisms that differentiates common pool resources from open access resources. Indeed, what the "tragedy of the commons" actually referred to were open access resources where there were no effective controls on access and use of a shared resource. By contrast, many traditional pastoral commons systems studied by anthropologists and ecologists are excellent examples of successful common property systems, and most of them include many, if not all, of the design features that Ostrom discusses.

Thus, by the 1990s, there was good evidence to support policies to shore up, not destroy, extensive pastoralism in East Africa. Ironically, it was at this same time that many pastoralists themselves were calling for privatization of their rangelands. Why this was the case in Samburu District will be pursued at length in later chapters, but a couple of factors deserve brief mention here. First, it should be acknowledged that the extensive pastoral systems analyzed by ecologists and anthropologists have undergone important changes over the last few decades, partly as a direct result of government policies and also due to population growth, increasing diversification, and sedentarization (Brockington 2001; McCabe 2003; Boone et al. 2005; Galvin et al. 2006). These studies draw varying conclusions regarding the capacity of changing ecosystems to support growing populations under different land-use systems, and there is a need for further empirical study in order to specify how these changes affect various groups (Lesorogol 1998). Second, Ostrom's and others' theories of how CPRs are managed tend to pay little attention to the differential benefits that accrue to various groups using the common resource (Agrawal 2003). There is a tendency to assume that benefits from CPRs are fairly evenly spread, but this may not necessarily be the case. In trying to identify the possible sources of challenge to apparently highly functional institutions such as pastoral commons, it is important to consider how benefits are actually shared and whether particular groups benefit (or are perceived to benefit) disproportionately from the maintenance of the commons. In the Samburu case, I argue that wealthier livestock owners do benefit disproportionately from common rangelands, and this provides one clue to understanding why particular groups are supporting privatization.

Given the bulk of studies over the last two decades affirming the value of pastoral production, it is perhaps not surprising that relatively few scholars have analyzed the breakdown of the pastoral commons. Some work has been done on this topic dealing primarily with political and economic processes. Peters (1994) analyzes privatization processes in Botswana focusing on how traditional water rights were gradually reinterpreted and extended into claims of land ownership by local elites. Galaty (1992, 1994, 1997) discusses the process of subdivision of group ranches among the Maasai of Kenya, concentrating on the role of government policy as well as the ways group ranch committees implemented privatization, which were often unfair and corrupt. Rutten (1992) provides a detailed analysis of the formation, functioning, and beginnings of subdivision of group ranches in Kajiado (Maasai) Kenya. His approach is mainly geographic and economic and, while it does have a wealth of data on some issues, includes relatively little detail on the particular actions and strategies of different social groups involved in the process. Mwangi's (2005) study of Maasai group ranch subdivision considers the incentives that motivated some individuals to seek private land ownership, especially the perceived benefits that would accrue from privatization. Other recent studies have begun to examine the effects of these processes among Maasai pastoralists focusing specifically on the ability of small land parcels to support livestock production (Kimani and Pickard 1998; Boone et al. 2005). Ensminger (Ensminger 1992; Ensminger and Rutten 1991) has analyzed moves to enclose common land among the Orma of Kenya from an anthropological and institutional perspective similar to that used here. In the Orma case, however, land has not actually been privatized, although access has been limited, and progress toward formation of group ranches is proceeding.

This study of privatization among the Samburu contributes to the debates over common property by tracing in detail the conflict over privatization that occurred in Siambu and analyzing the motivations and behaviors of the major players. Further, in chapters 7 and 8 the outcomes of privatization are considered, both in terms of their implications for household production and well-being and also at the level of individual behavior. This is done through a systematic comparison with another Samburu community,

Mbaringon, which has not undergone privatization. Using household-level socioeconomic data and experimental economic games, conclusions are drawn about the impacts of privatizing pastoral land on household wealth and well-being and on aspects of individual behavior.

Experimental Economics

Much of this book is devoted to explaining how and why individuals and small groups acted to transform the institution of communal land ownership into one of private ownership. It demonstrates how individual interests and actions aggregate to produce social change, and, in doing so, it contributes to our understanding of individual behavior and change processes. While I aim to show how individuals influence and drive change processes, the opposite question is also important. That is, when an institution such as property rights in land changes, what are the implications for individual behavior? What are the processes through which the new norms and values instantiated in the institution are inculcated in individuals? Is it possible to identify behavioral changes that may be traced to particular institutional shifts? Further, how does one go about studying behavior in a systematic way? These questions have relevance both to cases of undesigned institutions that emerge from social interactions and to those that are intentionally designed by governments seeking to engineer social change.

Anthropologists conventionally study behavior using techniques such as participant observation or more systematic methods such as time allocation studies. These methods provide qualitative and quantitative data about behavior and are a rich source of understanding of the cultural context of human action. However, they have the drawback that one only observes behavior that occurs "naturally" while one is in the field site, much of which may not have direct relevance for the questions being pursued. Further, it is difficult to compare these data across field sites due to their cultural specificity.

For these reasons, I decided to use methods from experimental economics that help overcome these constraints. Experimental economics games are designed to test the assumptions of economic theory about human behavior (Ledyard 1995; Camerer 2003). The games elicit certain types of behavior by asking people to make choices in particular bargaining situations. By keeping the games and procedures standard across field sites, and by abstracting the game from particular real-world situations, comparison across field sites is possible. It is also possible to conduct statistical analyses on the results.

While these types of games have not been used much in anthropology, there is increasing interest in their application cross-culturally (Ensminger 2000; Henrich et al. 2001; Henrich and McElreath 2002; Tracer 2003; Henrich et al. 2004, 2006). Findings from this experimental work challenge canonical assumptions about rational behavior by demonstrating that players from a wide range of societies behave in ways that show concern for social norms such as fairness, altruism, trust, and cooperation rather than narrow self-interest.

In this study, games were used to examine a number of characteristics of individual behavior in Siambu following privatization including fairness, cooperation, and trust. The behavior of participants in Siambu and Mbaringon was compared to detect differences that might stem from privatization of land. These experimental results, combined with the ethnographic evidence, suggest that an institutional change such as privatization of land does have implications for social relations in more general terms (as discussed in chapter 8).

Investigating Institutional Change

The next chapter introduces the Samburu, paying particular attention to their system of livestock production, and also includes information on the methods used in the study. More detailed explanations of methods for household surveys and experimental economics games accompany analyses of these data in chapters 7 and 8, respectively. Chapter 3 examines the historical context for land adjudication in Samburu District. Beginning with a discussion of colonial land policies in Samburu District, I move on to the postindependence policies of group land tenure and describe how these policies were implemented. In chapter 4, the history of privatization in Siambu is presented, emphasizing the roles and actions of various individuals and groups within and outside of the community. Building on chapters 3 and 4, chapter 5 is a theoretical analysis of the Siambu case. Drawing on the bargaining power theory of institutional change, I explain why privatization occurred in Siambu but not in other communities such as Mbaringon. In chapter 6, I present case studies of several individuals from Siambu whose experiences in formal education, employment, and military service shaped their attitudes and beliefs about private property and individual rights. These examples give further substance to the claims made in chapter 5 about the types of individuals who sought private property.

Chapter 7 addresses the outcomes of privatizing land. A systematic comparison of household-level socioeconomic data from Siambu and Mbaringon communities reveals similarities and differences between these two communities across a range of variables such as livestock wealth, income levels and sources, employment, education, and crop production. These are further analyzed in terms of their relationship to changes in land tenure. This chapter includes discussions of the livestock and cultivation systems in Siambu and Mbaringon as well as the scale and nature of land sales following privatization. Some of this information may be useful to readers while reading earlier chapters, and I have cross-referenced the relevant data where appropriate. Chapter 8 analyzes the implications of privatization through the lens of experimental economics. The comparison of Siambu and Mbaringon is extended in an examination of behaviors relating to self-interest, trust, and cooperation. Chapter 9 draws conclusions from the study and addresses theoretical and policy implications.

CHAPTER 2

Ethnographic Setting, Field Sites, and Research Methods

The Samburu, who number about 200,000, live primarily in Samburu District located in north-central Kenya covering an area of 20,000 square kilometers. In addition to ethnic Samburu who compose over 90 percent of the district population, the district is also home to small populations of Turkana, Ariaal, and Rendille pastoralists and traditional hunter and gatherer groups (Republic of Kenya 1997). In towns, other ethnic groups such as Kikuyu, Meru, and Somali live and carry on trade.

The Samburu are a Nilotic-speaking group believed to have migrated out of the Nile basin sometime during the first millennium after Christ (Spear and Waller 1993). Like most pastoralists in northern Kenya, their exact origins remain uncertain, although oral tradition claims they came from a place called Oto, somewhere to the north. Linguistically and culturally the Samburu are closely related to the Maasai, although it should be noted that ethnic identities in northern Kenya have been shown to be fluid and situational and should not, therefore, be overly reified (Sobania 1991; Lamphear 1991; Spear and Waller 1993; Straight 1997). Samburu and Maasai languages are mutually intelligible and they share many of the same customs, but there are also many differences between them. It is probable that the Samburu remained to the north during the Maasai migrations that extended southward into present-day Tanzania and, over time, gradually became a distinct group. Samburu call themselves *Lokop,* a term that translates as "murderers" and that they may have been given by the Maasai after Samburu clashed with the Laikipiak section of the Maasai in the late 1800s.[1] In common use, *Lokop* means "the people." They are also known by Maasai as *loibor nkeneji* (keepers of white goats) in reference to their having herds of goats, while Maasai predominantly keep cattle.

Two-thirds of the district is lowland scrub bushland dominated by acacia species with annual rainfall averaging about 150 to 300 millimeters. The southwestern third of the district comprises the Lorroki plateau—a highland region that forms part of the eastern boundary of the Great Rift Valley. Both of the communities involved in this research are located on Lorroki. Siambu, where privatization took place, is in the northern part of the plateau while Mbaringon is on the southeastern corner (fig. 1). Elevations on Lorroki range from 1,000 meters above sea level to over 2,500 meters at the highest point, in Siambu. This high elevation means higher rainfall—annual averages from 500 to 750 millimeters, with even higher amounts recorded at the highest points. Lorroki has cooler temperatures than the lowlands and lusher grasslands. Running north and south across the eastern edge of Lorroki are the Kirisia hills, which are covered in indigenous forest. Mbaringon is located at the foot of the southern portion of these hills. Parts of Siambu are also forested, and it borders the northern part of the Lorroki forest reserve, which has both indigenous and plantation trees (planted during the colonial period).

The semiarid environment of Samburu District, and northern Kenya more generally, poses numerous constraints on production systems. Rainfall is not only relatively low, but it varies both seasonally and spatially. Droughts are a recurrent reality. The predominance of mobile, extensive pastoralism throughout this region of Kenya is largely an adaptation to the environment. People and herds move seasonally according to the availability of water and forage resources. Freedom of movement and access to large areas of land are required for extensive livestock production, which helps explain why land has been managed communally by pastoralist societies such as the Samburu. In the past, households were truly nomadic, moving several times a year pursuing the best seasonal pastures. This is still true in parts of the drier areas of the lowlands. People who live on Lorroki plateau, however, generally have a semipermanent homestead, and only the livestock and their herders (older boys, young men of warrior age, and unmarried girls) migrate according to seasonal demands. Elder men travel back and forth between the home settlement and the cattle camps in order to supervise both. Increasing sedentarization is in part a response to government policies restricting the use of forests and protected areas that discourage pastoralism. Also, the establishment of towns and trading centers, health and education facilities, and the slightly better environmental conditions on Lorroki plateau are reasons people settle.

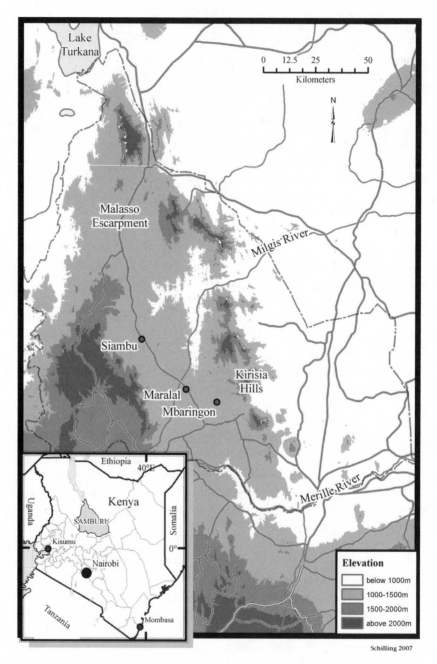

Schilling 2007

Fig. 1. Map of Kenya (Samburu District outlined in black)

During severe drought, however, the entire family might move, often separating the livestock into several herds managed by different combinations of household members as well as friends and relatives. The trend toward more permanent settlement has entailed many changes, including greater access to education, health services, markets, and the central government administration. Increasing population pressure resulting from sedentarization has increased health problems and led to localized environmental degradation (Fratkin 1999).

Samburu society is divided into two moieties, Nkishu Naarok (black cattle) and Nkishu Naibor (white cattle), which are further subdivided into eight sections, and further into clans, subclans, and lineages. Both Mbaringon and Siambu communities are predominantly from Nkishu Naarok sections, the Pisikishu and Lmasula respectively. The Lmasula section is by far the largest and is ritually senior, meaning that they go first in major age-grade ceremonies. They have not historically possessed formal powers over the other sections, although some Lmasula have attempted to parlay their ritual seniority into political capital in recent years by claiming a certain right to lead based on it. In this sense, some individuals are reinterpreting sectional identities in order to use them to form bases for political support, and institutions that had relatively little significance are becoming more salient.

Samburu are patrilineal and practice exogamy at the level of sections, although intermarriage among Lmasula is not very unusual and is becoming more common in the other sections as well. Residence is generally patrilocal although there are many exceptions to this rule. Sections and clans do not claim exclusive rights to particular rangelands, although it is common to find a preponderance of one clan in a geographic region. Efforts were made to geographically consolidate the clans during the colonial period, but there is still a relatively high degree of freedom to move, particularly to move herds in search of better pasture.

Paul Spencer (1965, 1973), the first ethnographer of the Samburu, characterized their society as gerontocratic, emphasizing the authority of older men who control livestock and women and who make most decisions at the household and communal levels. Indeed, the Samburu age-set system assigns particular rights and responsibilities to each male age group and does confer the greatest decision-making authority on elders. Holtzman (1996) has challenged Spencer's depiction, arguing that the warriors are not as alienated and disenfranchised as Spencer claimed and that elders' authority also has limits. In my view, warriors and women, though weaker than elders in terms of power and authority, certainly have many important roles in society and do influence decisions and events, often indirectly through their male relatives. In recent times, younger men have gained access to new sources of power that they are using to shift the balance between the generations (as discussed in chapters 4, 5, and 6).

Most Samburu make their living by herding livestock (chapter 7 includes details on livestock holdings and sales for Siambu and Mbaringon). Cattle are the most prized type of livestock, and Samburu culture is in many senses cattle-centric. Cattle are the basis of their livelihood and also have tremendous social and symbolic value. All important social relationships are mediated by exchanges of cattle, and all significant rituals involve their slaughter and consumption. Milk and, to a much lesser extent, meat and blood are the traditional dietary staples. However, Samburu can and do sell cattle to meet their growing needs for cash. While their production system has not been transformed into one that prioritizes beef production for the market, sales are common and represent a significant source of household income. Sheep and goats are also kept and are becoming increasingly valued due to their rapid rate of reproduction, hardiness, and salability. Camels are becoming more common, especially in the lowlands, as Samburu have come to realize their potential to resist drought.

Samburu live in settlements (*nkang*, pl. *nkangitie*) composed of several households. Houses are single-roomed, built of sticks and covered in a mixture of mud and dung. They are arranged in a circular fashion with the large cattle enclosure in the middle surrounded by a fence made of branches. A household includes a man, his wife or wives, and their children. Each wife builds and maintains her own house and has her own gate for livestock to enter into the cattle enclosure. Depending on the number of small stock owned by the household, they will have one or more enclosures for sheep and goats that are located near the house, adjacent to the larger cattle enclosure. Lambs, kids, and small calves are usually kept inside the houses at night, for warmth and protection from predators. Many settlements in Lorroki have five to ten houses and include several households. However, my household survey identified many settlements with only a single household, and my observations over the last ten years indicate a trend toward fragmentation of settlements. Sometimes this is a result of the natural progress of generational development: after the father dies, his sons separate and form their own settlements. At other times, households separate due to internal conflicts that may have to do with differences of opinion regarding livestock management or purely personal issues.

Population growth among the Samburu is about 2.5 percent annually, lower than among agricultural groups in Kenya whose growth rates can exceed 4 percent (Republic of Kenya 1997). Given the fragility of their semi-arid environment, though, this level of growth exerts pressure on the resource base. Combined with frequent droughts that wipe out large numbers of livestock, population growth is contributing to a trend of increasing impoverishment among the Samburu, attested to by falling per capita livestock holdings (Lesorogol 2000; Little et al. 2001). In response, many men are seeking employment within and outside the district to supplement their incomes, while women participate in small-scale trade in commodities from their homes or in small towns. Some are practicing agriculture for the same reason. Wildlife and tourism offer another potential source of income to local communities. Samburu Game Reserve, located on the banks of the Uaso Nyiro river (the only permanent river in Samburu District) in the eastern part of the district, is home to a high concentration of wildlife including elephant, lion, cheetah, hyena, leopard, buffalo, ostrich, monkeys, and many types of birds and antelopes. Some types of wildlife are unique to Samburu such as the reticulated giraffe, Beisa oryx, gerenuk, and Grevy's zebra. The concentration and diversity of wildlife and the natural beauty of this relatively small park draw many tourists to the area and supply much of the revenue of the local government, the Samburu County Council, which owns and operates the reserve. In recent years, there have been some efforts to distribute a portion of tourism revenues to communities adjacent to the park, and there are also a couple of community-based wildlife conservation and tourism efforts under way in the district.

Wildlife is an important resource for the Samburu, but there are also conflicts between humans and wildlife. Wildlife move in and out of the game reserve, and elephants, zebra, and antelopes are found throughout the district, albeit at much lower concentrations than in the reserve. Samburu are not traditionally hunters and are quite selective about which wild meats they consume. In general, they only eat the meat of cloven-hoofed animals such as gazelles. They do not eat elephant or zebra meat. These traditions and low population densities have meant that Samburu and wildlife have coexisted for centuries. However, as populations increase and access to range declines, partly due to the creation of game and forest reserves, human–wildlife conflicts are on the rise. Predators such as lions, hyenas, and leopards pose a risk to livestock, and elephants and buffalo occasionally injure and sometimes kill people. In areas where people try to grow crops, elephants, zebras, baboons, and even wild pigs often destroy crops. The placement of the game reserve on the banks of the only permanent river in the district also limits the surrounding community's access to this water supply, especially during dry seasons and droughts. Although hunting is outlawed in Kenya, the spread of guns in Samburu, mostly a response to cattle raiding by neighboring groups, coupled with rising poverty and food insecurity, has resulted in increasing hunting for food. Wildlife and conservation policies and programs have begun to address these problems by increasing community involvement in and benefits from conservation and tourism activities, but to date these appear to have done little to stem the decline of wildlife populations or substantially improve the living conditions of communities (Norton-Griffiths 2000; Western, Russell, and Mutu 2006).

It is also important to note that Samburu District, and northern Kenya in general, is considered, by other Kenyans but also to some extent by the inhabitants themselves, as a peripheral area of the country. For example, as a "hardship" area, government workers posted to Samburu draw a special allowance on top of their normal salary and benefits. Many of them view working in Samburu as a punishment (which it sometimes is when they are sent there on disciplinary grounds) and try their best to get out as soon as possible. People from "down country" (as the central parts of Kenya are referred to) perceive a place like Samburu as being very far away from them both physically and culturally (Lesorogol 1998). I was often asked by Kenyans how I could live in such a place. Most of them had never been there and were afraid to go. Some primary school textbooks referred to pastoralism as a "primitive" form of agriculture, and the common view was that pastoralists were living a backward lifestyle and needed to catch up with the rest of the country.

Ironically, I also sensed a certain degree of envy among many government personnel who came to work in Samburu. Partly, this stemmed from their misperception that all Samburu owned thousands of head of cattle and were actually rich, but I think it also had to do with the fact that in the face of pressure to change and conform to the norms of modernity, most Samburu maintain many of their customs and are proud to be who they are. At the same time, though most Samburu are proud of their heritage and highly value pastoralism as a way of life, as they gain more experience in other parts of Kenya they are increasingly understanding the differences and contrasts between where they live and the rest of the country. They don't lack for their own share of envy of some of the accoutrements of modernity that are much more in evidence outside of Samburu District. These beliefs about the contrast between pastoralists like Samburu and the rest of Kenya are important in understanding the process of privatization in Siambu and will be discussed in more detail in chapters 5 and 6.

It is somewhat ironic that while other Kenyans view Samburu culture as atavistic and unchanging, in many ways change is occurring very rapidly. As noted earlier, increasing settlement has altered the practice of mobile pastoralism, and greater access to education, health services, and markets has opened up new possibilities beyond pure pastoralism. Since the colonial period, Samburu have lost access to many of their rangelands through government demarcation and enforcement of administrative boundaries, as well as the creation of forest and game reserves. Increasing population on a decreasing resource base has intensified pressure on the environment, resulting in localized degradation and falling per capita livestock holdings. The change processes brought about by these and other factors are of central concern in this book.

Field Experience with the Samburu

Research for this book was conducted from July 2000 to December 2001. This was not my first experience among the Samburu, however. I had been living and working among the Samburu almost continuously since 1987. After becoming fascinated with the issues surrounding rural development as a university student, I traveled to Kenya on a study abroad program. There, I first visited Samburu District and became very intrigued by the challenges facing people living in such a difficult physical environment. I returned after graduation and spent two years teaching in a secondary school in Maralal, the district capital. After returning to the United States to earn a master's degree, I went back to Kenya determined to get a job in the development field. After several short assignments with development programs in Samburu and Marsabit (the neighboring district to the northeast) I was hired on a long-term program that aimed to enhance community and government capacities to plan and implement development activities.

I worked in the Samburu District Development Programme (SDDP) for six years. Over this time, I gained a wealth of experience working directly with Samburu communities all over the district. I also worked closely with many governmental and nongovernmental organizations during this time, primarily trying to encourage them to work in more participatory ways with communities. Through these experiences, I gained much insight into the functioning of these organizations, especially the ways they act on the ground, far from the capital city.

My development work was focused on facilitating processes of dialogue and decision making within communities and between communities and outside organizations that provide various services to the communities. The idea was to involve people (men, women, old, young, educated, uneducated, rich, poor, etc.) directly in the entire process of development. While I felt that we had considerable success in developing and testing innovative approaches for doing this, I continued to be curious about how decision making and change happened in these communities without the direct stimulus of an organization like ours. I believed that only by understanding these endogenous processes better could development practitioners hope to intervene in ways that not only were sensitive to local culture but also might bring about sustainable processes of dialogue and action toward change.

These concerns brought me back to graduate school where I looked forward to the luxury of thinking more deeply about and conducting research into these issues. The result was this research project that aims to understand changes in institutions, primarily by considering the intersection of individual action with political, economic, and cultural factors.

I've taken this opportunity to explain my own background since it has some bearing on the research process and also by way of situating myself in what follows. I do so also to comment on the concern with "reflexivity" and the politics of representation that has been prevalent in anthropology over the last ten to fifteen years. Many scholars have pointed out the importance of the role and position of the researcher in influencing the research process, its results, and their presentation (Rosaldo 1989; Marcus 1998; Jacobs-Huey 2002). For some anthropologists, this has led to a virtual abandonment of positive approaches in favor of the view of anthropological studies as texts and interpretations, accounts but not explanations.

I think that this challenge to the objectivity of the researcher has some validity, and that is why I have taken space here to sketch a bit of my own background and how I think it may have impacted on my research. However, I do not share the conviction that the subjectivity of the researcher in itself invalidates efforts at explanation or the use of a wide range of research methods, including those from positive social science. On the contrary, I concur with Salzmann (2002) that the validity and reliability of research depends on the quality and types of information gathered and the external validation of these methods, not merely the positioning of the individual researcher. I think that using a range of methods for data gathering and analysis provides better opportunities for cross-checking, or triangulating, information and thus enables a more rigorous analysis of the material and stronger explanations, even if these are not the only possible explanations or the definitive "truth." To this end, I incorporated a number of different techniques in this research (described later). There is a role for reflection as well, but I think it lies primarily in understanding how one's position enables or impedes the research process and being aware of biases that might impinge on the quality of research.

In my assessment, my years of interaction with Samburu people prior to this research facilitated the project, because I was already familiar with the district and its people, I could speak the language, and I had many contacts throughout the area. This was extremely helpful because I had numerous people whom I felt confident would share their knowledge and perspective freely with me. Of course, everyone has biases and selective memory, but I did not worry very much about these people deliberately deceiving me. On the contrary, they could assist in judging the reliability or veracity of the accounts of others less well known to me. Having lived there almost a decade, I found it relatively easy to meet people and interact with them in the context of the research. On the other hand, being so familiar with a place may have its liabilities, too. As a colleague pointed out to me, things cease to be "strange" after a long time in a place, and it may be difficult to perceive certain things precisely because they appear to be normal. I don't know how one can completely overcome this problem, but I hope that an awareness of it has aided me in not falling victim to it too often.

Another aspect of my experience with Samburu was that people were also familiar with me from my previous roles. In general, I found this to be a good thing because it made building rapport easier. On the other hand, I was also aware that my relationships with particular individuals, families, lineages, and clans could be perceived in different ways by the various people I met in the course of the project. I was aware of the reputations and statuses of these individuals and groups and how they might affect the reactions of others. While I could not completely overcome these associations, and they were often useful, I did make efforts to go beyond this group to interact with a wide range of individuals.

I did take pains to explain clearly that this was a research endeavor aimed at trying to understand the process of land privatization and that it was not a development project. People would only benefit in the sense of gaining some knowledge, but they should not expect any other types of material gains. I believe that over time people came to understand this distinction, especially since no development project was forthcoming even though I continued to live and work among them.

Selection of Field Sites

When I was employed in the development project, I had been curious to work in Siambu in order to see whether there were differences in the responses of people living in an area of private land compared to group ranch land or communal land. SDDP began working in Siambu in 1996. Although initial participation and interest from the community were high (over 600 people attended the first participatory planning workshop), over the next six months attendance at meetings fell dramatically and finally ceased altogether. At the time, we did not understand why this happened, but we had no choice but to stop working as people were apparently not interested in continuing. In fact, this was the only community, out of thirty-six that the project eventually reached, where this happened. I always wondered what went wrong, and I suspected that issues internal to the community had been the cause.

When I decided to focus on institutional change, specifically changes in land tenure, Siambu was the natural choice for a field site. As the only area in Samburu District that had been completely privatized (other areas have a mix of a few individual farms, group ranches, and unadjudicated common land), it was the place with the most radical change in land tenure and, therefore, the place where the process and effects of this change would be most notable.

Siambu, with a population of roughly 2,000 people, covers an area of about 16,000 acres and has two distinctive environments: the upland plateau (where most people live and where the flat land and good rainfall make agriculture possible) and the escarpment (drier, with rocky hills that plunge hundreds of feet to the floor of the Rift Valley).

The selection of Mbaringon as a comparative case, where land remained communally owned as a group ranch, was also a straightforward decision since this was the place where I had lived for over ten years. I knew the people there and already had a base from which to launch the research. I should note that although I had been living at Mbaringon for a long time, I had never worked there in the development capacity, as I had (so briefly) in Siambu. This project, then, entailed a shift from being just an inhabitant of the place, albeit an unusual one, to being a researcher.

The two sites are not identical, of course, so there is need to address the comparability of results between the two sites. There are historical and environmental differences between the two areas. Siambu is at a higher elevation and has higher rainfall and, thus, higher agricultural potential than Mbaringon, which lies on the cusp between highland and lowland regions within Samburu District. People began living semipermanently in Siambu, rather than using it only for dry season grazing, around the 1960s, whereas families had been using Mbaringon as a home base at least since the 1930s, probably earlier. People in Siambu are predominantly from the Lmasula section, Lotimi clan, while Mbaringon is mostly Pisikishu, Sitat clan. It also appears that people in Mbaringon have had greater livestock wealth than those in Siambu over the last twenty or so years (see chapter 7).

In spite of these differences, there are important similarities between the two areas. The people, though from different clans, share most aspects of culture and lifestyle. All of them are pastoralists, and livestock remain the mainstay of the economy, even in Siambu today. They share similar histories and views on many issues. Although I highlight the differences between the two places in order to trace the effects of institutional change, it is important to recall that there are broad similarities between them. An outsider traveling to the two places would not mistake them as different peoples.

Fieldwork Methods: Participant Observation

Participant observation was an ongoing part of the study. During the fieldwork period from July 2000 to December 2001, I was based at Mbaringon but spent at least two days a week in Siambu. At the beginning of the fieldwork I held public meetings in each place to explain the research and some of the methods I would be using. I felt this was necessary not only to inform people about what I was doing, but also to clarify my current role as researcher. I made it clear to people that the research was not a development project, and that I was not coming to give them something, but rather to spend time with them and to learn from them. I was candid that the research probably would not have any tangible benefits for them, but that it was an educational activity. This appeared to be well understood by most people, and I had no difficulties with overblown expectations during the research. I also let people know in the beginning that at a later stage (nine months into the research, as it turned out) I would be playing some games with them and that there would be a chance to win money. During the experimental economics games, people were quite pleased about the money they received; and at least in that sense, the research did benefit people in a minor way.

I believe that the initial meetings were very successful in the sense that people understood my role in the community and were prepared when I visited them or met them casually. I had excellent cooperation from people in both places. Only one or two people expressed reservations about participating in the household survey or being interviewed, and these were overcome with further explanation about the purposes of the research. The vast majority of people were very forthcoming and willing to discuss the issues raised in the project.

As a participant in daily life, I spent time with people in their daily routines and also during special occasions or ceremonies. I kept abreast of the *lomon* (news) of the community and the major issues that were currently under deliberation. I attended numerous public meetings on various issues. Chance meetings and car rides (usually me driving someone to Maralal, the district headquarters, located midway between the two field sites) were good opportunities to canvas opinion on the subdivision of land in Siambu and what it meant to people.

In-depth Interviews

In addition to informal discussions, I conducted in-depth interviews with forty-six people in Siambu and thirteen people in Mbaringon. These were mostly done during the second half of the research period after I understood enough about the issues to know which questions to ask. I used an interview checklist where I noted the key points I wanted to cover in the interview. This gave the interview structure without foreclosing opportunities to diverge or probe into different subjects. In Siambu, these interviews focused on the historical process of land subdivision, the strategies of the various groups involved, and the effects of subdivision on livelihoods and lifestyles. I selected people for interviews who had been key players in the historical process, such as land committee members, those who got individual land in the early stages, and those who opposed the subdivision of land. I also interviewed some people who were not deeply involved in the process to understand the views of those who were more peripheral to the process. This included a number of women who were largely left out of the entire land subdivision process.

Interviews in Mbaringon also focused on land issues, particularly the colonial-period grazing schemes and the transition to group ranches. Mbaringon had obviously not had the same process of individualization of land as Siambu, but they had undergone the adjudication process, and a few individuals did obtain private land during that time. Thus, in this case I was trying to discover why people had not objected to this privatization as they had in Siambu. The selection process in Mbaringon was similar in terms of trying to interview those who had been directly involved in adjudication of the group ranch and also people with good memories of the colonial period.

Most of these interviews were tape-recorded and transcribed. I made detailed notes of interviews that were not recorded as well as of informal meetings and discussions. I also interviewed government officials, particularly staff of the Ministry of Lands and Settlements, in order to understand the process of adjudication as well as the particular details of the Siambu case. Unfortunately, it was not possible to interview the particular officers who were there at the time since they have since left the district and in some cases have died or retired.

Archival Work

While it was not possible to interview all the relevant government officials, it was possible to read the files in Maralal that deal with Siambu and Mbaringon land issues. The Siambu file in particular was useful in reconstructing the major events and stages of the land adjudication process and the disputes it engendered. I also read general files relating to group ranches. In order to investigate the extent of land transactions I read the minutes of the District Land Control Board for the last ten years. All land sales, leases, and charges (using land as collateral for loans) must pass through the control board. In Nairobi, I read files in the National Archives relating to land policies in Samburu District. I also sought further information at the headquarters of the Ministry of Lands in Nairobi, especially to seek clarification on government policies pertaining to group ranches and their subdivision.

Household Survey

An important component of the study was to compare the socioeconomic situation of the two communities in order to detect differences that could be attributed to privatization of land in Siambu. To this end, a cross-sectional household survey was conducted with 100 households in each community, a total of 200 households. The households were selected at random from lists of group ranch members. In Siambu, all land owners in the privatized area are also members of Porokwai group ranch, the land that remained common after subdivision, so I was able to use the group ranch list here as well. Before selecting households, the lists were reviewed to remove minors who do not constitute household heads but who have been added to the group ranch registers. Having removed minors, there were 234 households in Siambu and 244 in Mbaringon. Using a random number table, I selected 100 households for inclusion in the survey. During the survey, a few households had to be exchanged because they were impossible to reach or unsuitable for the study (e.g., due to insanity). These were replaced with other randomly selected households. Random sampling was used to get the best representation of each community and to strengthen the validity of results.

The household survey consisted of eleven separate surveys including demographic data, livestock holdings, livestock sales, assets and debts, nonlivestock income sources, military service, annual and weekly expenditures, agricultural production, food consumption, and information about leaders, stock friends, and patrons. The surveys took two to three hours to complete and were conducted by myself and two research assistants. Participants' consent was obtained by having them sign a consent form. While this was a large amount of information to collect and required patience to allow participants enough time to recall detailed information, most participants actually said they enjoyed the survey. Many were pleased to have a chance to review their household situation, although a few wondered why such information was interesting to us.

Experimental Economics

A novel aspect of this study is the use of experimental economics to draw conclusions about the behavior of people in the two communities. One set of hypotheses was that changes in a critically important institution such as land tenure would lead to changes in people's behavior. For example, I hypothesized that people living on private land would tend to be more individualistic, even selfish, than those living on communal land. Conventional approaches in anthropology can provide insight into behavior from observation or interviewing, but it is difficult to generalize this kind of evidence to a population or to draw conclusions that can be compared with other populations with a high level of reliability or validity. The attraction of experimental economics is that it provides an alternative approach that enables generalizations to be made from controlled experiments with relatively small sample sizes. Games were selected that are designed to measure the types of behavior that were hypothesized to change due to privatization of land. Each game was played in both Siambu and Mbaringon, and the results were compared using statistical analysis. Details on the methods and procedures used in the games can be found in chapter 8.

Daily Life

In closing this chapter, I want to give the reader a feel for how pastoralists live day to day. The following is a description of a typical day in Mbaringon, like many that I participated in during my research. The rhythms of daily life revolve around the care of livestock, beginning with the morning milking of cows. We awaken to the sound of a cock's crowing signaling dawn followed quickly by the lowing of cows anxious to reunite with their young calves that have spent the night separated from their mothers in small enclosures within the main cattle enclosure (*boo*). The women emerge from their houses in the semidark, wrapped in cloths and blankets against the chill of a Lorroki morning, and head out to retrieve some of the cows who have managed to extricate themselves from their overnight confinement in the enclosure to partake in some nighttime grazing near the settlement. Luckily, there are not too many hyenas, lions, or leopards around to threaten the cows, and they are safely returned.

One woman opens the calf pen allowing out particular calves as women call out which cows they are milking first. Each woman has designated milk cows, her own or those borrowed from others. She also has a set of milk calabashes made from wood or gourds into which she milks directly by wrapping the leather straps around her left hand to hold the calabash in place as she milks with her right hand. The calf drinks simultaneously, and there is a constant need to keep the calf off the teats the woman milks. The process of milking constitutes a delicate balancing of the needs of the calf and the family members for milk and is one area of discretion that women have that is of vital importance both to children's nutrition and to the survival of calves and, by extension, herds.

After milking, women return to their houses and begin to prepare early morning tea. By this time, schoolchildren are preparing to leave and are given tea before they go. Tea has become a staple food for the Samburu in recent decades. Drinking tea, especially by children, was quite rare a generation ago, probably due to greater abundance of milk and less access to shops. Today, tea, ideally composed of about a fifty-fifty ratio of milk and water complemented by a generous amount of sugar (almost too sweet for my taste), is drunk by all family members, generally twice a day, once in the morning and again in the late afternoon. It is not surprising that purchases of sugar constitute a significant portion of household expenditures, and there is a pervasive habit of borrowing sugar and tea leaves whenever these run out. Many women also sell sugar from their homes and are able to earn a small but steady income as long as they do not succumb to too many requests for credit.

Schoolchildren leave to walk to school about two kilometers away while the children who remain home to herd livestock and help with domestic work begin to get moving. Men also emerge from houses and begin to look over the livestock, greet each other, and discuss the night, the weather, the condition of the animals, plans for herding, and other notable events. There are frequently visitors to the homestead who may be seeking assistance of some kind, or just visiting, and they will join the man of the homestead as he does his morning rounds among the livestock. Visitors are always welcome, even though their requests may not necessarily be. They bring news of other places that is often instrumental to decision making about herd movements as well as keeping up with friends or relatives that live in other parts of the district and beyond. In a community where radios and television are rare, and newspapers practically nonexistent, people rely on word of mouth for the vast majority of their news and information about affairs within their own community as well as the wider world. For this reason, people spend considerable amounts of time talking with one another to keep up with the *lomon* (news).

Around 8:00 a.m., sometimes earlier in the dry season, the cows leave for their day of grazing, their route having been determined by the head of the household. They are generally herded by older boys when they are at home, while the *lmurran* (warriors) play a more active role in herding when livestock are moved to cattle camps away from the home settlement, generally during the dry season or during droughts. Sheep and goats leave the settlement after the cows, usually between 9:00 and 10:00 a.m. Herders drink milk and may also eat stiff maize porridge (*loshoro*) to fortify them for the day of herding, during which they generally do not eat until they bring the animals home between 4:00 and 6:00 p.m. Boys and girls begin herding around age four or five by keeping an eye on the calves, lambs, and kids that stay behind just near the homestead when the older animals go out grazing. Children who do not attend school herd progressively more and larger livestock, moving from the baby animals, to the sheep and goats, to the cows and camels (if any are owned by the family). By the time he is twelve or thirteen, a boy is likely to be entrusted with his father's entire herd of cows, all day every day. Girls generally herd small stock (sheep and goats) but may herd cows if there is no boy available to herd. Ideally, several children herd together so they can help each other and keep each other company. Often, relatives combine their herds, and the children work together herding the larger group of livestock.

Shortages of herding labor are not uncommon, especially as more children are enrolled in school. To cope, families may request a herding-age child from a close relative, often the husband's sister's son, to come live with the family and herd livestock. These children often live in their grandmother's house and may remain with the uncle's family for years. Another common strategy in recent times is to hire a Turkana herder. The Turkana are pastoralists who live to the west of Samburu District. Turkana have long migrated outside their home territory in search of work, and older Turkana boys and teenagers frequently seek herding work with the Samburu. In some cases, these boys end up being essentially adopted by the Samburu family they herd for, including being circumcised (which is not practiced among the Turkana) and marrying Samburu girls. Samburu men and women also sometimes herd their own livestock, particularly when their own children are very young and additional labor cannot be easily found. This is not a preferred strategy, however, and significant efforts are usually made to recruit herding labor.

Once the livestock have left the homestead, women get busy with the many domestic tasks they carry out every day. Fetching water is an essential daily task. During the wet season, water is available in the stream about one kilometer away from the homestead, but during the dry season women may go farther to shallow wells where buckets are used to lift water from the well or to the school where there is a deep well powered by a wind pump that serves the school as well as the community. Water is carried in twenty-liter jerry cans that women carry on their backs supported by a nylon or leather strap that they tie around the jerry can and then over their forehead. Women collect firewood in the Kirisia hills forest, usually two or three times a week. This is an arduous task that takes two to four hours to complete. Firewood is also carried on the back using a strap around the forehead. In the lowlands, where water and firewood can be a day's walk away, women frequently use donkeys to carry these loads. On Lorroki, however, the use of donkeys is rare, and women carry heavy loads for kilometers. In addition to firewood, the forest has many products that women collect when needed including poles, branches, and fibers for building houses (which are constructed by women), medicinal plants for human and animal ailments, and wild foods such as berries and roots that are consumed especially during droughts.

At home, women do a variety of domestic and livestock-related tasks. They regularly clean the small stock pens using brooms made of small, leafy branches to sweep out the accumulated dung, which is heaped in a pile just outside the settlement. They also tend to young and sick animals that stay behind during the day, making sure they have feed and water and applying medicinal treatments, both modern and traditional. They take care of their own small children, often cooperating with other women in their settlement to watch each other's children so they can go to the forest or to the town (eight kilometers away) to purchase food and other items. Older women, the grandmothers, often watch young children for their daughters-in-law, and, in exchange, the daughters bring back firewood, water, and purchased items for them. Women do all the cooking and cleaning of the house, and they make many of their own beaded and leather ornaments, as well as fashioning the milk calabashes and preparing hides and skins for various purposes, including as sleeping skins. Thus, their days are normally relatively busy either traveling to the forest or to town, or spent around the homestead. Much of the time they spend in the company of other women, continuing a running dialogue of the local *lomon*.

Girls who do not attend school (still the majority among Samburu) help their mothers with domestic chores or with herding. Those younger than about six years are fairly carefree, even if they are supposed to be watching the baby animals. Like children everywhere, Samburu children love to play house, often constructing their own miniature Samburu houses, including having a real fire inside and cooking tea in tin cans. Another favorite game is making dolls and livestock out of mud and incorporating these into their games of house and herd. Older girls assume increasing responsibilities in herding, caring for younger siblings, and helping their mother with cooking, cleaning, and fetching water and wood. Girls are often married by age fourteen or fifteen, by which time they have a good degree of familiarity with the range of tasks required to run a Samburu household.

During the day, men have their own activities to attend to, and there is considerable variation among them in how they spend their time. Often, men will go out to visit the livestock during the day to check in with the herders or to help with tasks, especially watering the livestock if it is dry and they are using wells for water. Men are often engaged in meetings with other men to discuss community issues and to resolve disputes. These meetings may be large and formal or smaller and more impromptu, depending on the issue to be discussed and the range of people affected. Many men go to town during the day, either for trading purposes or to meet others and learn the news. Visiting friends and relatives is also common and may have numerous purposes. Maintaining social networks is important to men as their herds are built and rebuilt (following disasters) in significant part from social networks of stock-friends, with whom they have exchanged livestock, thereby entering into a lifelong reciprocal relationship. Men also tend to have some leisure time during the day. Many of them can be found in the heat of the day under the trees playing *dotoi*, a Samburu board game where stones are moved around a series of holes scooped in the board, or even in the ground if a board is not available.

By late afternoon, the livestock are heading back home. When they are close, the children herding will usually come into the settlement, get cups, and milk some of the sheep or goats to get milk for afternoon tea, which they are definitely looking forward to after the long day of herding. Women go out to meet the livestock and count them to make sure all are accounted for. It is not unusual for a few sheep and goats to be missing, especially in larger herds, in which case the herders and women will go searching for them. Animals that have been sick are checked and treated, if necessary, while the animals graze and rest near the settlement.

Afternoons, especially during rainy seasons, are also times when dances take place, often in conjunction with weddings. Warriors and girls are the primary participants in dances, although married women and men may also participate at times. Each generation of warriors has its own repertoire of songs, and there is a degree of competition both within age-sets (across clans) and across age-sets in terms of their skill and prowess in dancing and singing. This competitive element helps reinforce the solidarity of age-set members. The Samburu male age-set system is an important institution regulating men's social roles and responsibilities. Boys are initiated into an age-set in their mid- to late teens (though the age of initiation seems to be dropping, especially on Lorroki) through a complex series of rituals culminating in circumcision. They remain members of their age-set throughout their lives and develop their closest and most enduring ties with their age-mates. Each age-set has a unique name that also remains the same throughout their lifetime. The functions of the members of age-sets change over time, however, as they move through the age-grades. Thus, the first fourteen years following circumcision are warriorhood when the primary responsibilities of the young men are to protect the people and livestock and to build up their own herds in preparation for marriage and becoming household heads. In this capacity, they travel with the livestock during dry seasons and droughts in search of better pasture, and they provide protection to the livestock against predators, both human and wild. Traditionally, the *lmurran* were prohibited from marriage during the warrior years, but this tradition is changing. Many members of the last warrior group, the Lmeoli (initiated in 1990), married midway through their tenure as warriors.

Following warriorhood, men become junior elders, and they are allowed to marry and establish independent households. They are now allowed to join the councils of elders and participate in community discussions and decision making. The next age-grade is the firestick elders (*ilporon*), so-called because they have the responsibility to train and advise the upcoming warrior generation, including lighting the fire that symbolizes the initiation of the new age-set. Finally, there are senior elders who are respected for their experience and knowledge and who continue to play active roles in community affairs, especially presiding over important rituals like the age-set ceremonies.

The rainy season is often a time of relative leisure for warriors, since they are not required for herding, and they spend much of this time perfecting their singing and dancing as well as their elaborate, red-ochered hairstyles. Late afternoon and evening dances are also a time for warriors and older, unmarried girls to meet and socialize. Weddings are open to all community members and are very popular activities both because of the meaning of the wedding itself, bringing together different families, but also as a break from daily routine and chance to have fun and catch up with friends and relatives.

Cows come in around dusk, and the evening milking is conducted as the sun goes down, almost 7:00 p.m. Then, all the livestock are secured for the night—small stock in their pens, cows in the central enclosure, baby animals in pens or inside houses for warmth. There may be an evening meal, or just tea, depending on what food is available and on individual tastes. Evenings are taken up talking about the day's events, telling stories or singing songs, and schoolchildren trying to do homework by the light of the fire or a small kerosene lamp.

CHAPTER 3

Colonial and Postcolonial Contexts for Land Tenure in Kenya

The process of land adjudication in pastoralist districts such as Samburu was part of the Kenyan government's overall scheme for rationalizing land tenure. The system of group tenure planned for the semiarid areas of the country ostensibly secured rights of access and use for pastoralist communities. In fact, this process often skewed land ownership in favor of a few individuals who, being better acquainted with government procedures and their rights, were able to obtain relatively large private plots of land while the vast majority of people ended up as members of group ranches (Bates 1989). This was the case in all parts of Samburu District that underwent adjudication except for one: Siambu. The Siambu case is atypical because members of the community banded together to prevent a small number of individuals from acquiring large tracts of land as their private farms.

This chapter describes the beginnings of land adjudication in Samburu District. It is organized in two parts: the first provides the context for land adjudication in Samburu District by reviewing its historical precedents of colonial-era grazing schemes and the postindependence group ranch concept, and the second discusses the typical process of land adjudication as it occurred in Lodogejek adjudication section, out of which Mbaringon group ranch was formed. The discussion of Lodogejek highlights the features of the process that enabled individuals to acquire private land and the reasons why the community failed to effectively resist these acquisitions. In the next chapter, the Siambu case is presented, illustrating the particular circumstances and events that resulted in an equal distribution of land among all group ranch members.

Colonial-Era Grazing Schemes

During the colonial period, Samburu District was part of the larger Northern Frontier District (NFD), an area that was essentially closed off from the rest of the country in order to serve as a buffer zone between Kenya and Ethiopia to the north. The colonial regime's primary interest was to maintain security in this region, and, consequently, efforts at establishing markets or otherwise encouraging development were limited. As a result, the NFD lagged behind the rest of the colony in terms of the spread of formal education, development of socioeconomic infrastructure, and delivery of services.

In 1915, all land in the Samburu area was declared Crown land, meaning that it became the property of the state. The local population remained on the land and continued to practice mobile pastoralism. However, in the 1930s, schemes for controlling grazing were introduced in some parts of the district. The grazing schemes were established due to government fears that land, particularly on the Lorroki plateau, was being overgrazed by excessive numbers of livestock. To stem potential environmental degradation, numbers of cattle were limited on the plateau. Goats were completely prohibited from this area, while a small number of sheep were tolerated. In addition to stock quotas, grazing areas were demarcated, and a system of rotational grazing was established and enforced by armed guards. The grazing schemes may have had little impact on the condition of the range over the long term, but they appear to have had an important effect on Samburu people's attitudes toward the state.

This probably stems from two aspects of the grazing schemes. There was micromanagement of grazing land by outside authorities. For the first time, access to land was controlled by a government external to the people themselves. And these controls were stringent and thoroughgoing. For example, in Mbaringon, the grazing area was divided into several sections that were opened and closed on a rotational basis. Movements of animals were tightly regulated, and cows were prohibited from grazing in closed areas. Boundaries were so rigid that even to cross a closed area in order to access a water source required permission, and a specific path was marked out for the purpose. One elder, a young man at the time grazing schemes were introduced, described how the rotational system worked.

> During grazing guard when one side is closed, they close next to someone's [cattle] enclosure gate. When they come and notice that there is a

gate facing the closed side, they demand it be closed. We were being commanded by the grazing guard scouts. When the white man in charge came and observed that there was a lot of grass, he opened that area and closed another one. They closed the plains, too. During those days people obeyed rules.[1] (Rashaki Lonyuki)

In addition to grazing controls, herd sizes were limited through imposition of quotas on stock numbers. Each stock owner was issued a grazing permit specifying the number of cows he was entitled to keep on Lorroki plateau. Goats were completely prohibited from Lorroki, and only a limited number of sheep were allowed. All excess stock had to be moved off the plateau. In most cases this meant moving the animals a hundred kilometers or more to the lowlands (*lpurkel*) around Wamba where a separate settlement of the household would stay to herd these animals. One woman explained how households would split, keeping the quota of cattle on Lorroki and the rest of the animals in the lowlands.

Then the Samburu understood [the grazing schemes] and whenever the cows increased, they took them down to the lowlands. . . .Yes, the family would separate into two: the lowland one and the Lorroki one. You were not even supposed to keep goats here. If you wanted to slaughter a goat, you had to have a permit and go to the lowlands to bring it. After coming back, you had to take the permit back to report that you were through. You were only supposed to slaughter when you give birth. (Naanyu Loonyek)

Some of the excess livestock not taken to the lowlands were sold, although marketing was also tightly controlled by the colonial regime, and people were not highly motivated to sell since their cash needs were limited to paying taxes and buying small amounts of maize meal, clothing, and sundry goods.

The second aspect of the grazing schemes that was important was the way they were enforced. Armed officers, the grazing guards, patrolled the schemes and seized any livestock found grazing where they were not permitted. They also conducted spot checks on stock quotas by visiting homesteads, counting animals, and counterchecking with grazing permits. Anyone found with excess numbers of stock was liable to be arrested, fined, and/or the excess stock confiscated. It is this element of the schemes that was particularly irksome to the people. While they claim that the controls on grazing may have been beneficial in preserving pasture, they feared and resented the grazing guards and their draconian enforcement of the rules. These remarks by an elder reveal the close degree of monitoring and enforcement characteristic of the schemes.

> It [the grazing scheme] was introduced by the white government. The DC was a white man. He was in charge of all departments. They closed this side. They closed one side and told people to graze on another side. When cattle grazed on the closed side, the grazing guard scout [arrests you] and takes you to Maralal. Then they fine you. If one has no money to pay the fine, they take your cattle. And if they never caught you grazing in the closed areas, they could even close the forest. They could decide to close it for six months. When there is long grass, they opened it and let all people graze on that side, and the other one is closed. Later, they count all the cattle and record them according to the number you have. They branded all of them on the thigh, so that it is known that this cow is from Lorroki. We took the calves to the lowlands. When they catch you with calves, they arrest you saying that you brought the lowland cattle here. There was no limitation on cattle in the lowlands. When they count cattle and cross check with your permit and you are found with excess, then they arrest you. So, we were trying to keep the number allowed. There was a boundary between lowlands and highlands. When you take the excess cattle down to the lowlands, then you could relax. So, you continued sending the calves down. They also became adult cows there. It was like that during grazing guard. (Lopile Lemagas)

When asked whether the grazing guards were susceptible to bribery, most informants insisted that they were not, that they zealously carried out their jobs and that attempts to bribe them by giving them small stock usually failed. People explained that it really was not the fault of the guards, themselves, because they were at the bottom of a chain of command, and their work was closely supervised by their bosses. They would lose their jobs if found to be lax in enforcing the rules of the schemes.

Grazing schemes continued throughout the 1950s with only a few instances of significant resistance. However, as independence neared, and emboldened by a new generation of politicians who championed opposition to the grazing controls, the elders cursed the schemes and refused to comply with them. For Samburu people, the curse is a powerful sanction, normally employed against individuals or groups who commit serious violations of social norms. Most Samburu believe that the curse carries power to inflict real harm, even death, on those it is brought against. By cursing the grazing schemes, the elders were using one of the only means available to them to express their deep dissatisfaction against the controls. This mass defiance spelled the end of the schemes in 1961.

Samburu Attitudes toward Authority

The way people talk about the grazing schemes today is suggestive of their ambivalent feelings toward colonial authority in general. On the one hand, many people reflect on the grazing schemes as having had positive effects in terms of the health of livestock. They argue that limiting the population of cattle on Lorroki plateau and, especially, providing veterinary services, as the colonial regime did, resulted in fat, healthy animals. The fact that there was no major drought between 1930 and 1950 likely also contributed to this outcome. Informants often comment upon the good rains that prevailed over much of this period. On the other hand, they resented the limitations on movements and the militaristic implementation of grazing controls. However, they realized their impotence in the face of overwhelming British power. As one elder stated, "If you didn't like the schemes, you could move to the lowlands." This man actually did move away, to Wamba, but ultimately the schemes followed him even there.

Likewise, when discussing colonial authority more generally, many people refer to the benefits of order and efficient government services (veterinary and health) that they received during the colonial period. These feelings, of course, may be heightened by the lack of either of these today. At the same time, most people make it clear that they prefer an independent Kenya to colonial status—though, from their point of view, the independent government that replaced the British was almost equally as alien to them, in that it was dominated by other ethnic groups with different interests from those of the Samburu.

Thus, individuals' attitudes toward colonial authority were complex. While they appreciated some of the practical benefits provided by a strong state, they disliked the very force that undergirded that power. What is clear is that the first experience Samburu people had with an external government was one that interfered directly in the intricacies of their livelihood system and backed up its policies with the use of force. Accordingly, the costs of resistance were extremely high, and so most Samburu complied with the policies, or tried to.

Given this apparent acquiescence to authority, we may question why they finally cursed the schemes shortly before independence. A number of reasons explain this seemingly inconsistent event. First, political leaders emerged who assumed many of the risks of acting collectively against the schemes. Land and rights to land were major themes in the Kenyan independence struggle, and attacks on the grazing schemes were the closest proxy to the land question on which the new leaders in Samburu could focus in their bids for political support.[2] By mobilizing the population in opposition to the schemes, they stood to gain significantly in the electoral process. For the leaders, potential political gains outweighed the risks of challenging government policy. Second, by the early 1960s it was clear that British colonial rule in Kenya was ending and that the regime would be unable to enforce its policies. This considerably lowered the risks of punishment for flouting British authority. Third, cursing the schemes collectively spread the costs across the entire population, meaning that it was very unlikely that any individuals, apart from the leaders, would be punished.

However, in spite of their resistance to the schemes at the end of the colonial period, I contend that the Samburu people's experiences with the grazing schemes shaped their responses to postindependence policies as well, rendering them less likely to challenge policies emanating from central government. The conditions that enabled people to reject the grazing schemes in the early 1960s no longer existed when land adjudication policies were implemented in the mid-1970s: the independent government of Kenya was not going away, political leaders usually supported land adjudication policies, and individuals were likely to be punished for their opposition, as I will show later. Therefore, the fact that the Samburu collectively cursed the schemes at the end of the colonial period does not negate the fact that most individual Samburu had developed a habit of obeying governmental authority through their experiences with the strong British colonial state.

The Origins of Policies Favoring Private Property

While grazing schemes were in effect in Samburu District during the 1950s, moves toward private ownership of land were proceeding apace in other parts of the country. These culminated in the Swynnerton Plan of 1954 that established individual freehold title to land as the norm for Kenya. This set the stage for redistribution of white settler lands at independence, which secured the primacy of the title deed as the ultimate security for land ownership and entrenched a class of landed gentry at the helm of the postcolonial state.

It was acknowledged by government (colonial and postcolonial) that individual land ownership did not make sense in the arid rangelands. Instead, the Swynnerton Plan recommended expansion and intensification of the grazing schemes together with improved marketing channels to increase the off-take of stock and keep numbers below what was considered the carrying capacity of the land. Suggestions made in the Swynnerton Plan were further developed after independence in 1963. Rather than continue with government-controlled grazing schemes, the postindependence period saw the birth of the concept of group ownership of the rangelands.

During the 1960s, arguments emerged to the effect that communal land ownership resulted inevitably in the overuse of rangelands since no individual user has an incentive to invest in preserving the land while all users have incentives to exploit it. Reminiscent of colonial-era administrators, many academics argued that without some form of control, communal lands would become hopelessly degraded. This "tragedy of the commons" was most famously explicated by Garrett Hardin in a 1968 article and became the mantra of many working in the field of range management. While these arguments have since been challenged by a growing literature on management of common pool resources, they were critical to the 1960s genesis of the group ranch concept.[3] Indeed, this is a striking case of the rather direct translation of ideas generated in academia into government policy.[4] Certainly, the fact that the young Kenyan government sought donor support meant they were susceptible to policy prescriptions coming from donor agencies who were in turn influenced by academic research. Furthermore, because the Kenyan government was made up primarily of individuals from agricultural, not pastoral, backgrounds, and these individuals had been trained during the colonial period when grazing schemes were in effect, they were more sympathetic toward policies aimed at controlling and "rationalizing" pastoralism. Finally, there is evidence that the entire group ranch concept was viewed by many as one stage toward eventual privatization of land in semiarid parts of the country, which not only would be consistent with overall policy on land tenure but also provided the prospect of access to huge areas of land for a land-hungry agricultural population.[5]

In order to avoid the seemingly certain demise of the communal range-lands, the government developed a concept of group ownership of land, termed *group ranches*. Group ranches transferred rights in land from the government to residents of pastoralist areas through a process of registration of ranch members. The intention was that ranch members would cooperate in managing their jointly owned land. Although livestock would remain individually owned, planners encouraged ranch members to reduce livestock numbers in line with the carrying capacity of land and to reorient their production strategy more toward market production of beef animals and away from their traditional emphasis on milk production for home consumption. Regulating grazing areas and practicing rotational grazing was also part of the range management strategy developed by planners. Thus, the group ranches resembled colonial-era grazing schemes in their emphasis on market production and controlled grazing. However, they differed significantly from those grazing schemes in that ownership rights and management responsibilities were transferred from government into the hands of group ranch members.

It was felt that some type of shared land tenure was necessary for the success of group ranches, since without land as collateral, the groups would be unable to raise capital from banks to finance improvements to their land (Lawrance et al. 1966). With assistance from the World Bank and a consortium of donors, group ranches were established in the arid and semiarid rangelands, starting in the 1960s with the Maasai districts and extending, in the 1970s, into Samburu District and several other districts in the country.

The Land Adjudication Process

The idea of the group ranch is relatively straightforward. A geographic area is demarcated as an adjudication section. Within this section, all those individuals with legitimate claims to land in the area are registered as members of one or more group ranches. What constitutes a "legitimate claim" is difficult to discern from the records available on land adjudication in Samburu. As I discuss in more detail later, very little information was given to people about the registration process or the criteria to be used to select members of ranches. The Land Adjudication Act (Chapter 284) defers to customary law to make determinations about land claims but also empowers the staff of the Ministry of Lands and Settlements to make decisions regarding land claims. Relying on customary law is problematic for pastoralist communities who have no concept of land ownership and who are semi-nomadic. In Samburu, long-term residency in the adjudication area appears to have been the primary criterion for membership. Virtually all individuals who were registered were adult males. Women and minors were not included in the registration process. In some cases, if a man was deceased and had no adult male heirs, his widow could be registered. The number of group ranches established within an adjudication section depended on the size determined to be ideal. In Maasai areas, the first to be adjudicated, significant efforts were made to establish a feasible unit for the group ranch, based on both ecological and social criteria (Rutten 1992, 270–72). Finding a suitable land unit in Samburu was a more arbitrary process than in Maasailand, based roughly on geographic features and to some extent on clan settlement areas.

The adjudication process comprises several stages. First, a land adjudication committee of at least ten members is formed, made up of community members (elder males) from the adjudication section. Next, all adult males with a claim to land in the area are registered as group members. At this time, any individuals wishing to claim an individual parcel of land may apply to the local land committee. The committee deliberates on their request and either approves or rejects it. If rejected, the claimant can appeal to the District Land Arbitration Board, which hears the case and either approves or rejects the request.[6]

Once all members of the group ranch have been registered, the adjudication register is deemed complete and opened to the public for inspection. Objections to the register may be filed within sixty days of its completion. People may object in order to request membership in the group, to claim land, to challenge the inclusion of a member or to dispute a land allocation. Thus, someone whose claim for individual land was rejected at earlier stages could at this point file an objection to the District Land Adjudication Officer (DLAO) requesting land. These objections are heard and decided by the DLAO. Members of the local land committee are present at the hearings, as representatives of the group ranch, but the final decisions regarding objections lie with the DLAO alone. Parties not satisfied with the DLAO's decision have sixty days within which to file an appeal to the Minister of Lands and Settlements. These appeals are normally delegated to the District Commissioner for decision (see fig. 2 for a flow chart of the main stages of the land adjudication process).

When all these stages are completed, the group ranch is declared, and the members become shareholders in the group who are supposed to jointly manage the resources therein for their common benefit: "The group repre-

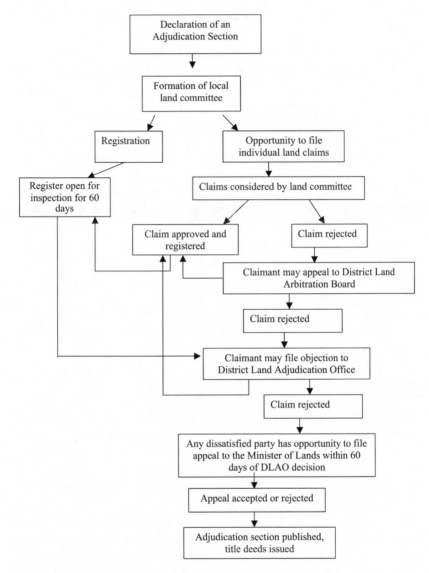

Fig. 2. Flow chart of stages in the land adjudication process in
Samburu District

sentatives shall hold the land and other assets of the group on behalf and for the collective benefit of all members of the group" (Republic of Kenya 1970). The fact that individual group members were conceived as shareholders intimated the possibility that shares could be divided at some later date, even though no concrete plans on how this would be done emerged until the 1980s, when groups in Kajiado District began to demand subdivision.

With title to the group ranch, its members could use the land as collateral for loans that, it was hoped, would enable them to develop their ranches by installing important production and marketing infrastructure. Initially, development assistance was made available through the donor projects and the Agricultural Finance Corporation (AFC) to help the groups get established and set up management structures and procedures. What was envisioned by the range planners was a rationally functioning commercial ranch that would produce beef for the national market. Not only would land be preserved, but productivity would increase as modern methods were applied. As it turned out, these expectations were hopelessly at odds with the reality of the existing pastoral systems.

Group ranches have never performed as they were intended. The failure of group ranches has been documented elsewhere (Hedlund 1979; Grandin 1981; Galaty 1992; Rutten 1992; Scoones 1994; Kimani and Pickard 1998), but suffice it to say that the entire concept of the group as a production unit wherein livestock would be managed jointly but owned individually was never adopted by the group ranch members, neither in Maasai areas nor in Samburu. The idea that stock quotas and regulated off-take would be implemented was abhorrent to people who had recently repudiated the colonial schemes due precisely to such practices. In Samburu, it appears that there was very little effort by government staff to educate people as to the rationale for group ranches as management units. Rather, the effort was geared toward registering members of groups. Many people agreed to register reluctantly, and this out of the belief that registration would secure their rights to the land they occupied. This defensive basis for membership in group ranches meant that they never behaved as management units at all. Further compounding their failure, the advent of group ranches set in train processes of social conflict still being played out today.

The Beginning of Land Adjudication in Samburu District

Following on progress made in the Maasai districts of Narok and Kajiado, land adjudication began in Samburu District in the early 1970s. At independence, Crown land, now termed *trust land,* had been transferred to the control of the County Councils, the local government bodies. In Samburu, the former clerk to the Samburu County Council recalled that a Maasai man who was Provincial Range Officer came to initiate land adjudication in Samburu. A committee was formed at district level to encourage the formation of group ranches. Prominent government officials including the clerk, a paramount chief, and a Samburu who was in the provincial administration were appointed to the committee. They traveled around the district trying to convince people about the importance of land ownership.

> To the committee, the main importance of forming group ranches was in order to secure title to the land. A tour to Kajiado showed them that the Maasai liked group ranches. Ownership was important in order to prevent others from encroaching on the land, particularly the [neighboring agricultural] Kikuyu. Encroachment from the Kikuyu was feared since Kenyatta [a Kikuyu] was still president and was resettling Kikuyu in many areas of Rift Valley Province. An MP, G. G. Kariuki, from Laikipia, had threatened that Kikuyus might buy land in Laikipia and then proceed to Samburu. Thus, these committee members, who were educated and had been more exposed to things outside Samburu District, believed that having group ranches was important to obtain ownership of the land and to protect it from outsiders. (field note 21, August 22, 2000)

While the committee members believed that owning land was important, it was not an easy task to convince ordinary people of this fact. Most people were not interested in owning land, which they viewed as a common resource without any owner, and they rejected the idea of group ranches. The committee's efforts to enlighten people on the value of title deeds were met with incomprehension (what is a title deed?) or resistance to the idea.

In spite of this lack of understanding among the general population, adjudication sections were established by the staff of the Ministry of Lands and Settlements, under whose responsibility the formation of group ranches falls. According to the former clerk, force had to be used to get the process started. The committee would visit an area, establish boundaries, and begin the process of registering members, with or without the consent of the local people.

As we saw in the discussion of colonial grazing schemes, people developed a tendency to go along with government policies, even when they did not agree with them completely. Since the group ranches were government policy, people felt duty bound to accept, even though they did not have a clear understanding of what was happening. In some cases, people believed that the group ranches were a transitory stage, something that would end, as the grazing schemes had. Lanyasunya (1990), in a study of the formation of group ranches in Samburu District, had similar findings. Eighty percent of the respondents in his study claimed that they accepted group ranches because it was government policy, and they believed group ranches would be short-lived (Lanyasunya 1990, 50). Not realizing the permanency of the institution, they did not accord it that much attention.

The fact that people did not comprehend the land adjudication process and that they perceived it as a temporary situation provided space for those who were seeking private land to obtain it without much opposition from the local communities. This happened in all the adjudication sections in Samburu. As we will see, it was only in Siambu that opposition to individual holdings was strong and successful.

Mbaringon: A Typical Case of Land Adjudication

Lodogejek (bloody legs) adjudication section was established on December 6, 1972. It was the first section established in the district. Located in the southeastern corner of Lorroki plateau, Lodogejek is primarily composed of open plains bordered on the eastern side by the Kirisia Hills and to the south by the Uaso Nyiro river that forms the boundary with Laikipia District. The land is punctuated by a series of springs, the largest being the salt springs at Kisima. The combination of plains grasslands, forested hills, and permanent springs provides an excellent site for extensive livestock production. The plains provide ample grazing during wet seasons, which is easy to access due to the openness of the land. In the dry season, cattle and small stock make use of the pastures in the forest. The springs provide water year-round, and the mineral salts at Kisima eliminate the need to take livestock far away for these essential nutrients. Six group ranches were eventually carved out of Lodogejek section, one of which was Mbaringon group ranch.

Mbaringon is nestled at the base of the Kirisia hills and is currently home to about 2,500 people. Most people are members of the *Pisikishu* (spotted cattle) section of the Nkishu Naarok moiety. In fact, the majority are from one clan within Pisikishu, called Sitat. Many families trace their origins to a Maasai clan, the Laikipiak, who were decimated during the Maasai interclan wars of the mid-1800s. In addition, there is a group of families that were traditionally hunter-gatherers. Called *Ndorobo* (poor) by the Samburu due to their historical lack of livestock, these people remain poor in livestock today and rely heavily on the resources available in the Kirisia forest such as honey and wild game. In spite of their differences from more "pure" Samburu, the Ndorobo, or Ndikiri as they call themselves, in Mbaringon are highly integrated into the community. They participate in daily affairs, intermarry with Samburu families, and share essentially the same language and dress as the Samburu.

When Lodogejek adjudication section was formed, a land adjudication committee of twelve members was selected, although there are no records available documenting meetings or decisions of this committee. In Mbaringon, the news that land was to be adjudicated and group ranches formed was met with surprise. Most people did not understand what was happening or what it meant to adjudicate land. In some cases, there appeared to be confusion between this process of adjudication and the colonial-era grazing schemes. Although the group ranch idea was new, people were reluctant to refuse since it was a directive from the government.

In Lodogejek section, five men sought individual land during the adjudication process. Two of them were members of the district land committee, mentioned earlier. Another was the member of Parliament for Samburu West at the time. These were men who were working in government and who understood the process of land adjudication. They were aware that during adjudication people were allowed to make claims for individual land.

In principle, the local land adjudication committee had the mandate to deliberate on these requests. If denied land by the committee, the claimant could appeal to higher levels. However, in this case, it is doubtful that the committee ever met to hear the claims of these individuals. There are no records of committee meetings, and the man who was chairman of Mbaringon group ranch at that time denies that the committee was ever called to hear these cases. Indeed, his description of events of the time highlights the fact that most committee members did not understand what was happening, nor were they properly apprised of the legal procedures for adjudication.

> People came who wanted to divide the land. It was as if now you say, "I'm taking that place to live," another says "I'm taking here," another says "I'm taking here," another says, "I'm taking here." . . . Now, these people who started this work, began doing it in secret. They picked some people to do this work secretly. . . .

Then they came and told the elders here, "We want a senior man to
be on the land committee." Well, all the elders from our area, the Lkili-
ako, the Lmekuri, the Lkimaniki [age-sets], they chose me. . . . Then, we
began to see that these people had something in mind. We saw. And we
said we should get involved. One day they came to my settlement and
said, "Come here," they said, "Now, the government has given some land
to L——." The government has given the land. You hear. The government has given the land, and this land is shown on the map. I asked
where was this land? They said at the stream of Lelamuriai. . . . So, I
asked if it was the map that knew how to divide the land, or the people of
the area? They said, it's the map. But they had already put a beacon at the
stream called Lekimenchu. They had gone and put a beacon there, like it
or not. They wanted to see what I would do. They told me to follow them
so that I can tell where the land is to be divided. But they had finished already. They told me to come and show them where the land should be divided. So, I then realized there was something going on. We went up to
the stream Lekimenchu where they stayed and showed the map. I told
them, "That's not the way it should be. Isn't that man a Loimusi?" "But
he's not from the side of Loimusi," they said. "How is it he's here," I
asked? (Letere Larari)

The chairman by this time realized that the land adjudication officers had
already marked off land for allocation to a prominent man who was not from
Mbaringon, not even from Pisikishu section. He was from the Loimusi section, though the officers were claiming that he still had rights to claim land in
Mbaringon. The chairman agreed to accompany the officers to their camp,
where he was surprised to find the very individuals who were seeking private
land. When these men heard that he was against their being allocated land,
they began to threaten him. The chairman recounts what happened when
they met at the surveyors' camp.

They [the land officers] said, "Here he is." They asked, "Is this him?"
They said, "Yes." I didn't want to be involved at all. I was standing at a
distance. They said, "Tell that man that the government has said that anyone who refuses [individual land allocations] will be taken to Nakuru [the
provincial capital]. If you refuse, you'll go to Nakuru. You hear. If you
refuse, you go to Nakuru." I told them, "Tell them I'm not going." I said,
"I'm not going." They said, "If you don't want the land divided, you'll be
jailed in Nakuru. If you don't want to divide land, you'll be jailed in

Nakuru. The government has said you'll go to Nakuru." I said, "Tell them I'm not going." They told them that. I said, "Since you've already agreed on that, then do what you want to do, do what you want to do." I'm telling you, how many other people would I be oppressing [if I agreed]? People who also wanted to benefit from their land. What was I looking for in Nakuru? If they could threaten me here, what about in Nakuru? So, I told them to do what they wanted, because I'm not going. They wrote my name in the book while I was watching. They asked me what my name was and I told them. Then, while I was standing over there, I watched them put my signature in the book. They just went on dividing the land. I went home. (Letere Larari)

In this case, the chairman's "consent" to the allocation of land to individuals was achieved by forging his signature on the necessary document. When he tried to object, he was threatened that he would be "taken to Nakuru," meaning that he would be arrested, presumably for interfering in the work of adjudication. While this appears to have been an idle threat, since as a committee member he had every right to object to an allocation of land, he took it seriously, realizing that the individuals seeking land had the backing of the government.

Other people soon found out that individuals were making claims to land in their area. Most people were against individuals being given land, while others did not appreciate the permanence of such land allocations and, thus, were not overly concerned about them. In any case, few complaints were voiced against these allocations. Only one letter was written challenging the allocations, but no subsequent correspondence or action on the matter is documented. An objection was lodged against one allocation. However, in the objection hearing, those who had brought the objection against the allocation reversed themselves and agreed to it.

Notwithstanding these few complaints, the majority of people feared to object to something being implemented by the government. Even those who admit that they wanted to complain say they did not know how to go about it. According to the former chairman of the committee, the land officers were involved in and supporting the individual claimants. They are the same officers whose duty it was to inform people of their right to object to particular land allocations. The language barrier also came into play in this connection. Several people noted in interviews that the government officers who came to conduct the adjudication exercise were not Samburu. Very few Samburu people at that time spoke Kiswahili, so even communicating with the officers was difficult, a point emphasized by the former chairman when describing how he was intimidated by the land officers and the individuals seeking land.

There is no evidence that people in Mbaringon were made aware of their rights or the basic procedures pertaining to land adjudication. Even registering their own names as members of the group was something they did with little or no cognizance of its significance. Thus, people who were already hesitant to challenge the government due to their experiences with the colonial regime also lacked the knowledge of how to go about it. The combination of these factors meant that no serious steps were taken to prevent allocation of land to individuals.

By 1974, Lodogejek adjudication area had been divided into six group ranches, including Mbaringon group ranch. The five individuals who had applied for their own land were awarded individual ranches, and other areas were set aside for public utilities. The total area of the individual ranches was about 1,500 hectares, 36 percent the size of Mbaringon group ranch, which had 307 registered members.

Lodogejek is a good example of the typical course of events in adjudication sections in Samburu District. Most adjudication sections resulted in several group ranches being formed and alongside these a number of individual ranches. Some of the individual ranches are sizable, up to four or five thousand acres in size, while the average group ranch size is about thirty-two thousand acres with an average membership of 242 (Republic of Kenya 1996).[7] As of 1999, there were 36 group ranches in the district. It is difficult to establish precisely the number of individual ranches. The Samburu land register lists 28 individual ranches, but this figure does not include the 239 individual parcels that were eventually registered in Siambu, and it may also be missing others since it appears not to have been kept up to date. One reason it is difficult to ascertain the number of individual ranches is that once land has been granted to individuals it no longer comes under the aegis of the department of land adjudication.

CHAPTER 4

Land Adjudication in Siambu:
The Struggle over Privatization

Siambu (which means striped) is a broad treeless plain cut through by river valleys lined with indigenous cedar and podo trees and flanked on its southern end by a series of hills that surround Poro trading center, the commercial and administrative center of the location. It lies at the northwestern end of the Lorroki plateau, about forty kilometers northwest of Mbaringon. At Malasso, on the edge of the Siambu plain, the land falls away over a steep escarpment. There is a panoramic view of the Rift Valley floor, and on a clear day you can see across the treacherous Sukuta Valley, desert hideout of cattle raiders, to Turkana District in the west. To the north, Mt. Nyiro and the Ndoto range, landmarks of Baragoi division, are visible. This is the highest point in Samburu District, and also the coldest. One hill is named *lalmarai* (the ribs), referring to the tendency of people to develop pneumonia here. Although it was frequented by Samburu herders at least since the latter 1800s, more permanent settlement in this area came rather later than in most other areas of Lorroki, mostly since the 1960s. By permanent, I mean that homesteads were established, and the area was used on a more continual basis than when it had just served as a dry season grazing reserve for cattle.

Besides the cold and wet weather, there was the additional risk of raids from the neighboring Turkana to deter permanent settlement. On the eve of land adjudication in 1978, most people had vacated Siambu proper and were living around Poro town due to incursions from the Turkana. Nowadays, people take pride in the fact that they are sticking fast on their land, now privately owned, and not running away, even when raids by Turkana in neighboring areas are intense, as in 1996.

The people in Siambu are primarily of the Lotimi (baboons) clan of the Lmasula section. According to legend, the founding ancestor of the Lotimi clan was lost as a boy, and he hid on some rocks where baboons lived. He was cared for by the baboons for a time before being discovered and adopted by people—thus the clan name, Lotimi. Another legend relates how the Lmasula clan was blessed by their ancestors to live on mountains and hills. These places are spiritually important to the Samburu, as places where God (*Nkai*) tends to reside. Certain key parts of ceremonies are conducted on the mountains, and the Lmasula, as the ritually senior clan, carry out these parts of ceremonies.

There are a few families from other Lmasula sections in Siambu, but Lotimi make up the vast majority of the population. Within Lotimi are two subclans (*ndipat*), called Kurpa and Siit. The population is about evenly split between the two subclans, and there is one very large family from Kurpa and another from Siit. The power relations of these two subclans are expressed in the fact that each subclan holds power in key institutions. For example, the chief of the area is Kurpa, while the councilor is Siit. The chairman of the group ranch (Porokwai) is Kurpa, while the vice chairman is Siit. It is not entirely clear whether these relations of power are consciously and explicitly chosen, but there is a definite tendency for balancing power between the two subclans.

While Siambu was one of the areas settled latest, it was one of the earliest places where people began experimenting with agriculture. A number of informants noted how people began farming in the area in the early 1960s. One man said that the reason he moved to Siambu from nearby Morijo was because he saw the promise of agriculture in the area and he wanted to try it himself.

> In that time [1960s], people started to grow crops. I came here, and I realized that this soil is good and rich compared to that of Morijo, which is hot. Then, I decided to move here. During that time nobody had power over another. So, people were free to move wherever they like. The community members living here are Lmasula. So, I stayed from that time till now when land subdivision was done. (Lopile Lemagas)

Those who dabbled in farming earliest had learned about it during military service or from other jobs that took them outside the district. Many people remembered how amazed they were when they discovered that maize came from planting something in the earth, a concept foreign to Samburu who traditionally disdain any activity that involves digging in the ground. One elder who had served in the army during World War II recalled the first farms.

> By then, when we came here, it was only Lerte who had a farm, then Lolgeeti also had one and planted some potatoes and pepper, and we asked ourselves about those things because we didn't know them. We came to know something called maize and we were really amazed. We even ate it raw! (Loyeku Ledonyo)

Most people retained their negative attitude toward farming, but a few became intrigued and decided to give it a try themselves. These individuals sought advice from the ones who knew something, and in this way a small group of people began to cultivate the land, albeit on a very small scale.

The relatively high rainfall and fertile soils of the area did attract some individuals to settle in Siambu. For example, one man who was originally from Baragoi, a dry, lowland area, was employed in the prison services. He learned about agriculture and was the manager of a prison farm for many years. It was partly by luck that he first came to Siambu, having been allocated a commercial plot in Poro town. However, when he retired he decided to settle permanently in Siambu largely due to his interest in agriculture. Today, he is one of the most active farmers in the area, cultivating eight acres and recently acquiring three dairy cattle, the first in the area. In spite of these early forays into agriculture, the Samburu in Siambu were, and still remain today, primarily pastoralists, and livestock are the mainstay of almost everyone's livelihood.

The Beginning of Land Adjudication in Siambu

Siambu was part of the Poro B land adjudication section. This section was declared in 1978, after Lodogejek and a few other sections had been completed. Land adjudication was still a new idea and unfamiliar to most people in Siambu. A local committee was selected by residents of the area, and, unlike in Lodogejek, its meetings were documented and reveal the kinds of deliberations that went on during the period of land adjudication and demarcation. Men appointed to the committee were chosen primarily due to their experience and leadership in the area. Some informants, including some committee members, contend that they were chosen because of their opposition to land adjudication. Presumably, it was believed that the land would be in safer hands if the committee members were against land adjudication. Perhaps this criterion was an indication that at least some people in the community already feared that land might be "lost" during adjudication. Although they were ostensibly against land adjudication, about half the committee members ended up requesting individual farms for themselves.

The early stages of land adjudication in Siambu look like a textbook example of the adjudication process as it is supposed to proceed. The committee was chosen, and residents of the area were registered as members of Siambu group ranch. At the same time, some individuals requested private farms from the local committee. The committee deliberated on their requests and approved ten out of twenty requests. Eight of those whose requests were denied appealed these decisions to the District Arbitration Board. The arbitration board, made up of twenty-five members selected by the provincial commissioner, granted three requests and denied five requests.

In 1982, the adjudication register for Siambu was completed. At this point, those individuals who disagreed with the completed register for any reason had a period of sixty days during which to file objections to the adjudication register. For example, if someone was a resident of the area, but their name had been left off the register for some reason, they could file an objection to have their name entered. Or, if someone wanted an individual parcel of land but had not been given one by the local committee or the Arbitration Board, he could file an objection to be given land. After the completion of the adjudication section in 1982, a number of individuals filed objections for individual parcels. Some of these were people who had been denied land by the committee and the Arbitration Board, but a number had never applied for land before. In late 1982, the District Land Adjudication Officer (DLAO) held hearings of forty-two objections, most of them requesting individual parcels of land. The DLAO granted all but two of the objections. With the addition of these people, a total of thirty-seven individuals had been granted land in Siambu.

Who Wanted Private Land?

Most of the men (and two women) who requested individual parcels of land in Siambu had either gone to school, served in the military, been employed as civil servants, or at least had some exposure to the world beyond Samburu

District. This was also the trend in other parts of Samburu District that were adjudicated at this time. However, the number of individuals seeking land in Siambu was higher than in most other areas, a fact that might be partly explained by the unusually high level of educational attainment in Siambu. Out of the thirty-seven individuals who were granted land, nineteen (51 percent) were in the household survey conducted for this study. Of those surveyed, eleven (58 percent) had some education, and seven (37 percent) had seven or more years of education. These are relatively high levels of education (e.g., compared with Mbaringon) considering the limited access to education in the 1960s and 1970s and the high dropout rates characteristic among Samburu. Indeed, only 44 percent of all adults in the Siambu sample had any education, and a mere 10 percent had more than eight years of education. Men in the Lkishili (forty-eight to sixty-two years) and Lkimaniki (over sixty-three years) age groups in the survey averaged only one year of education, whereas those surveyed who sought individual land (all but one of whom were from these two age groups) averaged 3.7 years of education (see chapter 7 for details on education and comparison with Mbaringon).

Just over half of those surveyed were engaged in business or employment. Six served in the military, comprising the total for military service in the entire sample for Siambu. That is, every man who served in the military in the household sample had also applied for individual land. Many of the earliest requests for land, made to the land adjudication office even before Poro B was declared an adjudication section, came from men in the army or civil servants working outside the district. Invariably they claimed that they came from Siambu and they wanted their own land for "development."[1]

Robert Bates (1989) has discussed the advantages that accrued to educated individuals during the struggle over property rights. His analysis of the Kikuyu during the colonial era appears equally applicable in the Samburu case.

> Certain social categories, then—rural entrepreneurs and the educated, sometimes called the *athomi* (those who can read)—were specially motivated to engage in the legal struggle to redefine entitlements to real property. . . . Not only did the educated possess strong incentives to demand legal changes; but also, within the context of the colonial order, they confronted lower costs in pushing legal claims. The educated spoke the language of the colonizers and the colonizers were dependent upon them for insight into local law and custom. (30)

Similarly, the educated and employed Samburu had a heightened understanding of the value of private land stemming from their experiences in areas of the country where private property was the norm (see chapter 6 for case studies). Furthermore, these individuals had gained knowledge and experience through their work that enabled them to understand the process of land adjudication, including the possibility of requesting individual land. The details of these procedures remained mysterious to most people within the district.

Not only were they aware that they could ask for private land, but some even used their positions as "faithful servants of the country" to assert their rights to land. This is evident in letters sent from the superior officers of some Samburu soldiers to the land adjudication office pleading the case of their juniors to be given land. In his study of African military service in the Kenya colonial army, Parsons (1999) argues that deliberate efforts were made to inculcate a sense of esprit de corps among army personnel. These efforts often led to feelings of superiority among soldiers. It also resulted in demands for special treatment and privileges, many of which were granted by the army (Parsons 1999, 5–6). In Samburu District, there is historical precedent for granting concessions to ex–army personnel. During the colonial period, retiring army men requested generous stock quotas on the grazing schemes in Lorroki. Efforts were made by the colonial administrators to meet these requests, apparently in appreciation of their service to the country (Kenya Colony 1943, 1945). Thus, it is not surprising to find demands for special consideration on land issues emanating from the armed services.

Indeed, it appears there was a conscious plan to settle retiring army personnel on private land in Samburu. One man who received a large individual farm in Poro A adjudication area (adjacent to Poro B but registered earlier) had been in the army, and he recalled how he was brought to the area and told to pick out the area he wanted, and this later was given to him as a private parcel.

> These group ranches were started in 1973. They gave us farms, all the people who worked in government or had been educated, because ordinary Samburu people did not want it. All those who were in the army, police and prisons, even businessmen; we were told [by the elders] that we can't make decisions about land. There was a land officer from Nakuru, known as Lesadera, a Maasai. He came and said, "You foolish Samburus, you're just staying and the land has gone. Strangers will come and take

the land. So what you should do is to get up and claim your land, and I'll sign for you, that's what I came here to do, because I'm a Samburu and a Maasai." We thought about it very deeply. Those among us who had jobs, because we had gone to many places, and we were somewhat knowledgeable about the management of land. . . . If you retire or resign from a job in those good days, you were asked what you wanted to do after going home. . . . I was with a Kamba man who was among the first people to get a piece of land in his home area. I was also with a captain in the colonial army. We came and roamed all over this place, and I chose to have a piece of land on these hills. It is just now that these people are envious, because the place was given to me and was also signed on my behalf by the Kenya Army during those days. (Parnas Leshampa)

These remarks reveal the extent to which those who sought private land felt they were only exercising rights that had been conferred on them by the government due to their particular position within it, in this case as soldiers. The fact that they were violating Samburu notions about land ownership was secondary, in their reasoning, to conforming to the expectations of the wider Kenyan society. In their minds, they were doing the Samburu a service by occupying and securing the land against outsiders who were poised to grab it, as the Maasai land officer warned.

Aside from becoming more aware of their rights and more conversant with government procedures regarding land, men in army service often had opportunities to observe and learn about crop farming. A number of informants told me how they had first seen crops during their army service in other parts of the country. This type of comment was typical.

I went through many places during my days as a soldier. I went as far as Ukambani, Nandi land and came across such [farming] activities, and I understood it. Then, I came and did it by myself. (Loyeku Ledonyo)

They were surprised to find people farming land equally as dry as many parts of Samburu, and they were impressed with the kinds of yields they obtained. These experiences piqued the interest of a few men in practicing agriculture. They began to experiment with growing crops when they returned to Siambu, but these experiments were not welcomed by their neighbors. Most people did not see any value in growing crops, and they resented land being used for that purpose since it interfered with the movement of livestock. One elder remembered, "When you told them do not graze animals in the farm, they ask 'what is a farm?' [a useless thing] and the owner of the farm hates that. When they saw you digging, they wonder why you are digging."

Others who requested private land were civil servants, such as chiefs and councilors of the area, people working in the land adjudication department and businessmen with shops in Poro town. These men were among the first generation of Samburu to enter the formal education system in the 1950s and 1960s. Education spread slowly among the Samburu at this time, and boys were often taken to school by force, over the protests of their families. The man who later worked in the prison system described how he first went to school, at age seven.

> They said that L _____ s will send one child, L _____ one child, then Ndoto area will send how many boys? Six. By force, no pleading. So, they came to my father's settlement, and they asked, "Whom have you decided to send?" and they said, "This one." When I was caught, my mother started to fight. She was fighting chiefs! I was taken up to school. Six of us were brought. (Jonas Lalbarta)

He was taken to a boarding school run by the Catholic mission about 50 kilometers from home. He remained at the school for most of the next four years, only visiting home during school holidays. After passing the examination after the fourth year, he went on to the next level, to another boarding school that was more than 150 kilometers from his home.

Each successive stage of education took him further away from home, not only physically, but also intellectually and socially. The curriculum was based on the British system and certainly did not inculcate an understanding of or appreciation for the intricacies of pastoralism. To the contrary, the bias was toward British standards and values with a vocational emphasis included so as to be more practical for the Kenyan setting. It is not surprising that these men, separated from their families at young ages and for extended periods, adopted many beliefs that were inconsistent with Samburu culture. Ideas about property and private ownership were only one set of such beliefs.

Not all the applicants for land were male, educated, and employed. Two sisters also requested land. They were uneducated, single mothers who realized that if they were left out of the adjudication process they would have difficulty securing their rights to land. Since membership in group ranches was restricted to adult males, they began by requesting membership in the group ranch, an exception that was reluctantly agreed to by the elders. Describing why she decided to seek registration as a group member, one of the women gave this explanation.

> When I was circumcised, I did not get married. I stayed in my mother's home and had two children. . . . When people were going to register themselves for farms, which Samburus were looking for, the first ones, God gave me knowledge and then I said, I will go be registered because I am a girl who doesn't have anything. . . . it's better to go so that they will include me in the register so that I can get a place where I will farm for my children. (Jane Letwampa)

In this case, the woman's mother was a widow, and only her two brothers were to be registered for membership in the group ranch. After the sisters realized that they could request private land, knowledge they gained through one sister's boyfriend, they filed objections to the DLAO and were granted land, over opposition from the local committee. The same woman described the objection hearing held at the DLAO's office this way.

> The committee was called [by the DLAO]. We discussed. It was like a case. They [the committee representatives] decided to keep quiet because they were asked questions. They were asked why they were saying that these ladies should not be given farms, because they are women. Yet, you know well that in other tribes they have right to get a portion because they are not married. They decided to keep quiet because they saw it was justified. By then, Lands [the DLAO] had already accepted. (Jane Letwampa)

In this case, as in many others, it was the DLAO that decided in favor of granting requests for private land, overruling the objections of local committee members who represented the group ranch in these hearings. Thus, those people who sought private land in Siambu found a sympathetic ally at the Ministry of Lands.

In trying to understand the motives of the individuals who sought private land, I have emphasized the ideological shifts that took place as part of their experiences in education, employment, and the armed services. These experiences were powerful in the sense that they provided an alternative set of norms and values relating to land use and presented the possibility of conceiving of land as something that could be privately owned. This is contrary to Samburu ideas about land that do not include a provision for private ownership. Land is there to be used by people, but it is not their possession and cannot be owned or alienated by them. Indeed, their aversion to crop production implies that interfering in the land, by digging, is inappropriate activity for human beings. Thus, these individuals' experiences served as a portal for new ideas, not just in the realm of land use and tenure but in a host of other areas as well. In this sense, they provided an alternative worldview to that of the Samburu, and to the extent that these individuals identified themselves with this view they distanced themselves from the Samburu community.

While education, employment, and military service opened up new avenues for thinking about land, it also provided access to new resources with which these individuals could pursue their interests. On the one hand, they gained literacy and language skills that gave them greater access to the state. On the other hand, they also gained economic resources that could be invested in productive enterprises. While most Samburu invest considerable income back into livestock production, many, including those who sought land in Siambu, diversify their investments. As noted, a number of applicants for individual land were investing in farming. Others had established small businesses in Poro and Maralal towns. Once they could conceive of land as an alienable commodity, it also gained value as an investment opportunity.

Individuals thought they could gain, economically, by owning land in Siambu. However, they were only able to come to such a conclusion after they had accepted the notion of land as a commodity that could be owned by individuals. To this extent, their experiences in education, employment, and military service were important in establishing the intellectual preconditions for investments in land. Differentiating the relative importance of these two forces, ideology and economic interest, is of interest in larger debates about the driving forces of social change. However, it is difficult to completely separate them in this case because both appeared to operate in the same direction. What is perhaps more interesting, and a greater contribution of this study, is how individuals took advantage of opportunities to act on their new preferences when conditions allowed and how they parlayed their access to the state into a more favorable bargaining position versus the elders. I develop this argument further in the next chapter.

How the Land Committee Worked

Government officers in charge of land adjudication were generally not forthcoming to communities about the purposes of and procedures relating to land adjudication, as noted earlier. This lack of clarity on policy issues, deliberate or not, had consequences for the operations of the local land committees that were charged with implementing adjudication policies. Lacking guidelines from above, I argue, the Siambu land committee forged its own criteria for considering individual land claims. Not surprisingly, these criteria drew on Samburu ways of adjudicating other types of cases: through consideration of personal characteristics, behavior, and history. Because the criteria they used remained implicit, the logic of the committee's proceedings is often hard to discern using the written record alone. For example, in the proceedings of land cases, seemingly objective reasons are given for accepting or rejecting requests for land, but from discussions with committee members and careful scrutiny of the records, it is clear that personalities and relationships were also important, even decisive, in making these decisions. Committee members stress that their decisions on land claims were based on whether the applicant "deserved" the land or not. In determining this, the committee members relied on their knowledge of the applicant, his character and personal history, much as they would in other cases that come before elders.

In the proceedings, the arguments used by applicants for private land emphasize a number of common themes. Claims for land are often based on long residence in the area and previous developments made by the individual in his locality. For example, if he had already farmed, fenced, built a house, or planted trees on land where he was living, these activities were brought forth as evidence that he was developing that particular area and it should be given to him. A few individuals claimed that they had already been given land by an earlier land committee for the whole Poro area, one that preceded the split into Poro A and B. Thus, they approached the committee to confirm this earlier allocation. Others asked for land based on their position as chief or councilor. They argued that they should be given land so they could serve as an example of positive development for others. People often claimed that, if given land, they had great plans for farming, introducing grade cattle, and so on. These, then, were the main reasons applicants gave for seeking land from the committee. However, while there was no applicant who failed to put forward such reasons, not all were given land.

According to the records of the committee's deliberations, people were denied land for a number of reasons. Very often, the committee that rejected land requests claimed that the land in the area was too small, or the population was too big. There simply was not enough land to give out. While this statement was often used as a general reason for not granting land, there were some cases where the committee refused requests for particular areas due to specific uses or planned uses of that place. For example, someone was refused land in an area that had a public water point. Other requests were rejected because they were in areas with salt licks or cattle dips, or in areas that the group planned to lease out for wheat farming. In these cases, the principle of private ownership was not questioned, just the specific area requested. However, the question remains why alternative areas were not given to those applicants if the one they first requested was deemed unsuitable.

The importance of personal history is revealed in some cases where requests are rejected due to the bad behavior of the applicant. In one case, land was denied to someone who was accused of having lied about his residence in the area. While he claimed to have lived in the area for a long time, the committee dismissed him as a newcomer and someone they hardly knew. The committee rejected another request arguing that the applicant had not developed his current area as he claimed. This misrepresentation was enough to dismiss his application altogether. A couple of applicants were chastised for not having had permission to cultivate land. Since they did not have permission to use land for crops in the past, their requests for individual land were denied. Ironically, while some applicants were rejected for having done too much without permission, another applicant was rejected because he had to date done no development in his area. Other applicants were told that they did not require individual land, since they could develop land within the group.

While there were many putative reasons given to reject applications for individual land, the fact that the committee approved about half of the requests means that something else was at work, since all applications could have been rejected for one reason or another. It is probably not a mere coincidence that four out of the ten individuals who got land from the committee were committee members. On the other hand, one committee member, also a local councilor, was not given land. Neither was the brother of the committee chairman. Neither was the area chief. Thus, it was not a simple case of the committee members, their friends, and powerful associates getting land. As noted earlier, the applicant had to be seen as deserving to get land, a calculation that included personal characteristics as well as objective considerations. Further, this determination had to receive approval from most, if not all, committee members.

Bribery of a sort may have played a role in the committee decisions, since applicants were expected to feed and brew beer for the committee members while they considered their case. Doing so, however, did not guarantee success. There were accusations leveled at the committee chairman to the effect that he had single-handedly given out land without the consent of other members, and that bribery may have been involved. Some of these accusations come from committee members and relate to a couple of specific cases. Others were voiced publicly by community members and appear to relate to the entire land adjudication process. The chairman, not surprisingly, denies these accusations.

Some of the dissatisfaction with the committee chairman may have emanated from his role in the objections process. This process was not well understood by the committee members and was a complete mystery to the average person. The committee chairman represented the group ranch in these objection cases where the DLAO gave out most of the land in Siambu. The fact that the chairman was at these meetings may have been construed as tacit consent or collaboration in giving away the land, even when it is clear from the proceedings that he was a vociferous opponent of most of those requesting land through objection. Many people also suspect that the land officers were bribed, not only to agree to give out land but to extend the boundaries of farms agreed to by the committee. While no one can provide definitive proof of bribery, there is a widespread perception that the adjudication process was tainted by it.

That the committee developed and employed its own unspoken and implicit criteria is understandable given the fact that they were given very little information about the land adjudication process and had only a partial understanding of its various stages. For example, the committee members did not understand the objection process and the role of the DLAO as judge in objection cases. Most of them were unaware that they had a right to appeal the DLAO's decisions to the Minister of Lands and Settlements. Overall, the procedures were not transparent to the committee members.

Perhaps more important was the fact that there were no clear and definitive guidelines from the ministry about what criteria should be used to allocate land. This was of particular significance considering that the Samburu lack a concept of individual ownership of land. It is interesting to note that applicants for land made claims based on elements of British common law such as adverse possession (the right to own land that one has long occupied). Such claims might be meaningful at the government level since Kenya's legal system is modeled on that of the British (Okoth-Ogendo 2000;

Delville 2000). Indeed, it seems likely that the applicants were advised by government officials (or their friends and acquaintances who owned land already) about the grounds they should use to make claims. Alternatively, many of them may have developed an awareness of these types of claims through their general contact with private property systems in other parts of the country. However, one would hardly expect Samburu elders on the land committee to have shared the same beliefs about the basis for rights to land when land was believed to be a communal resource. While it is true that the colonial regime attempted to instill territorial identification among clans by consolidating them into contiguous areas, this was only partially achieved and does not translate necessarily into individual entitlements to particular pieces of land. This conflict of understanding may explain why the committee was inconsistent in making judgments about the claims that were premised on notions that they did not value.[2]

In the absence of clear directives from the land adjudication office regarding how to determine land rights, and given the conflicts between ideas about land ownership from British common law and Samburu ideals of communal resource tenure, it was inevitable that the committee would have to use its own judgment in these matters. Their judgment centered on the personal characteristics and history of those requesting individual land. Individuals deemed as deserving, or worthy, got land. Those whose character was questionable, who misrepresented themselves or were considered outsiders, were not given land.

The Pro-Private Bias of Government Policy

Although group ranches were the form of land tenure officially designated for pastoral areas, the land adjudication officers in Samburu demonstrated a predilection for granting land to individuals. This divergence from government policy suggests that ideals about private land ownership remained at the forefront of their thinking. This can be seen in their decisions in objection cases during land adjudication in Poro A and B. As previously noted, in Poro B, the DLAO heard forty-two objection cases and granted forty of them. Thirty-four of these cases were requests for individual land; the rest were for permission to be admitted as members of the group. Indeed, only one request for individual land was rejected, and that was from a man who already had been granted a large individual farm and asked for more land. Therefore, the DLAO did not reject any new request for individual land. In

Poro A, the DLAO granted six out of seven requests for individual land. In several cases, he defended the interests of individuals who had been given land by the County Council before the onset of land adjudication. In these cases, the local land adjudication committees had filed objections challenging the early allocations, but the DLAO found in favor of the individual land owners.

The proceedings of these land cases reveal the underlying rationale for the decisions, which centers around two main themes: modernity and development, and individual rights. These themes pervade discourses about politics and policy in postindependence Kenya. Concepts regarding the primacy of individual rights, including the notion of private property, derive from British common law, the basis of the Kenyan legal system. These ideas permeate the educational system and the operations of bureaucracies and form part of the worldview of governmental decision makers. Similarly, notions of modernity and development are a constant in discussions about government policy and the broader goals of the Kenyan state.[3] For example, the motto of the first government of President Jomo Kenyatta was *harambee,* a Swahili word literally meaning "let's all pull together." The idea was that all citizens of the country needed to work together toward the betterment, the development, of the nation. Political leaders are often judged on the degree to which they are "development conscious" and the extent to which they channel patronage resources toward local development projects such as schools, roads, and health facilities. The most important committee at the district level is the District Development Committee, which has powers to approve all projects carried out in the district. These are just a few examples that illustrate the ubiquity of the concept of development and progress. In the case of Samburu (and other pastoral areas), the idea of private property, undergirded by concepts of individual rights and development, is viewed by "modernizers" (such as DLAOs) in opposition to common property, which is associated with concepts of communal rights, backwardness, and resistance to change. For land adjudication officers, dismantling common property is often believed to be a progressive move and one sanctioned by the state, regardless of its policies on group ranches.

Such an interpretation is supported by the decisions written by DLAOs in land cases. They frequently claimed that private land ownership was critical to enabling the Samburu people to develop themselves and join modern life. In one decision in Poro B, the DLAO writes, "the court feels it is the right of every individual member to choose how to live and develop according to the modern life" (Poro B Objection 23/82). A woman in Poro A whose land claim was granted was praised for putting up a permanent house and farming. She should keep her land, the DLAO writes, because she is a good example to others (Poro Objection No. 2/75). In another case in Poro A, two brothers had been given a large piece of land by the County Council before land adjudication started. Their claim to the land was challenged by the local committee through an objection. The DLAO found that they should retain ownership of the land.

> This particular area had been given to the defendants by County Council who informed them to carry out development on the land in order that Samburus can see and start settling down to leave nomadic life. . . . they have been living on this particular land for the last 21 years, without wandering from place to place . . . they started putting up proper dwelling houses. (Poro Objection No. 6/75, November 12, 1975)

The biases of the DLAO are clear: settling permanently, farming, building "proper" houses; all are manifestations of modern life and development, and should be encouraged by granting individuals land, regardless of the views of the local land committee or government policies advocating group ownership.

The basic right of individuals to land was also cited on many occasions by the DLAO. For example, in finding for the single woman who requested land in Poro B, the DLAO noted that individuals have a right to land for development, even women (Poro B Objection No. 19/82, December 30, 1982). In granting land to the councilor of the area (whom the committee and arbitration board had both rejected), the DLAO pointed out the importance of him having land so that he, as a local leader, could set a good example for others (Poro B Objection No. 34/82, December 30, 1982). Thus, in these decisions, individual rights prevailed over the rights of the group, reflecting the larger context of land tenure in Kenya and the primacy of individual freehold title.

These tendencies among the land officers may also be partly explained by the fact that they were not from pastoral areas and appear to have shared the common antipastoral biases of many government officers hailing from agricultural regions. Their preferences for farming, modern life, and individual rights, I have argued, were at odds with the views of most Samburu people for whom private land ownership was a new and foreign notion and for whom individual freedom is kept in check by communal pressures to conform. The fact that they found in favor of private land ownership in virtually all cases may also explain the resistance against these allocations that soon emerged in Siambu, resistance that came from the land committee as well as from the community members at large.

In 1985, there was a flurry of interest in subdividing group ranches in areas considered to have significant potential for crop farming. Letters were exchanged between the Samburu DLAO and the district commissioner (DC) discussing the importance of encouraging these group ranches to subdivide. The DLAO held a meeting with these groups where he clearly and forcefully suggested that they should subdivide their ranches. He stressed that they should become independent and produce their own food, noting that if their crops should fail the government would certainly understand and bail them out. He pointed out that the Agricultural Finance Corporation (AFC) was ready and willing to give them loans, using their land as collateral (Minutes of DLAO Meeting, July 12, 1985). As a result of this discussion, however, only one group ranch, Lpartuk, expressed interest in subdivision. Twenty-two years later, Lpartuk still has not completed the process of subdivision because of disagreements about how to allocate land coupled with rising costs imposed on communities desiring subdivision.

While the DLAO in Samburu was urging groups to subdivide, the central government was reconsidering the wisdom of that policy. In September 1986, a circular was sent to all DLAOs cautioning them that subdivision could lead to problems and, citing fears about unequal subdivision of land, ordering them to suspend this practice until procedures were worked out (Director of Lands circular, September 25, 1986). To date, no firm procedures on subdivision of group ranches appear to have been put in writing, at least not officially. Ironically, this circular coincided with the decision to finally subdivide Siambu.

Given the fact that government policy was geared toward dismantling customary land rights in favor of individual freehold tenure, it is rather surprising that it backed away from subdivision of group ranches. The proximate cause for this adjustment appears to have been the difficulties that subdivision was occasioning in the Maasai districts (Galaty 1997, 1992, 1994; Rutten 1992). Profligate land sales there raised the specter of huge numbers of landless pastoralists on the doorsteps of the capital, Nairobi, where they could easily have become a political problem, particularly for the Moi regime that was seen in some sense as being pro-pastoralist. Even though concepts of individual rights, modernity, and private property were pervasive at national level, this did not mean that customary systems of land tenure ceased to exist or to matter at a practical level.[4] The risk of widespread dispossession of pastoralists due to privatization of their land seems to have set off at least a few alarm bells in the government, which appeared to value order and control over conceptual consistency.

The Beginnings of Opposition to Individual Allocations

By 1983, thirty-seven individuals had been granted private farms in Siambu. Together, they took up virtually the entire fertile area of the upland plateau. This is where the story of Siambu diverges from that of other adjudication areas in Samburu. Rather than passively allowing land to be taken by individuals, opposition to these allocations began to build until it became a formidable force ultimately leading to the nullification of the original land demarcation in favor of equal subdivision of land among all group members. How and why this opposition emerged is the subject of the rest of this chapter.

Opposition to the individual allocations of land was centered among the traditional elders of the area, or what Samburu nowadays call the elders of the blanket, referring to the fact that they still wear traditional clothing such as blankets. Early in 1983, people began to realize that land had been given out to individuals in their area. While the local committee had been responsible for some of these allocations, as we have seen, it was the DLAO who granted the bulk of the land during the objection process. Furthermore, not only had land been given to individuals, but it was the best land in the area, the fertile plateau area, where most of the people lived.

Once it was understood that land had been granted in this area, people began to ask themselves where they would live. This was not an idle question, since some of the individual land owners began to evict people from their newly acquired but not yet titled farms. One elder described the situation this way.

> Many people had seen what was going on. So, they said, this can't happen here in our place. When those people took those big farms people saw that they were taking all the land, almost finishing this place. Now, many people saw that it was true that the land had gone, because if you're told, this is my farm, you'll certainly be told to move. Now, people started to fight, to say no. (John Lembaaso)

The enclosure of some individual farms and the eviction of people from the land was an affront to the values and lifestyle of mobile pastoralists and was not taken lightly. In earlier times, when a few individuals had dabbled in agriculture, others had grazed their livestock on their fields as a demonstration of their disdain for farming activities. Once individuals began to enclose their newly acquired farms, the reaction was more severe. For example, one elder related how a man given land by the DLAO enclosed his farm and prevented people from passing through it with their livestock. He closed off all the paths and personally confronted anyone trying to bring their cattle through. One day, he attempted to stop a warrior from passing with his cattle. The warrior was so infuriated by this action that he attacked the man, killing him. While extreme, this action indicates the seriousness with which people took the matter of privatizing land and preventing livestock from moving freely.

Elders began to meet among themselves to discuss the situation. Interestingly, even the land committee members were not happy with what was going on. In February 1983, they wrote to the DLAO complaining that land had been given out without their consent in an area set aside for development. This reflects their lack of understanding of the adjudication process and the authority of the DLAO to allocate land through the objection process, with or without the consent of the committee. They also complained to the district commissioner, who held a meeting in Poro in April 1983, at which time he announced that the adjudication was to be nullified. On what authority he made such a statement remains obscure, but a newspaper report of the meeting certainly got the attention of the Ministry of Lands personnel in Nakuru and Nairobi. Within days, both offices wrote to the DLAO demanding an explanation for this so-called nullification and an account of what was going on in Poro B (LA.14/3/3/30/278, April 19, 1983; LA/RVP/ 80/4, April 22, 1983).

The DLAO wrote back in May 1983, defending himself and the process (LA/SEC/2/252, May 10, 1983). He explained that the committee only gave out a few individual parcels and that he had awarded others during the objections, because he could find no reason why people should be prevented from having individual parcels. He further argued that the dispute over the adjudication process was political, but he did not elaborate what he meant by that. After this incident, no action was taken by the ministry. In December 1983, the Land Adjudication Committee complained again in writing, this time to the provincial director of lands in Nakuru. They again argued that land had been given out without their permission, in a wheat-growing area. They listed the names of those individuals to whom the committee had given land, and claimed that no other land allocations were legitimate. Curiously, these names differ from those given in their earlier letter, and they do not entirely correspond to those given land in the committee proceedings. This may be another indicator of the partial understanding that the committee had of the process—they were even unsure exactly who had been given land. Again, no action was taken in response to these complaints.

The Role of Wheat Farming and Land Leases

The fact that wheat growing had begun by this time, on land leased from the people in Siambu, is also quite significant. In 1981, a commercial wheat farmer from another part of Kenya decided to try his hand at farming in Samburu. He had been farming in Narok, a Maasai district in southern Kenya, but since that area was crowded with farms, he decided to strike out to a new place where more land was available. He found the land he wanted in Samburu and first settled in Siambu where he tried to persuade people to lease land to him for wheat farming. There was resistance to this idea at first. The former clerk to the County Council, who was asked to help convince the local community of the advantages of modern farming, recalled making strenuous efforts to persuade the people in Siambu to co-operate. He saw this as a test of the viability of commercial farming in the area. As in other matters having to do with land, the former clerk had to re-sort to force to get the people in Siambu to agree. He remembers going to the extent of jailing the area chief and councilor for a couple days to induce them to lease out the land. This technique was apparently successful in persuading them to prevail on the elders to abandon their resistance to the idea.

The wheat farmer himself remembers the hesitancy of the people who, he says, were unfamiliar with farming and feared that the land would some day turn black and not grow anything. However, once the payments from the leases started coming in, he claims, the attitude changed dramatically. His views are confirmed by most informants who said that while they did not un-derstand the wheat farming at first, they began to appreciate the value of the land once they received the payments for the land leases. The single mother, who applied for group membership and later, individual land, pointed out that the main benefit she expected to derive from membership in the group ranch was access to the wheat money.

> I saw it was wise for me to be registered, even if it was money, I would still get it, because they used to get money from the wheat; then, when it was a group ranch. If you were a member, it was your right to get money from wheat. So, that way I could get money to help my children. That's what made me struggle to be included in the register. In the past, I used to get money from the group, I was just given equal shares, like the men. (Jane Letwampa)

The advent of wheat farming and, more specifically, the opportunity to lease land out for wheat farming increased the value of the land, and it made this value transparent and tangible to the local people. Of course, in the early 1980s, the adjudication process was still under way in Siambu. The group ranch had not been declared, yet it was entering into leasing contracts with the wheat farmer. It seems clear that at least some of the individuals who requested individual farms in Siambu did so in order to take advantage of this opportunity. Why share the profits from leasing with all group members if one could get them for himself? The timing of the requests for land is significant when considered in this light. The first twenty applications for land, ten of which were rejected by the local land committee, were made in 1979 and 1980, before wheat farming began in the area. A further thirty-four requests, all approved by the DLAO, came between 1982 and 1984, after wheat farming was established. Also, the early applicants, those approved by the committee, received rather modest plots of land. The really big farms (two hundred acres and more) were granted by the DLAO to the later applicants during the objection phase. It seems plausible, then, that at least some of the later applicants were motivated by the promise of easy profits from land leasing in Siambu and that this prospect was also the reason they wanted large acreages, beyond what any of them could have farmed independently.

This possibility was not lost on the rest of the community. Their letter of December 1983 clearly pinpoints the fact that some people had been given land in the area set aside for wheat growing by the group. The fact that these individuals were going to reap all the benefits from land leases raised the pitch of the opposition. Not only were people being evicted from their land, but those doing the evicting were going to take away the opportunity that land leasing provided. Such treachery could not be allowed to succeed.

Tactics of the Opposition

I will demonstrate in this section how the strategies of those opposing privatization of land were in keeping with their social positions. Elders opposed to privatization mobilized the population through public meetings where they discussed the issues and made plans. They drew on the organizational strength of age-sets by allowing the warriors to meet as a group and plan their own actions. They also resorted to the use of the curse (*ldeket*), traditionally the strongest sanction available to Samburu elders.

It was not difficult to convince the local community that much was at stake if a few individuals were allowed to take all the fertile land in Siambu. At public meetings, elders emphasized the problems. The land being taken was the best land in the area and had potential for agriculture, from which group members were already benefiting through the wheat leases. All these benefits and potentials would be lost if individuals were allowed to take the land. Furthermore, the people would be forced to move down the escarpment to drier and less desirable land. This was a serious problem, since not only was this land dry and drought prone, it was also insecure. Only a short time before, people had been forced to retreat from the lowlands, and even the end of the Siambu plateau, because of raids by the Turkana. Being confined to the lowlands meant being constantly under threat from the Turkana and having nowhere to retreat to. The only other relatively safe area was the forest that, as a gazetted forest, is owned by the government. Anyone living there permanently risks eviction. Thus, when people asked, "where shall we go?" it was not a rhetorical question. All other areas of Lorroki plateau were undergoing adjudication at the time. People from Siambu would not be admitted as members, particularly since they still retained the lowland portion of their own land. Through their meetings, the elders instilled the message that Siambu had to be retained as community land.

The elders' appeals to concrete livelihood issues were supplemented by the invocation of communal norms about property. The elders articulated how individuals seeking private land were violating ideals of common access and use rights relating to land. They were appropriating resources that belonged to the group as a whole and threatening to exclude people who had as much right as they did to the land. The refrain "where will the people go?" that was frequently repeated by informants seems to encapsulate their feelings of moral outrage at what the individuals were doing. Thus, elders raised the community's awareness not only of the material consequences of individual land allocations, but also of their moral repugnancy.

Clearly, the elders, at this stage, wanted to retain the land in common; but how to do this? The warriors, who were meeting on their own, in secret, in the forest, had their own ideas on this score. They were preparing to do battle with those claiming individual land. These plans were not empty threats. When the wheat farmer attempted to plant on the individual farms, a group of warriors confronted the tractors and chased them away. One woman vividly recalls this incident.

> There was a day when some tractors came and ploughed the land at Lolngojine. A group of warriors saw the tractors and wondered who had told them to plough there. They resolved to find out what was going on, saying they could not just sit watching people sell the land. They would defend the land with the spear as they do the cows. They asked the chairman of the land committee about it, but he said he didn't know. The warriors declared that they will start a war. . . . They said to come the following morning and see, because blood will be shed, for we'll not just stand aside and see our own land being taken. The chairman pleaded with them that they should not take the matter into their own hands, but give [the matter] to the government. The warriors turned a deaf ear and held a meeting that they should take immediate action before the land goes out of their hands. Early the following day, the warriors went straight to where the tractors were ploughing. . . . The tractors' owner disappeared immediately, but I think they were informed by the elders that whenever they see warriors they should vanish because they were in danger. (Naina Lemarkat)

This example contrasts the approaches used by the different age-sets. While the warriors were organizing themselves to fight, the elders wanted to take up the issue with the government. All informants agreed that the elders' first course of action was to go to the government, to see whether their problems would be heard and addressed. If this failed, then they were also willing to consider fighting for the land.

These different strategies reflect the characteristics of the age-sets themselves and the styles of behavior that are considered appropriate for each. Warriors, as the name implies, are supposed to be ready to fight, to defend the people and their livestock. This is one of their most important functions.

While it may appear to be outmoded today due to the advent of the modern state with its police force and army, this role has not completely disappeared. On the contrary, the need for warriors is actually on the rise in recent years as government forces are unable to deal effectively with the scale and ferocity of contemporary cattle raiding. During the 1990s, the warriors have often been pressed into service to follow their stolen cattle, which they now do with guns as well as spears.

Elders, by contrast, are more moderate, working through negotiation and discussion, reaching decisions by consensus. Theirs are the cooler heads. They are supposed to rein in the excesses of the warrior group, as the chairman tried to do in the preceding example. It makes sense that they would try to resolve the land issue through peaceful means, taking their complaints to the government and writing letters. They began by approaching the government officers within the district, but it eventually became apparent that these officers were not in a position to reverse a process that had progressed to an advanced stage. The elders then wrote to the provincial level, in Nakuru, but there was, again, no clear response. Ultimately, they had to find ways to take their complaints to the highest level, to the capital, Nairobi.

While elders normally resolve most conflicts and disputes through reasoned discussion, they can also employ the curse. Most Samburu people still believe in the power of the curse to cause misfortune and even death. Many calamities are explained with reference to the curse. Whether or not the curse was used by the opposing elders against the individuals who got private land is a subject of dispute among informants. A number of them insist that the curse was used, while others deny this. Discussing this subject with people is somewhat delicate, and I had the feeling on a number of occasions that people were intentionally evasive when it came up. They did not want to admit that the curse had been used. However, some of the people who had individual farms recalled the particular meeting where they were cursed. One of the sons of a leader of the opposing group discussed in detail how the curse was used. He also added, however, that once the situation was resolved by subdividing the land equally among all members, the curse was revoked through a blessing ceremony.

This attempt to restore harmony to communal relations is a theme that pervades all discussions of the conflict over land in Siambu. All informants are anxious to emphasize that the conflict was resolved in a fair way and that people are now living together peacefully. Their recounting of the story is remarkably similar among informants and always stresses the happy ending.

The development of a shared narrative may be one way in which people have brought closure to what was a very difficult period for the community, an issue I return to in chapter 5.

To summarize, the initial strategies of those opposed to individual farms were consistent with their roles and their age-set proclivities. Elders and warriors organized themselves and used approaches and arguments that served to mobilize the population against the individuals getting land. The elders' determination to work with and through the government is also a reflection of their experience with external governments up to that time. Their authority had been severely undermined during the colonial era, and they had become used to playing a subordinate role to the government authorities. In terms of reining in the warriors, the elders had at times been the active collaborators with the colonial regime in their attempts to suppress the aggressive nature of this age-grade.[5] Although there were many aspects of government rule that they disagreed with, the elders still respected the power of government, particularly relating to land issues. They were hopeful that the government would find in their favor, once it was convinced of the righteousness of their cause.[6]

Building Alliances

In late 1984, land adjudication commenced once again in Siambu. A new DLAO had arrived and met with the people to discuss the situation with the individual farms. At this point, complaints centered on a few farms given to certain "bad" people, but no action was taken to nullify the original allocations. Indeed, by February 1985, provisional maps were produced for the adjudication section showing forty-nine plots: one for the group ranch, eight for the County Council (public purpose), and forty for individuals. The section was then published, which is one of the last stages of the adjudication process before incorporation of the group ranch and issuance of title deeds. A meeting was held in March 1985 at the DC's office to discuss the contentious issue of wheat leases. At this meeting it was agreed that the land currently under lease now belonged to individuals, but the farmer was instructed to complete the 1985 lease with the group ranch and then to commence with the individuals from 1986 (LND/16/35/172, March 26, 1985). At this stage, then, the individuals were recognized as owners of the land they were allocated and were on the verge of being issued with title deeds.

Around this time the elders opposing the individual farms realized that their efforts at stopping the allocations were not working and that they had to go beyond the district and even the provincial level to seek redress. A group of them decided to pay a visit to one of the most powerful Samburu men in the country who at that time was a general in the army, based in Nairobi. He is their clansman, although hailing originally from the Mount Nyiro area in Baragoi division, about 150 kilometers north of Siambu. He was also among the group of individuals who had been given their own farms in Siambu. The local land committee had given him a piece of land when he approached them in 1980 requesting land in the area. While he had been granted that land, his primary residence, apart from his station in Nairobi, was on his sizable private ranch in Laikipia District, just south of the border with Samburu District. Here he was developing a dairy herd in addition to beef cattle.

They decided to seek his help because they believed that with his seniority and power in the government he would be able to take their grievances to a high enough level to reverse the process of adjudication that was nearing completion. That he had been given a farm in Siambu did not appear to deter them very much, since they felt that once he fully understood the situation, he would realize the injustice being done and the problems that were being created. There was the difficulty of how to reach him, though, since he was sometimes in Nairobi and sometimes in Nakuru, and it would take some funds for a group of elders to travel and stay there. In that connection, they went to see the wheat farmer. The wheat farmer was also against the subdivision of land. He says that he opposed subdivision because he feared that the Samburu would end up losing their land to outsiders through sales. He had seen this happening in Narok where the Maasai were selling off their land once it was divided into individual parcels, and he figured that the same thing would happen in Samburu. Thus, when the elders approached him for assistance, he gladly supported them by providing transport to visit the General, as he is often referred to by Samburu.

The General, now retired, recalls those elders visiting him and his reaction to their complaints.

> When I heard their complaints, I went there, to the survey office. I saw the people in land adjudication. I went to Poro. I listened to people's views. I knew those people who were getting land first. I knew the ones who hadn't received [it]. So, I went with those men who were complaining. Then, I saw there was a lot of tension. So, I went there to calm people so they wouldn't fight until I had taken their issue to the govern-

ment, and then we would see. In this, God helped us and we succeeded. Then, each person got [land].

The General put emphasis on the tension he sensed in the community. People were close to physically fighting. The two groups had become so polarized that they were barely on speaking terms with each other. In some cases, families were being torn apart by the issue because some of them were getting individual land and others not. One of the men who had received an individual farm put it this way.

> They [the opposers] were strong such that even you could see that it was better that this thing be nullified. Even for my life. Even we ourselves came to reason that it wasn't good for me to take this land and my other brothers stay without. (Michael Lesoito)

Another man whose two brothers had individual farms noted how he attended meetings of the opposition group because he had no land while the others did. Although he did not harbor particularly negative feelings toward his brothers, it was only sensible for him to look after his own interests by joining the opposing group. In other cases, relationships among members of the family on opposite sides of the issue were openly hostile.

One event that heightened tensions even more was the murder of a man from the Siit subclan. This man was a watchman hired by the wheat farmer to guard the wheat fields. Although no one witnessed the murder, a common account of what is believed to have transpired is as follows. One day, walking back from Poro town, he was killed near a stream, and the body was dumped in the water where it stayed for a day. The next day the body was moved and finally discovered near the Poro police line. One of the individual land owners, who had had a dispute with this man over land they each claimed, was arrested and accused of the murder. He was jailed for a time, but the case was dropped. No one was ever tried for the murder.

There are diverse interpretations of this event. A few people claim that it was not important to what was going on at that time over land. They argue that this man was killed for other reasons, not because of the land issue. Some speculate that he might have caught people stealing from the wheat farm and been attacked by them. For whatever reason he was killed, they contend that it did not contribute to the worsening situation in Siambu. On the other hand, the majority of people I spoke to felt that the murder was significant and that it was an indicator of the potential for violence to escalate in the area. Most of them are convinced that the man originally accused did indeed commit the murder, even if no evidence could be brought to bear against him. They also refer to another dimension of the murder that has cultural relevance. This is the fact that this man was from the Siit subclan while the one accused of murdering him is Kurpa. Murders between two subclans are unpropitious and require that compensation (*nkiroi*) be given to the family of the deceased. If no compensation is proffered, then relations between the subclans will remain troubled, and the cycle of murder may continue. One informant described the conflict between the subclans.

> I think the conflict between Kurpa and Siit is due to murder, and it is not only from Lkiroro; there was another murder during Kiliako time. Yeah, so that conflict came long time ago. There was someone in Kurpa family that was killed by [a] Siit, and during this time [a] Siit was killed by a Kurpa, so it's like they're paying [back] the conflict and there's nothing that can save that problem because it's within, generation to generation. (Margaret Lekwe)

The perception that this murder was part of an underlying conflict between the two subclans must have contributed to the unease in the area, even if it was not a direct result of the land issue. There is no strong evidence that the conflict over land corresponded with subclan affiliations. Members of both subclans were among the group of individuals getting big farms, and both were represented in the opposition group. Thus, there was no cleavage directly along subclan lines. It may be, though, that this murder, coming at the time it did, raised people's fears that the conflict might spread to encompass inter-subclan hostilities. In any case, while he is among those who dismiss the importance of the murder, the General was worried enough about the situation in Siambu to personally take up the matter and make arduous efforts to resolve it.

This leads to the second aspect of the matter that was particularly relevant to the General—the fact that this problem was happening among his clansmen, his close relatives. Therefore, he felt an obligation to intervene.

> Where would the other people go? If those twenty people took the whole area, where would the others go? And, you know those people are my relatives. Now, where would they go? Then I got involved because I saw they were going to have big problems. . . . Yes, people were going to fight.

And if those people got title deeds, maybe they would have been killed. . . . Those few people were soon to get title deeds. And it was very hard for me to stop it. I almost looked for a lawyer. I was almost defeated, ready to get a lawyer. Then, when I talked to the director [of the Ministry of Lands], by good luck, he said he'd go to see the place so he could decide. I was happy. So, the director came. When he came he listened. He saw that this thing was not done properly. So, he used his authority, as the director, he nullified this thing and started afresh, to count the number of people and the acreage.

Once he understood the gravity of the matter and the injustice of it, the General says that he decided to do all in his power to get the adjudication process nullified, including disowning his own plot in Siambu. He convinced the director of the Ministry of Lands to come to Poro to meet with the people and to make a decision on the issue. This meeting is well remembered by the local people as the "helicopter meeting" because that was the mode of transport used. Certainly, a helicopter landing at Poro town was no everyday affair, and neither was this meeting. After three years of vacillation on the part of the government, the final decision to officially nullify the adjudication and to subdivide the fertile plateau area among all registered group members was made.

In this meeting, which went on for two days, October 8–9, 1986, the main grievances of the opposition group were aired once again: the committee was not involved in the objection process; people extended the boundaries of their farms without permission; and the boundaries of the farms given out by the DLAO were not specified (meaning they were too big). This time, resolutions were made that determined the future of the adjudication process. The director of lands declared the entire adjudication process null and void and directed that a new adjudication process be initiated in which all household heads would be given equal-sized plots on the fertile plateau. The lowland area remained as a group ranch.[7] There was also discussion of the role of the former DLAO who had granted the individual farms in Siambu. He was brought back from his new post to attend this meeting, because allegations of corrupt dealings had been made against him. However, he was publicly exonerated from wrongdoing at this meeting, perhaps a sign of the relief people felt that the issue appeared to be finally resolved in favor of the majority. By the end of the month, a new committee was installed to assist the land officers with the new adjudication process.

Strategies of the Individual Land Owners

While the elders of the blanket were organizing and building alliances with powerful individuals to take their grievances forward, those individuals who had been granted private farms were also actively working to protect their interests. The extent to which this group worked as a cohesive unit is debatable. It appears that the original impetus to request individual land was something that people came to on their own, not something stimulated by membership in a particular group. As noted earlier, many of these men had experiences in the army, employment, or public office that exposed them to the concept of private land ownership and helped them begin to appreciate the value of having one's own land. Furthermore, the introduction of wheat farming in Siambu raised the value of that land as a commodity that could be leased out. They had also witnessed other people in the district, in other adjudication sections, successfully applying for land. So, they followed suit, each applying for his own land from either the committee or the DLAO through objection.

As opposition to their claims rose, however, this group became more cohesive, meeting together to strategize. In contrast to the tactics used by the elders, this group attempted to use their knowledge of the modern systems in Kenya and their access to local organs of government to influence the course of events. For example, they used the power of the area chief, who was one of them, to break up the meetings held by the opposition group. Besides the aspect of intimidation involved, this forced the opposition group to meet in secret, sometimes in the forest. They also worked with the land adjudication officers to try to secure their claims. In 1986, when the opposition appeared to be gaining ground, all of the individual land owners wrote to the land adjudication office requesting copies of the proceedings of their cases. The proceedings constituted evidence of their ownership of the land, which they used to counter attempts to nullify their claims.

They also wrote letters to various departments, including one to the district commissioner, copied to the director of lands, warning that violation of their land rights would have dire consequences. This was in January 1986, when the wheat farmer met with the people in Siambu and announced that he would be leasing land from the group that year (contrary to what had been agreed upon in 1985) since he had been told by the director of lands that there were no more individual farms in Siambu. The individual land owners wrote, in reference to this meeting, that:

The wazee [elders] became wild wanting to spear the land owners. Please as a matter of urgency please confirm the situation as the trouble maker is [the wheat farmer]. And we would like to know what is going on about lands at Poro B otherwise things will go wrong at Poro if no actions will be taken. As from the date of this letter, we the individuals of Poro land we warn [the wheat farmer] not to step to those lands as we don't want him until we wait the instruction from the DC or the director of lands. . . . We kindly request the government to step in to this matter as quickly as possible so that more blood may not be shed again as last year, 1985.

While their language is polite, the implicit threat of violence is not subtle. The reference to bloodshed in 1985, I believe, refers to the murder of the watchman, strengthening the contention that this murder did play a role in heightening tensions. In response to this letter, the district commissioner took swift action, directing the wheat farmer to suspend payments to "avoid any uprising" until the issue could be resolved (LND 16/35/Vol. 1/122, January 20, 1986). In the event, after a public meeting on the issue in early February 1986, the wheat farmer was told to lease from the group, not the individuals. The tide was turning against the individual land holders.

Some informants also believe that this group of individuals was responsible for the death of two of the elders of the blanket who were leading the opposition. They claim that these two elders were either bewitched or poisoned and that they died within about two weeks of each other. As with the question of whether or not the opposition elders employed the curse, this is a controversial accusation. While some find in the coincidence of these men's deaths support for the argument that they were the victims of witchcraft or deliberate poisoning, others disregard this, insisting that they had contracted malaria while on a visit to their settlements in the lowlands where they went together to attend a ceremony. There is no proof, but again, even the perception that this group was resorting to such methods added fuel to the growing conflict among the people. If true, it means that even this group of apparently modern men were not beyond using traditional means to fight for their cause.

Finally, one informant, the son of a prominent opposition elder, claimed that he and his father were offered land in exchange for abandoning their opposition to individual land allocations. They refused these offers since their goal was a fair distribution of land for all. Attempts to buy off the opposition do not appear to have been widespread as this was the only case that was reported.

The main difference between the tactics of the group of individuals and that of the opposition was their appeal to the wider public. The elders of the blanket focused their efforts on unifying people against the small group that was taking land, and then on taking their grievances to the highest level possible. They mobilized the people against individual allocations by articulating how these violated both the moral and material interests of the community. In contrast, the individuals concentrated their efforts on using the government machinery and legal system, which they understood better than the elders, in order to secure their claims. This strategy had worked in other parts of the district, where individuals had obtained land with little or no opposition. However, this strategy did not bear fruit in Siambu due to the ability of the elders to mobilize the opposition and make alliances with parties whose power rivaled and even exceeded that of the individual land owners.

The Aftermath: Equal Subdivision

After the meeting of October 8–9, 1986, the process of subdividing the land moved forward relatively rapidly, although it was not entirely free from conflicts. The new committee worked with the land officers to measure the amount of land available for subdivision and to confirm the membership among whom the land would be divided. It had been decided that only the fertile plateau area of Siambu would be divided, while the area down the escarpment would remain a group ranch. All of the members who got land in the upper area automatically became members of the group ranch, which was named Porokwai. It is somewhat unclear who actually made the determination to divide the upland area and leave the lowland as a group ranch, but it seems likely that the idea originated with the General. He emphasized that he felt this was the best solution as it would enable all members to have some of the good land where they could farm, but it would still leave a large area where the cattle could graze. While the elders opposing the privatization of land would have preferred to leave all the land as a group ranch, they realized that doing so would not resolve the conflict, as individuals would still attempt to get individual farms in the fertile area. Therefore, in order to head off future conflicts over land, they agreed to the compromise solution of dividing Siambu and leaving Porokwai as a group ranch.

One contentious issue at this time was the determination of membership in the group. The adjudication register had earlier been completed, but the new committee was charged with the task of reviewing the register and confirming the membership. At this point, a certain number of people were removed from the register and others, some of whom had been in the group of individuals, were threatened with deregistration. In the end, however, it appears that only a small number of people were deregistered, though it is difficult to be definitive on this issue since there are hardly any records of the work of the second committee. It was also decided at this time to remove anyone from the register who was under eighteen or did not have a national ID card. This meant that the current age-set of warriors, still boys at that time, were not registered. Today, many people cite this as one of the few mistakes made during the final subdivision. However, the young generation has been promised that they will have opportunities to get their own land in Porokwai, and there are plans to subdivide part of this area, though they are progressing only slowly.

Once the membership had been confirmed and the land measured, each member was allocated about twenty-three acres of land. The allocations are fairly equal, but there is some variation due to topographical features, such as slopes that are not included in the acreage. Also, the two single women who had been included in the register were given one farm to share rather than two separate farms. It was argued that, as women, they did not require as much land as men. Rather than allocate the plots randomly, the committee decided to distribute them according to where families were already settled. This reduced the distances that people had to move and ensured that close relatives remained neighbors. The intention was to reduce the likelihood of disputes between neighbors, a strategy that appears to have succeeded.

Records of the adjudication section were completed in April 1989 and forwarded to the director of lands. The section was republished in 1991, and the original publication of 1985 was thereby canceled. In December 1992, the adjudication was certified complete, and title deeds were issued for the individual plots in Siambu while Porokwai was registered as a group ranch. It is estimated that about half of the land owners have actually collected their title deeds from the land registry office in Nyahururu.

Reactions to Privatization

Discussions and interviews reveal a highly positive reaction of the people in Siambu to the final subdivision of land. Everyone, whether they originally supported or opposed privatization, extols the value of owning their own land. The first and foremost advantage, universally claimed, is that owning private land gives one control over his affairs. You can do as you want without the interference of others. Comments like these were typical.

> After subdivision, nobody can control you. If you want to farm your land, you just decide on your own like other forms of development. Nobody can control your land and nobody can tell you what to do on your land. (Lopile Lemagas)
>
> Now, everybody has rights over his own land and one can restrict his own land and put paddocks for his own livestock. (Loyeku Ledonyo)
>
> If you have your own property, you have authority that protects you and your property. Nobody will interfere with you. (Michael Lesoito)

Besides having control over one's affairs, people also speak of the cessation of conflicts among people. Now, everyone knows the boundaries of their land, and there are no disputes over who owns what. This is a great relief to people. They also emphasize the possibilities for farming and of making money by leasing out land for wheat farming. Through leasing, they claim, people with little or no livestock are able to improve their situation. They also speak of the potential for improving livestock productivity by introducing modern production methods. The only real disadvantage noted by many people is the danger of land sales. Most people say they are against selling land, and some moves have been made by the elders and the area chief to discourage sales. Land sales are feared because they may leave people without (good) land, and they may also enable outsiders to become established in the community.[8] Changing land use patterns and the socioeconomic impact of privatization will be discussed in detail in chapter 7. What is important to stress here is the overwhelmingly positive reaction of people in Siambu to the final outcome of the subdivision.

Sanctioning the Individual Land Owners

I have emphasized here that once the decision was made to subdivide the land, it was met with relief and satisfaction by the people. It is also true that, when discussing the issue of land subdivision today, people uniformly emphasize the positive and harmonious outcome. However, not all reactions to the decision to subdivide were innocuous. Indeed, the elders who had opposed privatization of the land took this opportunity to sanction some of the men who had received private farms initially. These actions were a way of punishing these individuals for flouting the authority of the elders and of demonstrating the continued power that the elders possessed.

The sanctions consisted of destroying fields that these men had cultivated. In one case, the wheat farmer was instructed to plough under maize and to plant wheat there, instead. In the other case, fields were invaded by livestock on their way to a cattle dip. These two events happened on the same day in 1987 and were organized by the opposition elders. One of the men, Lalbarta, describes what happened on his farm.

> You know, the farm that cattle entered was of the group; that is when we were still a group ranch. Since I was a person who liked development, I took six acres near Baba Regina's farm, then I fenced. I planted maize and it grew well. Since it was a property owned by the group, it wasn't personal property, people were unhappy about this. One Saturday, about 400 cattle that were coming from the dip were driven into the farm. The fence was destroyed and scattered all over. They were divided into groups. One man told the hundred or so people, "stop this, isn't this man yours?" . . . He asked them, "Isn't this boy yours? Can't you give him one chance to harvest and then he won't plant again?" But they didn't listen. They went on to destroy the farm. Later I realized that everybody has their own people. I was very angry, but then, one person can't kill the whole world.

As this event happened in 1987, it was during the time that the decision to equally subdivide the land had been made, but the new farms were not yet demarcated. Thus, this man had decided to go on with his farming activities as he had been doing earlier. This time, however, the opposition elders decided that his farm would not be allowed to succeed. The fact that the farm was on the way to the cattle dip was significant since one of the main complaints against farming in the area was that it blocked livestock movements. After his farm was destroyed, he went to the district commissioner to complain. He reports that his grievance was dismissed because this had been a mob action and, therefore, no particular individuals could be charged. However, he suspects that the elders had earlier met with the officer and convinced him to stay out of the case, perhaps even bribing him.

The same day that the cows invaded that farm, the wheat farmer took his tractors to the farm of the man who had been accused of murdering the watchman. The tractors ploughed under several acres of maize and planted wheat in their stead. Again, the rationale behind this was that the land had reverted to the group, at least for the time being, and the individual's claims had been voided by the decision to re-demarcate the land. However, there was more to it than this. The wheat farmer himself admits that he was very upset by the murder of his employee, and he shared the community's suspicions that this man was responsible for the murder. Thus, his own emotions about the issue in part dictated his actions. Certainly, the community was also unhappy with this man who not only was widely believed to be a murderer but who was still clinging to his earlier land claim. Thus, this incident was an attempt to demonstrate that he would have to abide by the will of the larger community. In contrast to the first example, the victim in this case ended up filing a court case against the wheat farmer seeking compensation for his destroyed crops. The case dragged on for ten years until finally the wheat farmer paid the compensation.

An interesting aspect of these cases of sanctioning is that both victims were perceived as outsiders, people who had come to the area relatively recently. In contrast, those who had individual farms but were from the area, originally, suffered much less from this sanctioning. I think that is what Lalbarta was referring to when he says that he realized later that "everyone has his people." That is, these were not his people, after all, and he had no way of seeking redress since he was still considered an outsider, even after years of residence in Siambu. In his case, however, he has gone on to establish himself as a leading farmer in the area and is much admired by many people. However, he has not attempted to enter into any leadership positions; his efforts are at the level of apolitical development activities. The second man sought relief outside the community, through the courts, and after a long battle that appears to have nearly bankrupted him, he won compensation from the wheat farmer. Though he won in court, he remains a pariah in the community, a subject of derision and ridicule by almost everyone.

Conclusion

The conflict over land in Siambu displays in microcosm the clash of interests and ideologies that began in the colonial period and continued after independence between those seeking to set Kenya on a course of modernization and development and those defending their cultures and livelihoods from assault. This conflict did not take the form of a simple dichotomy between the West and the indigenes, however. We have seen how individual experiences, strategies, and interests shaped the behavior of various groups. Among the Samburu, those with exposure to education, employment, or military service came to think of land as something that could be owned individually. These same experiences furnished them with additional economic resources that they frequently chose to invest in agriculture or business in addition to live-stock. The growing value of land in Siambu due to wheat leases provided strong impetus for increasing investment in land, the benefits of which could only be monopolized through private ownership. Literacy and linguistic competence gave them greater access to the organs of the state, enabling them to take advantage of opportunities for individual land ownership pro-vided by the land adjudication process.

Elders in Mbaringon, and many other parts of Lorroki, failed to prevent individual land allocations precisely because they lacked understanding of and access to the state. Instead, their inclination to follow government man-dates was heightened by the paucity of information provided by land adjudi-cation officers and the intimidation tactics employed by those seeking land. The elders in Siambu, though, overcame these limitations. In the face of very high stakes, potential eviction from their land, they compensated for their weak understanding of the state by mobilizing the community against the al-locations and making alliances with other actors who possessed intimate knowledge of the workings of the state machinery and the power to influence decision makers at the national level.

Actors within the state were not monolithic in their behavior, either. The district-level land officers failed to provide adequate information on which land committees could base their work in land adjudication. As a result, the land committees deployed implicit criteria for making decisions about land claims, based on methods they use in other sorts of disputes. In the Mbaringon case, officers clearly sided with the individuals seeking land and participated in their deception of the committee members. Even if they did not gain materially from this complicity, it is clear from their decisions on in-dividual land cases that land adjudication officers valued privatization ideo-logically, and they favored the individuals who sought land during the adju-dication process. While this was the pattern at district level, the national-level officials backed away from subdivision of group ranches in the 1980s, probably fearing the larger political implications of land sales and dis-possession of pastoralist groups. When pressure was brought to bear in the Siambu case, they acted to nullify the adjudication, even though there ap-pears to have been no legal basis on which to do so.

This examination of events reveals how individuals and groups acted in pursuit of their goals, both ideological and material. It also demonstrates that the equal subdivision of land in Siambu was a compromise solution to the conflict of interests between the group of individuals who sought private land and the elders who defended common property. While neither side achieved their original goals, the compromise satisfied enough of their interests to gain acceptance. In turn, by settling the land issue, the community was able to return to a state of relative harmony and social order, both of which had been undermined over the course of the conflict. Positive reactions to the subdivision, even among those who were initially against it, reflect at least in part the high value individuals place on order, stability, and predictability in their social relations.

CHAPTER 5

The Political Dynamics of Privatization

The process of subdivision of land in Siambu constitutes an important institutional change. The transformation of land tenure from a communal system to one of individual freehold land tenure transferred rights in land from the community as a whole to individual land owners with implications for economic production and social relations. The previous chapter laid the foundation for understanding how land was privatized in Siambu by describing the key historical events and processes that led to this change.

In this chapter, I provide an analysis based on the dynamics of bargaining power that explains why privatization occurred in Siambu as it did. Three factors are central to this explanation. First, those seeking private land had experiences that convinced them of the value of private property and provided them with new sources of power enabling them to challenge the status quo. Second, government policies and practices regarding adjudication of common land provided opportunities for those seeking land to do so—they lowered the costs of raising a challenge against common property. Third, the strategies used by the elders to counter individuals seeking private land proved pivotal to the outcome of the dispute. In the end, relatively equal bargaining power between the two sides resulted in the compromise of equal subdivision.

I will contrast the Siambu case to that of Mbaringon to show why people there failed to prevent individuals from obtaining land at the expense of the group ranch. The Mbaringon example serves as a counterfactual account, "what would have happened if . . ." (or, more appropriately in this case, if not) and aids in assessing the critical factors that explain the Siambu case.

A Theory of Institutional Change

Institutions encompass a wide range of social arrangements that facilitate interaction and exchange by providing information about the probable behavior of others. They may be thought of as the formal and informal "rules of the game" (North 1990) and include laws and constitutions as well as informal social norms, codes of conduct, and conventions. While they may yield numerous collective benefits, it is important to understand that these benefits are not evenly distributed across all members of a society.[1] That is, some individuals or groups stand to gain more from particular institutional arrangements than others (Bates 1989; Knight 1992; Ensminger and Knight 1997). For example, in the case of Samburu pastoralists, I will show how communal land ownership, while ensuring access to resources for all pastoralists, differentially benefits the wealthier members of society. The fact that institutions have distributional consequences is critical to understanding why and how they change.

If individuals understand that institutions distribute benefits differentially, then they may choose to work toward the establishment of institutions that benefit them disproportionately. Since many individuals will behave in this way, conflicts will emerge over the form and content of societal institutions. It is out of these conflicts that new institutional arrangements emerge. Further, it is the parties with greater bargaining power that are likely to be victorious in such conflicts (Knight 1992). Those with access to resources that confer power, such as land, capital, authority, information, knowledge, skills, and so forth will bring these to bear against those who seek alternative outcomes (Bates 1989). Weaker parties, in turn, may accept a particular outcome as the best they can do, given the current constellations of power (Knight 1992). However, this does not foreclose future opportunities for them to work toward changing institutions in their own favor. Indeed, it is the fact that institutions confer benefits unequally that accounts for their instability over time.

Those who are less favored by particular institutions have an inherent incentive to challenge them to the extent they believe (1) that their challenge will be successful and (2) that the resulting institution will benefit them more than the status quo. On the other hand, those who benefit disproportionately from extant institutions will tend to resist change unless they are confident that such changes would be even more beneficial to them, all things considered, than those obtaining under the status quo (Ullmann-Margalit 1977,

139). To understand why change occurs at particular times, then, it is important to consider the variables that influence actors' perceptions about the risks and benefits involved in challenging or defending the status quo. These would include, for example, factors that lower the cost of challenging the status quo or increase the potential benefits of change for specific groups. Similarly, a shift in the relative power of individuals or social groups would make challenges more likely as groups gaining power use their newly acquired resources in efforts to strengthen their positions (Ensminger and Rutten 1991; Ensminger 1992).

In Siambu, all of these factors came into play in the early 1980s and influenced the course of change. The land adjudication procedures put in place by the Kenyan state created choices—between group ranches and private land—and opportunities—to challenge common property or defend the status quo—for the members of Samburu communities. Laws imposed from above produced conflicts among community members as they struggled between alternative institutional arrangements defined by the state. Which system of land tenure was selected had further ramifications in terms of locally constructed ideals about land use and ownership of property.

This approach to the study of institutional change assumes that actors behave according to their perception of their interests. This is not to say that actors are able to accurately perceive their objective interests, nor that these interests must of necessity be narrowly material. On the contrary, a modified rational choice approach grants the fact that individuals lack access to complete information in forming their preferences (Ensminger 1992; North 1990). Furthermore, preferences may extend beyond material interest and include such noneconomic motivations as social status, prestige, or approval from others, to name a few (Chong 1991; McAdams 1997). The critical assumption is not that actors have particular preferences but rather that their actions are guided by their perceptions of their interests as well as their expectations about how others will respond. That is, they behave strategically, working toward an outcome that they desire, yet working within the constraints posed by internalized systems of norms and values as well as the perceived interests of other actors in the environment.

Internalized norms and values, what we might call culture, define the range of actions that individuals will deem acceptable in their pursuit of their interests. The previous chapter illustrated how elders tended to work in ways that were consistent with their roles, statuses, and self-perception as elders in Samburu society. Warriors, however, acted in quite different ways, but their aggressive behavior was still considered appropriate for them. Thus, we may think of norms, beliefs, and culture as providing the outer limits on what types of behavior are considered suitable, or, in the Samburu case, respectable, both by oneself and the wider society.

By the same token, one is subject to the sanctions of the community if one violates norms and standards of acceptable behavior. Enforcement of social norms is critical to their maintenance and, by extension, to social order (Taylor 1982). While much enforcement is internal to the individual in the form of a guilty conscience, third-party enforcement is very commonly deployed to discourage people from violating norms. These sanctions can range from disapproving looks, to negative gossip, to fines and punishment, or to more extreme modes of censure such as banishment, ostracism, or—for the Samburu—the curse. Most individuals want, and need, to maintain their standing and reputations in their communities and will, accordingly, work to avoid sanctions by complying with norms (Chong 2000, 49). Enforcement mechanisms discourage challenges to institutional arrangements, since such challenges will initially be met by not only resistance but also sanctions. This may account for the fact that many successful institutional changes originate from more powerful social groups who are less likely to be sanctioned, or at least are better able to withstand sanctions (Ensminger and Knight 1997; Henrich 2001).

However, there are cases in which these underlying norms and beliefs are the subject of more fundamental challenges. I will demonstrate how the individuals who sought private land often did so as part of their effort to gain entrance into the larger community of "modern" Kenya. In order to do so, they were able, even required, to violate many of the norms of acceptable behavior of Samburu society. At the same time, they became less vulnerable to communal sanctions against their behavior, since they had less need to safeguard their reputations among Siambu people.

Once a challenge has been mounted against an existing institution, as it was by those seeking private land in Siambu, parties to the conflict not only will rely on their prior resource endowments but will work to enhance their bargaining power. This implies that actors are able to do more than choose among a fixed menu of choices, as in game-theoretic formulations. Instead, they are able to shift the game itself to a new level by altering their bargaining position and by so doing opening up a new realm of strategic options. It is this aspect that makes the analysis of institutional change dynamic. Endowments of power are never fixed but are subject to change. Some of these changes may be the unintended consequences of earlier courses of action. For example, in the Siambu case, educating children (especially boys) gave them access to new resources of information and knowledge that they later put to use in challenging common property. Similarly, experiences in the army or employment exposed young men to other parts of Kenya where they encountered alternative ideas about how land should be used and how the state operates. These experiences conferred on them ideas, information, and skills that both motivated and facilitated their challenge to common property. These shifts in power were by-products of experiences that had other primary purposes.

Once the conflict over land began, both the elders and the individuals seeking land sought ways to enhance their power positions. The elders did this by organizing collective action against the individuals claiming private land. The need for collective action to achieve change is one barrier standing in the way of those challenging status quo institutions. Later I will discuss how the ability of the elders, and the inability of the individuals, to motivate collective action was important to the outcome in Siambu. Their ability to achieve collective action also set Siambu apart from other Samburu communities undergoing land adjudication.

The emergence of strong, charismatic leaders in Siambu was another, related, way that elders increased their bargaining power vis-à-vis the individuals. The ability of elders to invoke social norms and to provide credible commitments to their course of action partly explains how collective action was achieved. In addition to organizing collective action, the elders in Siambu also sought alliances with powerful parties who were well positioned to advance their interests. These alliances enabled the elders to bypass the state at the district level and take their case directly to the center of power in the capital, further increasing their bargaining power. As we saw in chapter 4, the General played a pivotal role. Although his presence alone does not explain the course of the conflict in Siambu, he did much to shape the contours of the final compromise solution.

By 1986, the bargaining power of the two opposed groups was nearly equal. This power equivalence was important to the outcome of the conflict, because it moved both parties toward a compromise solution that satisfied most members of the community. Such an outcome may be particularly desirable in a small-scale community where the costs of social disruption caused by struggles over institutions are far-reaching and can severely undermine social order. The multistranded and complex social ties that exist in such a community are critical to survival in an uncertain environment. This may explain the great relief experienced by Siambu people at the resolution of the land issue. Equal subdivision of land established a new equilibrium in terms of land ownership. In doing so, it restored the order and predictability that are necessary to the functioning of a community.

Having achieved a new institutional status quo, the denouement of the Siambu story illustrates how social actors work to repair damage done to their prior positions of power and authority. To this end, the Siambu elders appropriated the rhetoric of private property to reassert their authority and to make claims for the superiority of their clan. They have done their best to translate a second-best solution, privatization of land, into a reinforcement of their social status.

In this section I have briefly discussed the critical components of a theory of institutional change. While drawing on earlier work on the role of bargaining power in bringing about institutional change, the Siambu case adds several dimensions to our understanding of these processes. Of particular significance is the way leaders acted to enhance their power when challenged and how they sought alliances to make up for gaps in their own capabilities to deal with the state. This case also brings to the fore how social sanctioning mechanisms may fail when those being sanctioned are no longer concerned to maintain their reputations in the community. We often speak of the breakdown of society or the erosion of social norms. The Siambu case enables us to pinpoint how and why such a breakdown can occur. Finally, the elders ultimately made use of positive rhetoric about privatization, which shows how actors try to make the most out of compromises concerning institutional arrangements. Rather than viewing privatization as the demise of their traditional base of power and authority, the elders worked to reassert both in a new language of control and development.

The Initial Position: Who Benefits from Communal Property?

Pastoralist societies have often been portrayed as egalitarian (Schneider 1979; Salzmann 1999, 2001). In recent years, there has been increasing debate among scholars of pastoral societies regarding this assertion. Many authors have pointed to increasing economic diversification as proof of the existence and growth of inequality among pastoralists (Ensminger 1992; Fratkin 1991, 1998; Fratkin, Galvin, and Roth 1994; Little 1985, 1992; Anderson and Broch-Due 1999; Roth 2000). Some historical work also suggests that differences in wealth have a long history, even if there has not been a permanent class of poor pastoralists (Waller 1999). Others maintain that pastoralists remain highly egalitarian in a political sense, in spite of economic differentiation (Salzmann 1999, 2001). This suggests that the debate may be over two incommensurable conceptions of egalitarianism: political equality that exists in small-scale societies where all adult men participate in decision making, and inequalities of wealth in terms of livestock or other assets. While these realms may be related, for example, wealthier pastoralists having greater say in ostensibly egalitarian political structures, there may still be value in separating the two for analytic purposes.

The absence of a centralized hierarchical authority among East African pastoralists and the relative freedom of individual herders to access land, water, and other natural resources support a view of pastoral egalitarianism. Decision making is decentralized, and all the elder men of a locality have the right to participate in the councils that adjudicate disputes and make other important communal decisions. At the same time, the "moral economy" created by dense networks of reciprocal relationships serves as a social insurance system that historically enabled many pastoralist households to remain pastoralists even in the face of devastating droughts and other disasters (Scott 1976; Dahl and Hjort 1976). Among the Samburu, the concept of a moral economy is embodied in the social norm of respect (*nkanyit*) that encourages generosity and mutual assistance as signifiers of appropriate behavior (Spencer 1965; Fumagalli 1977). The frequency of disasters implies that household wealth is likely to rise and decline over time, preventing the formation of a stable class of wealthy herders (though this is changing, a point I return to later). Thus, it is in one's interest to assist those impoverished by drought since you may well require the same assistance in the future. The oscillation of wealth caused by the boom-and-bust nature of the pastoral economy serves to buffer extreme wealth differences. Thus, there is much evidence supporting the notion of pastoralist egalitarianism in both a political and, at least historically, an economic sense.

On the other hand, there is an inherent tension between individual freedom and equality within male age-sets and the hierarchy of authority between age-sets. Rigby has pointed out this contradiction for the Ilparakuyo Maasai, and the same exists within Samburu culture (Rigby 1992). Elder age-sets have a high degree of authority and control over the younger age-sets. This authority is particularly strong between the firestick elders (*olpiroi*) and the warriors (*lmurran*), two age-grades their juniors. The firestick elders have a duty to inculcate proper behavior and understanding among the warriors: to instill a sense of *nkanyit* in them. Along with this social duty comes their ability to sanction the warriors, even to use the curse to keep them in line, if necessary. It is this authority that Spencer referred to when he characterized the Samburu as a gerontocracy (1965). The ritual and moral authority of the elders is further enhanced by their control over livestock and wives, both of which are monopolized by the elders, while the warriors are required to delay marriage until the end of their warrior service, a period of fourteen years.

While a number of authors have discussed this aspect of inequality for the Maasai and Samburu,[2] there has been less attention to inequities of wealth and their implications for land use. The literature on common pool resources (CPR) has increased our understanding of how groups of resource users overcome collective action problems in order to manage communally owned resources in ways that limit their overuse and degradation. By developing rules, monitoring systems, and sanctions, large groups of users have avoided the "tragedy of the commons" by specifying the community of users, the conditions for use, and the penalties for abuse of the resource (McCay and Acheson 1987; McCabe 1990; Ostrom 1990; Bromley and Feeny 1992). While these arrangements certainly exist among the Samburu, they tend to mask differential access and power that accrue to wealthier members of society. By emphasizing the collaborative aspects of decentralized resource management, there has been inadequate attention to the effects of wealth differentials on resource use (for an exception, see Ruttan and Borgerhoff Mulder 1999).

Among the Samburu, all herd owners have access to the range as long as they abide by the restrictions on use put in force by decentralized councils of elders. These usually mean that certain key resource areas such as forests, highlands, or permanent water points are restricted for use during part of the year. In addition, herders who are migrating out of their home area are expected to negotiate access to the pasture where they want to move. Access is rarely denied. There is virtual equality in terms of access to resources. However, it is also the case that wealthier herd owners exploit the resource base to a greater extent than those owning few livestock. Thus, the maintenance of the open range is more important to a wealthier herder than to a poor one since the wealthier herder has more animals to feed and requires a greater area of land than a poor pastoralist. While making greater demands on the resource base, the wealthier herder is not under any obligation to contribute more to the preservation of that resource base. For example, he does not have to provide more labor for enforcement tasks such as scouting to identify those breaking grazing rules. Nor is he necessarily subjected to higher fines for his own transgressions. As long as he abides by the established rules and regulations regarding access and use of resources, more is not expected from the wealthier herder than the poor herder in terms of resource management or conservation. Declining access to rangeland through government policies has reduced Samburu territory by more than half since the colonial era (Lesorogol 1998). This situation highlights the disproportionate advantages of wealthier herders. When land was seemingly unlimited, there was little need for concern about the absolute demands livestock placed on the environment. As land available for Samburu herders has decreased, the situation becomes closer to a zero-sum situation where the grass consumed by the wealthy herders' animals may be seen as a true loss to the poorer ones.

While this fact is not highlighted in the literature on CPRs or pastoral commons (Behnke, Scoones, and Kerven 1993; Scoones 1994), it is a subject for concern among some Samburu, particularly younger and poorer ones. In explaining why they desired privatization of the range, these individuals frequently argued that wealthier men were at an advantage in the communal system, for the reasons just explained. They felt that privatizing the range would be to their benefit since they would be able to exclude others from their land and develop it as they saw fit. Some of them believed that they would do better economically in such a system of private ownership, even if land parcels were small. The feasibility of these possibilities notwithstanding, the important point is that wealthier pastoralists have a disproportionate advantage under the system of common property.

The communal property system among the Samburu is not necessarily the most efficient and collectively beneficial way to manage range resources, as is sometimes posited by proponents of the "new thinking" about pastoralism (Scoones 1994). Rather, this system advantages those who are wealthy in livestock, and it is therefore in their interests to defend and maintain this system. This said, it is not the case that there are no benefits for the poorer livestock owners from the communal system. Indeed, the fact that the system has been relatively stable for several centuries implies that it does serve the needs of most pastoralists much of the time. If it did not, we would have seen more challenges posed to the system by those who were disadvantaged by it. Stability is an indicator that even poorer pastoralists internalized norms regarding common property and its management, because they recognized that this was the best they could do given the constellation of power relations obtaining in the society (Knight 1992, 140). After all, poorer members of Samburu society still enjoy access to all the key resources and are able to make claims for reciprocity from the richer groups.

Motivations to Change the Institution of Common Property

If the norms relating to management of common range resources were stable and provided some, albeit unequal, benefits to all social groups, why was there an impetus to move toward privatization of the range? Poorer pastoralists who benefited less from common land might be motivated to challenge the norm if they believed they could succeed in shifting it to one that would favor them more. In the past, recurring disasters meant that wealth was a temporal phenomenon that did not necessarily last over generations. Thus, those who were poor at time A could hope to become wealthy at time B and therefore had a stake in upholding a system that might well benefit them in the future.

However, evidence from the last few decades demonstrates a trend of increasing economic stratification: the wealthy are remaining wealthy, while a class of poorer pastoralists is becoming entrenched (Ensminger 1992; Little 1992; Rigby 1992; Fratkin 1998; Anderson and Broch-Due 1999; McPeak 2006). There are various reasons for this. Wealthier pastoralists preserve their assets during difficult times by moving their herds far away to better areas, purchasing supplementary feed, or selling animals and banking the money. They also invest in livestock with proceeds from trade, business, or employment. They are often the ones buying stock from poorer pastoralists during droughts. The fact that livestock still die during droughts while the human population survives through relief food distribution means that there are many stockless pastoralists at the end of droughts who may never be able to recover their losses. These factors help explain why there is growing awareness of the inequities of the common property regime among those who are at risk of being perpetually poor.

A particular subset of this group that was important in the Siambu case were those individuals who had begun small-scale agriculture in the 1960s and 1970s. These individuals perceived farming as a new activity that, while it would not displace livestock production entirely, could supplement their household food production. In order to grow crops, they had to assert quasi-private land rights over their cultivated fields. This move was resisted by the majority in the community who did not share their enthusiasm for agriculture, viewing it as a violation of pastoralist ideals about the relationship of people to the earth. That is, digging in the ground was seen as beneath the dignity of pastoralists, an activity suited to lower classes of people. Wealthier livestock owners were particularly unhappy with farming since it threatened to block stock routes, impede the freedom of movement of their herds and, if it caught on, reduce the overall size of the range.

Another group that had an interest in changing the norm from communal to private land ownership was the group of Samburu who had been more exposed to modernity through education, employment, or military service. These men had often undergone an ideological shift as a result of socialization into a different set of attitudes, beliefs, and social norms that lauded all things modern and developed and disparaged traditional society as backward and inept. Many of them had traveled extensively in Kenya and even outside the country and thus been exposed to different ways of life beyond pastoralism. Within Kenya, land ownership was, and remains, crucial to survival in a country with limited land of agricultural potential and a burgeoning population. Among agricultural groups, the attachment to land and the struggle to own land are on a par with the Samburu propensity to own livestock. Beyond the mere utility of land or livestock to food production, land for farmers is a defining characteristic as is livestock ownership for a pastoralist.

Thus, having come to adopt many of the values and norms of "down Kenya," as Samburu refer to the rest of the country, land ownership became a signifier of entrance into the community of modern Kenya. For many of these individuals, gaining entrance into and acceptance among modern Kenyans became a goal, and land ownership a means to achieve it.

Furthermore, access to education and employment provided these men with new resources in the form of economic and human capital that they would ultimately deploy in their attempt to gain private ownership of land. Compared to Mbaringon, for example, more men from the Lkishili age-set were educated in Siambu, a fact that may partly explain why more men sought private land in Siambu than in Mbaringon (chapter 7 presents details of educational attainment in the two communities). While not all men who requested private land were exceptionally wealthy in terms of livestock, most of them had some cash income that they could use to invest in new ventures. Some had been given commercial plots of land in town by the County Council, and a few had started small businesses. Their greater familiarity with the cash economy enabled them to imagine the possible benefits that might accrue from owning land such as farming, leasing, or selling it. In these individuals, ideological and material interests converged around a desire for private ownership of land.

Conditions That Lowered the Cost of Challenging Common Property

The advent of land adjudication provided an opportunity for groups with interests in changing the norm to act by lowering the costs of challenging a pervasive, stable, and generally beneficial land tenure regime. The goal of the Kenyan state in the land adjudication process was to fix and formalize rights in land. In most of the country, this meant the establishment of individual freehold tenure. As we have seen, in the pastoral areas, this process took the form of the creation of group ranches where all residents of an area would become joint owners of the land. However, the provision that enabled individuals to make claims to land during the registration process created space for those interested in obtaining private plots of land to challenge communal ownership. The fact that this loophole existed suggests that the state anticipated the ultimate privatization of pastoral land, even if this was achieved through a gradual process.

The role of state policy was important in another way, because it established the parameters of the conflict over land tenure in Samburu District. Communities had an implicit choice between group ranches, private land, or a mix of the two. I say implicit because these choices were not explicitly communicated to the people prior to land adjudication. Indeed, if people had had a clear understanding of what the choices were, then the communities might have acted to preempt individual land claims before they were ever made. The fact that the possibility for private land ownership only became apparent to the majority of community members after land claims had already been made (and granted, in cases such as Mbaringon) meant that either the claims were grudgingly accepted (as in Mbaringon) or were contested in a rearguard action (as in Siambu).

The state's preference for private land ownership was revealed in the actions of its personnel, particularly the District Land Adjudication Officers (DLAO). The DLAOs granted claims to private land due to their belief that individual land ownership would further the modernization process. Support from these state actors within Samburu District was important to those claiming individual land rights, because it gave them confidence that they would prevail over elders supporting communal ownership. The power of the state to impose its will on the community had been thoroughly demonstrated during the colonial period, and most Samburu had a tendency to accept state-sponsored directives whether or not they agreed with them. This explained the relative lack of resistance to individual land claims in other parts of Lorroki adjudicated prior to Siambu. Individuals seeking private land in Siambu knew of the success of others in obtaining land, since they were often part of the same network of friends and acquaintances.

In addition, their differential access to information and clearer understanding of the land adjudication process and the roles of state officers in general conferred an advantage on those seeking private land, particularly at the objection stage when their claims went directly to the DLAO, not the local land committee (see Ensminger and Rutten 1991 for a discussion of a similar phenomenon among the Orma; Hedlund 1979 for Maasai). Armed with superior knowledge of and access to the state through their connections gained through employment, education, and military service, these individuals were well placed to seize the opportunity to obtain private land. They understood how to appeal negative decisions made by the land committee, and they could speak the language, both literally and figuratively, of the DLAOs. Thus, even those individuals whose land claims had been rejected by the elders in the committee, succeeded in getting land through objection to the DLAO. The fact that they were able to override the decisions of the elders on land is a clear demonstration of how they made use of their newly acquired human capital.

Since a legal process was available for those seeking private land, collective action was not initially required in order to challenge the communal ownership norm. It is clear in Siambu that, in the beginning, each person desiring land independently applied either to the local land committee or, later, directly to the DLAO. While there was a certain amount of communication and discussion among applicants, they did not attempt to act as a group until much later when their claims were challenged. Thus, rather than a concerted effort to shift the norm from communal to private ownership, what occurred was a series of uncoordinated actions emanating from individual motives supported by a legal environment conducive to change. Rather than a case of formal institutional design, the aggregate of individual choices ultimately amounted to a challenge to the status quo of common property.

In addition to the existence of a land adjudication process that favored private ownership, another important factor in the Siambu case was the sudden change in the value of land. Land adjudication began in Siambu in 1978. By the end of 1980, twenty individuals had applied to the land adjudication committee for individual parcels of land. Ten were approved and ten were denied. Nineteen eighty-one was the first year that land in Siambu was leased for wheat farming (see chapter 7 for more information on wheat farming). Between 1982 and 1984 a further thirty-four individuals sought land from the DLAO, and all of these applications were successful. Interestingly, a few of these applications were for extensions of land already granted by the land committee. The fact that almost twice as many people requested private land following the start of wheat leases supports the notion that the rising value of land was at least partly responsible for this upsurge in land claims.

The economic benefits to be had from leasing out land broadened the appeal of private ownership beyond those interested in small-scale cultivation or in land ownership as a marker of modernity. In interviews, some individuals were very clear that it was the possibility of making money from leasing out land that convinced them to apply for it, while others lumped this together with the general possibilities for development that would accrue from private land ownership. The dramatic rise in applications for land following the beginning of leasing illustrates clearly how changing relative prices, in this case a rapid rise in land values, may advance a process of institutional change.

Resisting the Challenge: From Leveling to Collective Action

The rising value of land in Siambu was apparent to the elders of the blanket. The first land leases were negotiated between the (yet to be registered) group ranch and the wheat farmer. Once the additional individuals were granted private land (all of it in the wheat-growing area) by the DLAO, the elders realized that they would lose the wheat revenues to these individuals. The impending loss of wheat money was a powerful motivator for the elders to resist individual land claims. Indeed, it is arguably this aversion to future losses that emboldened the opposition even in the face of state power. Literature on cognitive function shows that people perceive a threatened loss as of greater significance than a comparable possibility of gain (Tversky and Kahneman 1987). Accordingly, we would expect people to resist a potential loss more vociferously than they would fight for the comparable potential gain. This aspect of the land issue in Siambu differentiates it from other areas of Lorroki, like Mbaringon, where those opposed to privatization of land did not have such powerful incentives to resist individual allocations.

Two other factors that were important in this connection were the quality and extent of the land being claimed and the presence of dynamic leaders. First, the land that individuals were given in Siambu differed dramatically from the arid land over the escarpment that was to be left for the group ranch members. As noted in the previous chapter, not only was the land over the escarpment much drier and rockier, it was also insecure, since it borders Turkana and Baringo districts, home to Turkana and Pokot cattle raiders. This same diversity in land quality was not present, for example, in Mbaringon where the land allocated to individuals did not differ significantly from that left for the group ranch. While people in Mbaringon were unhappy that individuals were given land, they did not face eviction to a greatly inferior area as was the case in Siambu.

Second, a group of dynamic elders emerged to lead the opposition against individual land allocations in Siambu. These men were motivated to act by the impending loss of critical grazing resources and wheat revenues. As wealthy elders, they benefited most from the status quo and, therefore, had most to lose by a change in the norm. Again, the magnitude of the potential losses is important in understanding why elders here acted whereas those in other Samburu communities failed to act. While all wealthy elders should have been similarly motivated, discussions with numerous informants indicate that there were four elders who were particularly charismatic and were able to bring the community together to act against the individual land allocations.

The presence of such leaders is important since they enabled the group to overcome barriers to collective action. Acting collectively is costly and, as Mancur Olson (1965) has argued, the rational course of action for individuals is not to contribute to collective action but, instead, to free ride on the contributions of others, as Chong notes about the civil rights movement.

> If the rest of the group does not contribute, the public good will not be obtained, and the individual would be wise to conserve his resources. If, on the other hand, the rest of the group does contribute, the public good will be obtained *whether or not* the individual contributes, so he may as well refrain from contributing under this contingency also. Therefore no matter what the rest of the group decides to do, the individual should not contribute to collective action. (1991, 7)

One way the barriers to collective action are overcome is the existence of leaders who are so highly motivated to act that they will bear very high personal costs to initiate action. In the Siambu case, these leaders emerged, I would argue, because the stakes were very high for them materially and also because their position as authority figures and respected elders was on the line. If they allowed individuals to seize the land, they would be condemning the entire community to serious hardship. The concern for the fate of future generations that was echoed often by informants in such statements as "where would the children go?" indicates an awareness of the predicament of the community. If the community was in jeopardy, then so were their leaders. Inaction on their part in such a situation could have led to their rejection by the community that looked to them for guidance. So, they acted in order to preserve their positions, not only as wealthy livestock owners but also as leaders. As with the individuals who sought private land, ideological concerns—their status and identity in the community—meshed with material interests for those elders who led opposition to privatization.

The strong motivations of the leaders, however, do not automatically translate into collective action. They still had to organize collective action among the mass of the people. In Siambu, this was achieved by providing information around which many community members could coordinate their actions. R. Hardin discusses the pivotal role of leaders in stimulating coordination or initiating the tipping phenomenon that leads to collective action.

> We might simply fail to coordinate at all in any active sense, even if we have language, religion, and ethnicity in common. Whether we coordinate might turn in part on whether there is someone urging us to recognize our identity and coordinate on it. I may fully identify with my group but take no action on its and my behalf until an Alexander Herzen, Adolf Hitler, Martin Luther King, or Ruhollah Khomeini mobilizes those of us with similar identifications. (1995, 51)

While he is referring here primarily to ethnic or national movements, the generalization applies equally to this case. Indeed, it was the presence of strong, charismatic leaders in Siambu who were willing to galvanize the population against land grabbing that facilitated collective action in this instance, while it was absent in the other parts of Lorroki where such leaders failed to emerge. As discussed in chapter 3, colonial history and intimidation tactics successfully stifled the leaders in Mbaringon, but Siambu was different in this respect.

The elders urged people to act against the individual land allocations by holding numerous public meetings at which they made it clear to the people what was going on. Providing this information alone was very important and clearly lacking in other cases of privatization in Samburu. In many communities, individuals already had obtained ownership of land before other community members realized what was happening. Furthermore, in Siambu, the knowledge that the individual land owners would evict them from the land once their title deeds came through made this threatened loss very real. Again, this was not the case in other communities where individuals who gained private land rarely evicted their neighbors. In Mbaringon, for example, only one of the five individuals restricted access to his land, and this occurred years after the adjudication process was over. The other individual owners were nonresident and left the land available for communal use.

In Siambu, not only would the individuals have gained private parcels of land, but they would also gain the benefits from land-leasing arrangements with the wheat farmer. Thus, they stood to gain materially, while the others would lose absolutely. In addition, their triumph would probably have boosted their status as they joined the community of modern land owners in Kenya. Their status gains would have implied relative losses for the other community members. Once community members realized how high the stakes were—that they were in danger of losing access to their most critical natural resource, land—action to resist individual land ownership was forthcoming. In order to safeguard both their material and status interests, and with the urging of their leaders, individuals joined the opposition.

The initial strategy of the elders was to use conventional social sanctions to dissuade the individual land holders from their course of action. These techniques comprise what anthropologists call "leveling tactics" and are similar to the "weapons of the weak" discussed by James Scott (1985). These behaviors are aimed at discouraging individuals from upsetting the status quo by keeping them in their place through social pressures. They are designed to keep individuals in line, encourage them to follow existing social norms, and conform to communal expectations. Negative gossip about the individuals who had been allocated land was one such technique, as was criticism of them at public meetings held by the elders to discuss the land issue. More powerful sanctions included the threat of cursing those who had been given private land.

The use of leveling tactics is often effective in enforcing adherence to social norms. They work in large part because members of the group seek to preserve their reputations among their peers. Especially in a small-scale society such as Samburu, more so a subset of it like Siambu, where multisided relationships are pervasive and contacts among group members are frequent, one's reputation is of prime importance to maintaining status in the community and reaping the benefits of group membership. For the Samburu in particular, an individual must show himself to be worthy of esteem by cultivating a sense of *nkanyit,* or respectability. Certainly, depriving fellow community members of critical land resources was viewed as behavior lacking in *nkanyit.* The elders invoked social norms such as *nkanyit* as part of their effort to mobilize collective action against privatization. On top of the fact that these individuals were taking away prime land from their own community, they argued, they were violating the very essence of community by behaving contrary to its shared ideals. While these arguments from social norms were effective in raising the consciousness of the community about the risks that privatization entailed, and in stimulating them to counter such moves, they were not effective in reversing the behavior of individual land claimants. The outward response of the individuals claiming land was to seek assurance that their claims were secure. They did so by requesting copies of the documentation of their claims and writing letters to the district administration seeking a rapid resolution of the land issue in Siambu.

The reason that leveling tactics were ineffective, I argue, is that the majority of individuals seeking private land had become impervious to social pressure from the Siambu community. They were no longer overly concerned to maintain their reputations among Siambu people, because their reference group had shifted away from their local community toward those of modern Kenya. They could afford to resist the pressure exerted by the Siambu community, because they were concentrating their efforts elsewhere, on gaining entrance to the community of modern Kenyans. Leveling tactics are only successful when the one being "leveled" cares about what others think of him. If he no longer shares the same norms and values, is no longer tightly bound by the multisided ties that make small communities work, then he will not respond to leveling. In many ways, the men who wanted private land were seeking it as part of an overall strategy of separation from the confines of Samburu society.[3] They no longer wanted to be bound so tightly. Rather, they wanted freedom to pursue their own interests.

This perspective is revealed in the way the individuals who sought land discuss the issue of privatization. Most of them contend that by claiming individual land they were simply exercising their rights according to Kenyan law, as one Lkishili man, a junior elder in the 1980s, told me.

JL: You know the worst they did was to throw dry wood at us.

CL: To curse you?

JL: To curse us, yet they know very well that we weren't at fault, we were just after our rights.

In this way he deflects the fact that those seeking individual land were violating communal norms. In his mind, they were justified since Kenyan law allowed, even encouraged, individual land ownership. His comments indicate that, in his mind, in a competition between Kenyan law and Samburu norms, Kenyan law ought to prevail. Of course, this could simply be a way to rationalize unpopular and selfish behavior, but his further comments reveal the extent to which a rift was developing between "traditional" people and those aspiring to be "modern."

> Yes, we had different knowledge from them, because they just stuck to one thing, just cattle alone and we saw that cattle alone is not enough for us, we wanted to farm. That's where we didn't understand each other. They say cattle and we say development. Moreover, if you see the people who were the leaders of wanting farms and those who wanted to stay in the group, they are just sleeping. Father of L ____ , L ____ . If I tell you, all the thirty-seven [individuals] are doing development. Those who were for the group are fools. That's the way it is.

While unusually blunt, his statements were echoed by many informants who had made claims to land. Land ownership, for them, was a sign of their personal advancement and growth away from the customs of the Samburu, some of which they had come to despise. The way in which the discussion is framed in legalistic terms with an emphasis on individual rights reflects the fact that these individuals had been influenced by the modernizing project of the Kenyan state.

In some cases, the urge to identify with the forces of modernity and the state overlapped with dissatisfaction with the power relations obtaining in the status quo. Resentment against the wealthier and more influential families, who opposed privatization, provided additional motivation to flout their authority and get even. In this sense, acquiring one's own land was a strategy to reduce the power of the wealthier groups.

When leveling tactics failed to bring about any change in the behavior of the individuals who had been granted private land, the elders had to find other ways to prevail. This meant challenging the state head-on and required increasing their relative bargaining power. They did this in two ways. First, they threatened retaliation against those who were challenging the norm. Knight argues that threats can be an effective way of establishing a power relationship among two parties.

> Here threats mean the actors' capacity to affect the benefits derived by others from their own choice of action. For example, A may threaten retaliation against B if he fails to choose L. The effect of the threat can be to increase the pressure on B to adopt his less-preferred alternative. The reason is that the threatened retaliation (if carried out) would increase the costs of adopting R. (1992, 135)

The elders opposed to privatization threatened the individuals who were claiming land that if they did not give up their claims they would be cursed or even killed. While the threat of the curse may not have been very effective since its credibility had lessened among the modernizing individuals, the threat of violence was still potent. Groups of warriors had been meeting in the forest plotting violence, and these plans were well known in the community. The growing tension was capped in 1985 by the murder of the watchman, which was widely perceived to have been linked with the land issue. The murder took on added significance because it brought to the fore underlying tensions between the two subclans, Siit and Kurpa. Playing up these latent clan hostilities could have escalated the conflict over land into a more encompassing issue with a potential for even greater violence. It appears that it was unnecessary for the elders to accentuate the clan issue, since the murder alone provided a signal to all of the tenuousness of the situation and the real possibility for a breakdown of social order.

Beyond the threat of retaliation, the elders built up their bargaining power by forging alliances with powerful third parties. As discussed in chapter 4, the General came to support the elders' opposition to individual land allocations. The General occupied a pivotal position due to his ability to influence government policy and practice. Not only was he a senior officer in the army, but he had been instrumental in foiling the attempted coup d'état against President Moi in 1982. This meant that he had access to the highest levels of governmental decision making. Although he was one of the individuals claiming private land, he came to understand that the struggle over land in Siambu threatened to descend into chaos if action was not taken to change the course of events. It is also important to recall that he was a clansman of the Siambu people, and their support would be important to him in his future endeavors. In fact, as it turns out, his cousin made his first attempt at the Samburu West parliamentary seat in 1987, the year following the resolution of the land issue in Siambu. It is likely, then, that he acted at least in part to preserve his good relations and reputation for wise leadership among this important constituency.

The elders also approached the wheat farmer and asked for his assistance. The wheat farmer supported the elders because he, too, wanted to preserve communal land ownership. When interviewed, he emphasized his concern that if land was privatized it would be sold off rapidly to non-Samburu, and Siambu residents would be left landless. He had reason to believe this might happen since that had been the result in some parts of Maasailand that had been privatized. He was also motivated to act, he says, to avenge the murder of his employee. On the other hand, it would also benefit his wheat farming operation if he only had to deal with one lessor, the group ranch, rather than thirty or forty land owners. Some more cynical informants suggested that he preferred dealing with the group ranch since they were unaware of the acreage of their land and could easily be duped into accepting unfairly low lease rates.

A few informants claim that the wheat farmer was promised a farm or at least free access to lease land anywhere, in exchange for his assistance, but others deny this. It probably does not matter whether he was offered any specific incentives. The possibility of leasing land from the group was incentive enough for him to act, since his interests already overlapped with the opposition's. The wheat farmer provided transport and funds for the elders to travel outside the district to visit the General to try to gain his support. The wheat farmer also claims that he brought up the matter with President Moi, whom he believes followed it up personally.

These strategic alliances ratcheted up the power of the elders so that it approximated that of the individuals. While the individuals had the backing of state policy and the support of the government officers within Samburu District, the wheat farmer and, especially, the General were able to bypass local officials and work directly at the national level, where exceptions could be, and were, made to the standard land adjudication process.

A Failure of Collective Action

Once the elders began organizing in earnest, the individuals who were claiming land began to meet together more often to discuss their common problems and to strategize. I will refer to them at this stage as the Group of Thirty-seven to denote their attempt to act jointly. While they did coordinate their actions aimed at securing their land claims and demanding a favorable resolution of the land issue in Siambu from the district administration, their coalition remained limited to themselves. They failed to build a following among the ordinary community members for their cause. In fact, there is little evidence that they even attempted to do so.

There are several reasons why the Group of Thirty-seven failed to cultivate followers. First, ideologically, most people in the community either did not comprehend the idea of private land ownership or, if they did, were against it. The Group of Thirty-seven did little to change this view. Although there was talk about the advantages of private land, this was rather ineffective in convincing most people, especially since the best land was going disproportionately to a few people. Second, since the majority of these individuals obtained land against the objections of the land committee, they were of necessity keeping a low profile and not revealing their activities, making it difficult to attract supporters. Third, the Group of Thirty-seven did not provide selective incentives in the form of side payments or promises to potential followers. I learned of only one case in which the Group of Thirty-seven apparently tried to buy off one of the elders leading the opposition. The effort was rebuffed. Their attempts to get land stemmed almost entirely from self-interest or, occasionally, from genuine feelings of entitlement. It was not in their interest for too many people to get private land, since the fertile land on the plateau was limited. Unlike the elders, they could not appeal for support on the basis of social norms, since what they were doing was in violation of a number of these. Initially, they did not anticipate opposition and so did not see a need to build support for themselves as a hedge against this possibility. Their confidence was not surprising given the ease with which people had obtained individual land in earlier adjudication sections.

In short, they were not acting as leaders who were trying to build a following that would then push through a change in land tenure that would be viewed by most individuals as superior, as a collective good. Rather, they were using their knowledge and abilities to obtain land with or without the consent of the other community members. Thus, they did not attempt to head off opposition or to attract followers through selective incentives, as would be expected if they had been trying to stimulate collective action, for example, to encourage a voluntary shift toward private land ownership as the norm. At the same time, most of them were not genuine community leaders.

Some were appointed officials, accountable to the central government, not the community. They did not require the approval of the community to retain their status. As pointed out earlier, most of them were working to gain entrance into the modern Kenyan elite, not to curry the favor of the Siambu people.

By the time the elders' opposition coalesced, it was too late for the Group of Thirty-seven to build a following among community members. Once their activities were made public, they were branded as grasping individualists, ready to sell out their clansmen to get access to the best land.

Compromise: An Outcome of Equal Bargaining Power

Once the General intervened on behalf of the elders, the bargaining power of the two groups was nearly equal. The bargaining theory of norm change posits unequal power as the general case and predicts that outcomes will favor the more powerful party. But in a case where bargaining power is virtually equal, then compromise is the logical result as each side gets some of what it wants, but not everything. While I am arguing that the power of the two groups was nearly equal, this was due, at least in part, to the General's individual preferences. In principle, he could have influenced the outcome so that it would have entirely favored the elders (i.e., a return to communal ownership in the form of a group ranch). Legally, that outcome would have been acceptable since it was the normal result of the land adjudication process in pastoral areas. However, the General opted against this solution and in favor of equal subdivision of the land among all the members. He did so because, although he understood the stance of the elders and the risks for the community posed by the stalemate over land, he was at heart a modernizer and believed deeply in the value of private land ownership and development. He suggested the solution of equal subdivision of land on normative grounds since he felt it was better for each person to have access to some land for farming. This move also enabled him to retain a modicum of support from the Group of Thirty-seven who, though they would lose acreage, would still get land.

The compromise was accepted by both sides, but for different reasons. For the elders, equal subdivision secured their rights to the land and preempted any further attempts by individuals to grab large parcels of land. This solution was perceived as fair since all were treated equally, but it was also a victory since they had prevented the individuals from obtaining the whole plateau area and relegating the rest of the community to the lowlands. Equal subdivision preserved their leadership position and restored order and calm to the community. The individuals who had made land claims also accepted the compromise, and most of them were satisfied because they still got private land under the agreement, even if the parcel sizes were smaller than what they would have received. The compromise was also a victory for them in that the norm of land ownership was effectively shifted from communal to private, in spite of the opposition from the elders. Thus, each group won something, even if it was not what they had anticipated. Overlaying their individual outcomes was the possibility to restore order and a degree of harmony to a community that had been seriously rent by the conflict over land.

Can Laws Change Norms?

In the end, the institution of land tenure was changed from communal to private, not out of an ideological shift or a simple triumph of more powerful modernizing interests, but rather through a complex conflict in which bargaining power was gained and lost, ending in a compromise that satisfied most members of both groups. Given the way privatization occurred in Siambu, we may wonder to what extent the advent of private property has altered the informal norms surrounding land ownership. Does the fact of private land ownership lead to the internalization of private property as a good in itself? Does the norm change from describing what is to the realm of what ought to be?

The ability of law to create new norms is a subject of debate among legal scholars who study social norms. On one side, there are those such as Scott (2000), Posner (2000), and Ellickson (2001), who argue that law, by putting into place sanctions against certain behaviors, modifies the incentives of actors engaging in those behaviors. Using the tools of rational choice, Scott traces the effect of law on incentives and, through these, on behavior. He assumes for the purposes of analysis that preferences, or internalized norms, remain constant. We change our behavior to conform to a law because there are costs attached to breaking it, not because we have internalized a norm against the particular behavior sanctioned by law.

On the other side are scholars such as McAdams (1997), Lessig (1996), and Sunstein (1996), who argue that law plays a role in shaping preferences. They contend that law has an "expressive" function that influences the formation and internalization of norms. McAdams (1997), for example, claims that law has the effect of publicizing a social consensus about a norm that may not be accurately perceived by members of the society. Once they become aware of the consensus, individuals may change their behavior in order to conform to that consensus, thereby reaping esteem from others. Seeking esteem, McAdams argues, is the basis of adherence to social norms in the first place. He goes further to say that law may lead to the internalization of new norms to the extent that a law makes concrete an already internalized, abstract norm. As an example, he cites the abstract norm of "being a good parent." Many possible behaviors might qualify to make one a good parent. If a new law, say, for using child safety seats, becomes perceived as a concrete expression of what it means to be a good parent, then it may be internalized and followed. This may have been the case, for example, with those individuals who applied for private land. Private land was one instantiation of what it means to be "a modern Kenyan." Obtaining land was a concrete means for them to fulfill what they had already internalized as an abstract norm.

Applying this debate to the Siambu case, the question becomes whether individuals are adhering to the new norm of private property merely because it would be costly to diverge from it or because they have internalized the norm of private property in a deeper sense. The evidence is equivocal. Private property in the area is generally respected. People know where the borders are between their plots, and they do not infringe for the most part on the freedom of action of individuals on their own land. When land was divided, families moved to settle on their plots, fragmenting the prior settlement structure where extended family groups often shared a single homestead. Title deeds have been issued for the land and carry the backing of third party enforcement by the state.[4] In addition, the elders do enforce rights to private property under some circumstances. For example, if livestock encroach on cultivated land and cause damage to crops, the owner will be fined by the elders. This is in stark contrast to the earlier practice of elders organizing invasions of cultivated land in order to punish those trying to start farming. Land is also leased out and sold by individual owners, and the community, while generally against land sales, has not intervened directly to prevent them. In these ways, private property is upheld not only through the threat of state enforcement but also through enforcement from the elders.

Even though private property is recognized, other aspects of land use suggest that the land remains in some senses a commons. Traveling through the area, a casual observer would probably not realize that the land was privately owned since it remains almost wholly unfenced. Only 2 individuals, out of over 230 owners, have recently enclosed their entire parcels. Most people only fence the area of land they are cultivating, which averages about two acres, out of a total plot size of about twenty-three acres. Livestock still move across the land relatively freely. It appears that the imperatives of Samburu livestock production, the need for extensive tracts of pastureland, outweigh the prerogatives of private land ownership. This was not a necessary outcome, however, since there are other places for livestock to graze outside the privately owned area. In addition to the lowlands over the escarpment that remain a group ranch, Siambu also borders a national forest where livestock grazing is ubiquitous in spite of its illegality. Siambu people do utilize the forest, taking their cattle there particularly during dry seasons and even establishing temporary cattle camps (*lale,* pl. *laleta*) within the forest boundaries. Thus, the fact that people continue to graze animals in the privatized area is a choice, not a true necessity. It is a choice that is generally tolerated among community members. Other resources continue to be shared as well. Women claim that, aside from firewood, which they may have to buy from their neighbors, they have access to other natural resources, particularly water, on others' land.

To understand if a norm has been internalized would require situations in which individuals adhere to the norm even when there is no risk of detection or punishment. If, in such a circumstance, they felt guilt or shame about violating the norm, then we could conclude that the norm had been internalized and that conformity to it was not just due to fear of sanctions. In Siambu, people violate private property often (e.g., by grazing on and collecting firewood and other resources from others' plots) and in full view of other community members. They can do so due to the hybrid nature of land use: recognizable and potentially enforceable private boundaries coupled with continued sharing of pasture and other key resources.

Although apparently contradictory, the norms of private and communal land use and ownership coexist in Siambu. Which norm is enforced varies depending on circumstances. Thus, private ownership is enforced when it comes to the cultivation of crops and their protection from livestock. Firewood also appears to have made the transition to commodity status, with individual owners selling it to their neighbors. Recently, a community member purchased a chain saw and has started a business of cutting and selling timber. Individual land owners contract the chain saw owner to cut selected trees on their land and sell the timber in Maralal town. In these cases, land

and its products are privately owned commodities, and owners assert their rights to monopolize the returns flowing from these resources. When it comes to livestock grazing and access to water, though, communal access is still the norm, although those individuals with the ability to fence their entire parcels may do so, effectively curtailing this access. Most people believe that the trend is toward greater enclosure of land, not the opposite.

This situation is not very surprising given the history of how private property became established in Siambu. As shown here, the shift was not achieved through a consensus on the superiority of private property. While they accepted subdivision of land, this did not imply that the elders and their supporters suddenly became converted to the views of the modernizers but that they realized they could do no better than to divide the land equally and stave off further land grabs.

In addition to the fact that most people were initially opposed to privatization, we would also expect that it would take considerable time for a new norm, particularly one introduced through formal law, to become internalized. It has only been fifteen years since title deeds were issued in Siambu, probably not long enough for the new norm to become fully entrenched. While the extent of true internalization of the norm of private property remains opaque due to the hybrid nature of land use in Siambu, the existence of the new norm has been incorporated into a shared rhetoric that, I argue, has been instrumental to restoring a sense of community among the people of Siambu.

Revisionist History and Group Status

Over the fifteen years since the resolution of the land issue in Siambu, a rhetoric regarding the virtues of private land ownership has developed with which virtually everyone, regardless of which side they were on during the conflict, concurs. This rhetoric takes two forms. First, there is a shared narrative about the process of land subdivision. During interviews, when asked to explain how land came to be privately owned, all informants started with a nearly uniform account of the process. This summary account included the main features of the conflict: land adjudication started, a few people wanted their own land, they were about to get this land, the community complained, and the government divided the land equally among everyone. What is interesting about the narrative, aside from its striking uniformity among informants, is the downplaying of the conflict and the emphasis on the harmonious solution brought by the government. In some cases, informants started by omitting the conflict altogether and skipping forward to the equal subdivision. When probed, they did give the account of the conflict but always returned to the happy ending of the story.

The other aspect of the rhetoric is the enumeration of the positive attributes of private land ownership. The key words here are control (*aitore*) and development (*maendeleo*). Private property is good, people say, because the owner is able to control what he does with his land. No one can interfere with him, or tell him what he can or cannot do on his land. This is in contrast, they go on, to the situation in communal lands or on group ranches where one is subject to the rules of the community regarding land. You may not be able to farm or even build a "modern" house on a group ranch. This hinders development, they say. You cannot develop if you do not have control over your affairs, including, especially, your land.

The narrative serves the purpose of restoring social harmony that was almost destroyed during the conflict over land. By simplifying events and emphasizing the final outcome, the narrative constitutes a collective representation of what happened in Siambu that is easily recalled and recited by community members. In glossing over the negative events, these details may ultimately be lost to future generations whose understanding of this history may come primarily from the narrative. Indeed, even my research assistant, whose father was a land committee member and had told him much about what happened, had not heard some of the details elicited during our interviews. The emergence of this standard narrative has assisted the community to come to terms with what happened and reestablish relatively harmonious relationships among themselves.

Similarly, the rhetoric about control and development serves a specific purpose. Control and development are significant emphases when considered in light of Samburu social structure and the history of privatization in Siambu. As noted earlier, there is a tension between individual freedom and equality among men in Samburu society and the hierarchy of authority embodied in the age-set system. The senior age-sets have a degree of control (*aitore*) over their juniors that puts them at an advantage. When Siambu people speak of having control (*aitore*) over their land and affairs, they are at once implicitly challenging the authority of senior elders and at the same time asserting their superiority over communities practicing communal land ownership. While they may not openly flout the authority of elders, they are putting a limit on it—it stops at the boundary of their land, since no one can dictate or interfere with what an individual does on his land. By contrast, in an ordinary Samburu community, one lacks this control. He may be dictated to even within his own homestead.

Their feelings of superiority vis-à-vis other communities are clear in the tone of their pronouncements about their higher level of development, deriving again from land ownership. Ironically, they have adopted many of the clichés about development—such as the superiority of cultivation, iron-roofed houses, and Western-style clothes—that were used by the land officers as justification to grant individual land in Siambu. These same ideas were inculcated into the individuals who sought private land initially, and they used them to set themselves apart from the rest of the Siambu community, as in "they say cattle, we say development." These markers of modernity are now being claimed by virtually the entire community whether or not they practice "development" themselves.

These statements about control and development mesh together with the shared narrative about privatization. Where the narrative serves to reestablish social harmony, the control/development discourse elevates the status of the community relative to the rest of Samburu society. Thus, not only did the events in Siambu not destroy the community, they actually made them better than their neighbors. For people of the Lotimi clan, occupying a superior position to other Samburu communities is not without precursors. After all, Lmasula are the largest and the ritually senior section among Samburu. They live on mountains or high places where the Samburu believe God is more accessible. Accordingly, they tend to view themselves as more blessed than the ordinary Samburu. They have also been the first to abandon certain traditions, such as clan exogamy. While marrying within one's section is becoming more common in other sections, it has been acceptable among the Lmasula for many years.

Viewed against this background, it makes sense that the conflict over privatization would be reinterpreted as further evidence of Lmasula, or more specifically Lotimi, superior social status. In fact, it revamps their ritual superiority in the more updated garb of modernity. After all, rituals are on the decline. To maintain superiority will require fresh justification, and the trope of development might just meet this need. This effort, however unconscious, to revise clan status helps explain why the rhetoric is espoused by people who were against privatization, as well as those who do no farming and engage in no activities that could be interpreted as development.

In retrospect, it also clarifies why people were so willing to participate in this research project. Having some idea of the gravity of the conflict over land in Siambu, I had expected some reticence on the part of community members, and I even anticipated that there might be resistance toward my conducting the research. On the contrary, I believe that some people felt that the research was an opportunity for them to tell their narrative and share their rhetoric. Perhaps they hoped that the comparison with Mbaringon would confirm their higher level of development.

While it is possible to delineate the function played by the narrative and the rhetoric, it is more challenging to identify their source. Like most social norms, institutions, or shared values, these have arisen in a decentralized manner and not as a result of conscious design. The evolution of the narrative probably began as the natural simplification that occurs with the retelling of historical events, something like the creation of a myth or a legend that distills the broad strokes of what happened while simultaneously winnowing out extraneous details. However, the coupling of the narrative with the themes of control and development bespeaks a more instrumental agenda.

I argued earlier that a powerful motivation of the elders was to preserve their position of authority. If they had allowed the individuals to take all the fertile land they would have been condemning their community to a harsh fate, and their position would have been jeopardized. It turned out that everyone got land, but at the same time a new regime of private land tenure was established. By appropriating the terminology of development and control, the elders, as well as other, younger leaders, have been able to turn this situation to their advantage. Rather than threatening disintegration of the community, the division of land became a way to reassert the cohesiveness and strength of the community based on their very independence and progressive tendencies. Through this reversal, the clan remains at the pinnacle of Samburu society, not just due to their ritual seniority but due to their forward-looking values. And the leaders, even if they were not the originators of the narrative or the rhetoric, remain leaders by articulating and disseminating these ideas. By providing focal points for communal identification, they make it easier for members of the Siambu community to see themselves as a group and to perceive their relative status among other Samburu communities.

Conclusion

Institutional change emerges out of conflict among parties struggling to establish institutional arrangements that will serve their interests best. The role of the analyst is to understand the positions of various social actors, not only at the commencement of the conflict but over its entire course. People act from given endowments of power, but they also work to enhance their power. While there is considerable scope for choice and agency, some choices are harder to make than others due to the costs involved in violating acceptable norms of behavior and culturally shared values. On the other hand, when individuals free themselves from these restraints by associating themselves with another community, as the Group of Thirty-seven did, they may push their opponents to seek new sources of power. In the Siambu case, the elders were up to the challenge. Subdivision of land was not the end of the story, either, as elders worked to make the most of an outcome that promised to reduce their authority.

CHAPTER 6

Experiences in Education, the Military, and Employment

The individuals who sought private land in Siambu were predominantly people with experiences in formal education, the military, and employment, as shown in previous chapters. Furthermore, I have made the claim that these experiences were significant for a number of reasons. First, they exposed individuals to the practices of agriculture and private land ownership, both of which were relatively unknown among the Samburu. Second, these individuals came to value agriculture and private property not only as economically valuable activities but as part and parcel of becoming modern. This association of property ownership with modernity and with gaining entrance into the class of Kenyans considered developed was an important reason these individuals wanted private land. They sought land not only for economic purposes, though this was usually the case, but also as a way of identifying with another society beyond that of Samburu. Through their experiences, these individuals had been socialized, or enculturated, into a new set of beliefs and values, including the notion of private property and cultivation as necessary components of being a modern Kenyan.

In this chapter, I present vignettes of a few of these individuals as further illustration of the significance of experiences in education, the military, and employment. By describing some of their life history, including the way they themselves present it, I hope to clarify the particular ways in which their experiences shaped their beliefs and values. These personal stories do not represent a random sample of those who sought private land, nor are they meant to be comprehensive life histories. I chose these examples based on my knowledge of the individuals and the opportunities I had to interact with them in some depth. However, I do feel that their stories are indicative of the experiences of many individuals who were part of the first group of Samburu to enter formal education, military service, and employment.

Case One: Formal Education and Work in the Prisons—Jonas

I first met Jonas in 1996 while I was working in the SDDP development project. I remember it well, because after our meeting he invited us to visit his plot in Poro town where he showed us the orange and lemon trees he was growing. Seeing citrus trees in Samburu is extremely unusual (the only other place I've seen them is in the compounds of a couple of Catholic missions), and his trees were large and productive. He explained to us that he had learned how to grow these trees while working in the prison service. Kenyan prisons often have large farms where the prisoners work, and he had been a farm supervisor in a number of prisons during his twenty years of government service.

His agricultural skills extended beyond the orange trees, however. His maize farm was relatively large for the area (indeed, at eight acres, it was the largest farm in our household survey), and his maize was well tended. That year, he was experimenting with growing wheat on a small scale. Instead of leasing out his land to the commercial wheat farmer, as many of his neighbors did, Jonas wanted to try growing wheat on his own, by hand. He was also involved in trials of pasture development that our project was coordinating along with the Ministry of Agriculture and Livestock Development. The aim was to introduce pastoralists to the idea of planting fodder grasses for their livestock. Jonas was one of the first to volunteer to try growing grass, and he had considerable success with this.

His farm was one of the few that ministry staff used as a model farm in their extension work. In 2000, the ministry and a UN agency, the World Food Programme, held their World Food Day celebrations on Jonas's farm, to expose other Samburu to the potentials for agricultural development. In addition to his well-tended fields and livestock, Jonas's homestead itself exhibits many of the characteristics often associated with development in Kenya. Unlike the typical Samburu house that is a low, rectangular structure made of sticks and mud with a flat, mudded roof, his house showed the influence of agricultural groups. It was large and square in shape and roofed with corrugated iron sheets. It had several rooms, and the walls were plastered with red clay on which his children had painted attractive designs with white and blue clays. While this housing style is becoming more popular in Siambu, Jonas's house stands out for its size, its iron roof (most are thatched with cedar bark), and the elaborate wall decoration as well as the furniture (tables, chairs) inside it. In his town plot, he has built a number of buildings of cedar pole construction with corrugated iron roofs. This style of construction is typical of town buildings, and proof of a significant monetary investment. Jonas's buildings, with their plastered and painted facades, were more elaborate than most in Poro.

Other signs of modernity in the household were the fact that all family members wore Western clothes, apparently at all times. In many cases, Samburu men own a pair of trousers, shirt, and jacket that they don on trips to town, but at home they retain the Samburu wardrobe of a cloth around the waist and a T-shirt. I never saw Jonas in a cloth, even when I passed his place early in the morning on the way to other homesteads. His wife also did not conform to the usual dress for Samburu women. She did not shave her head, did not wear layers of beads around her neck, and did not wear cloths. Instead, she wore a Western-type dress and had her hair in short braids. For a Samburu woman to dress this way immediately identifies her as nontraditional: someone who has gone to school (as she had) and/or a Christian (which she is).[1]

In addition to the furniture in their house, it also had framed photographs of family members, mostly Jonas himself at various points in his academic and work career, hung on the walls about a foot under the roof line. This arrangement of family photos is ubiquitous in modern Kenyan homes across the country and is often the only adornment of walls. The size of the photos and the elaborateness of the frames appear to correlate positively with wealth. Who appears in the photos may also be significant. Usually, it is family members, often in formal portraits or during significant occasions such as school graduations or weddings. However, some go beyond family affairs. For example, in homes of a few elite Samburu I've noticed pictures of the husband with prominent political personalities, including President Moi himself. The display of these pictures seems to be a not-so-subtle statement about social position. While they take up the most wall space, these photos are often displayed together with plaques or wall hangings with religious content such as "Jesus is the head of this household" or "May God bless this house."

I point out these details of Jonas's household to make the point that there are many physical markers of modernity that can be easily observed like dress, hairstyle, language, house design, and decoration. These are also perceived by Samburu people as signs of development. This was brought home to me when, in the course of SDDP's work with communities, we asked people to draw what they thought of as development. Invariably, across more than thirty communities, what they drew were things like corrugated iron roofs on houses and buildings in towns, schools, Western-style dress, vehicles, electricity, tarmac roads, and farms growing crops. Discussions of development and change usually began with emphasis on these kinds of physical changes—people would no longer wear their traditional dress, their housing style would change, children would go to school, they would farm the land. The extent to which people connected these changes with different value systems and beliefs varied, though most had a notion that change implied more than just outward signs and involved some degree of loss of traditional values. In what follows I discuss the more intangible aspects of development or modernity by considering the attitudes, beliefs, and philosophies of individuals all of whom display, more or less, the physical trappings of change.

Jonas attended many of our early meetings in Siambu and was an active participant. As I noted in chapter 2, SDDP was unable to continue working in Siambu after about six months due to decreased participation by community members. After that, I occasionally saw Jonas when I was passing through Siambu or sometimes in Maralal, the district headquarters. After I began my research in Siambu, however, I saw him frequently and visited his farm several times. During these visits I had an opportunity to learn more about his life experiences and philosophy.

Born in the Ndoto mountain range north of Baragoi (about 100 kilometers north of Siambu) around 1949, he began life as a typical Samburu boy, herding his father's cattle. This did not last long, though, since he was selected to go to school at age seven. At this time, the colonial government was beginning to provide some formal education in Samburu District, mostly through the Catholic mission. Families were encouraged to send at least one son to school. Due to widespread disinterest in formal education among Samburu, this encouragement often amounted to coercion. Jonas reports that there was a quota of boys to be taken to school from the Ndoto area.

They said that our family will send one child, Lealmusia one child, then Ndoto area will send how many boys? Six. By force, no pleading. So, they came to my father's settlement, and they asked whom have you decided to send, and they said this one. When I was caught, my mother started to fight. She was fighting chiefs! I was taken up to school. Six of us were brought.

Although he was forced to go to school in this fashion, when he talks about the process he reveals his admiration for the government-appointed chief who sent his own sons to school: "[Chief] Lesokoyo said, personally, instead of sending those children who are poor, I will send my children as an example." Jonas also pointed out that Lesokoyo was a wealthy man, but he differed from most wealthy men of the time who disdained formal education.

Thus, at seven years of age, Jonas was taken far from his family to a boarding school run by the Catholic mission in Baragoi. He and the other boys had difficulty adjusting at first, but the sweets they were given by the Italian nuns helped convince them that this was not such a bad situation.

What changed our minds about school was when she [the nun] brought us a whole package of sweets. Imagine, you were crying, then you are given a sweet. She was speaking poor Samburu so we couldn't understand what she said. After one week of being bribed with sweets, we saw that this place was not bad. Then later we became eager to learn. We started learning and we saw things are not bad.

Candy was only the first in a long chain of incentives and gifts from the mission that enabled Jonas to continue his education through the secondary level. He noted several times that without the Catholic mission he would never have been able to get an education.

Jonas describes the educational process as a series of weeding-out exercises, an account that will be familiar to any Kenyan who has gone through this system. Terminal exams at the end of primary school (eighth grade) and secondary school (twelfth grade) are indeed terminal for the majority of students who do not pass or, even if they do, are unable to continue to the next higher level of education due to shortages of schools or money for fees. For Jonas's cohort in Baragoi, the first weeding out came even earlier, after fourth grade. Out of six boys from Ndoto, four passed the exam and were sent on to Maralal DEB (District Education Board) school. The other two went home.

In Maralal, they joined boys from all over the district for grades five to eight. At this point it was not only the demands of academia that led to the end of academic careers but the lure of becoming a warrior (*lmurran*). Of his group from Baragoi, only Jonas withstood the attractions of "moranism" (as educated Samburu refer to this life stage) to remain in school. Two left to live the warrior lifestyle, while another one who tried to leave was found by a priest and convinced to come back and join the Rural Training Center, a vocational school in Maralal. But Jonas stayed the course, successfully passing the Kenya African Preliminary Examination (KAPE) and gaining entrance to Mangu Secondary School in Thika, just outside Nairobi. Like the other schools he attended, this one was run by Catholics and his teachers were Catholic brothers. Going so much further away, about five hundred kilometers from Samburu District, posed new challenges for him.

> If it was not for the Catholic mission, we would not have gone to school. . . . They were the ones who took us to school, then back home. When the school opens, the father in charge of Maralal would take us up to the father in charge of Nyahururu; the Nyahururu father takes us up to Nyeri; the Nyeri father takes us up to school. Sometimes Nyahururu father offers a vehicle straight up to Mangu High School. When we want to go up to Ndoto, we had to stay in the mission until the vehicle that goes to Baragoi comes.

In addition to transportation, there was the problem of paying for school. School fees were KSh 420 per year, the equivalent of five cows at the time. After one year, Jonas's father told him that he could no longer afford the school fees, but the Catholic mission again assisted by providing him with employment during school vacations.

> My parents only paid school for one year. When they saw that five cows were sold for school fees, my father said, "Son, it's up to you." The priest said, you can work during the holidays so you should come here, then I will pay you. I came to quarry the stone, nine-by-six-inch blocks. When I completed, I was given school fees and even pocket money.

Working in a stone quarry to earn money may not strike us as unusual, but for a Samburu it was quite unusual. As I noted in chapter 4, digging in the ground to grow crops was considered a demeaning practice by Samburu. Digging for stones would fall into the same category, perhaps even worse since it might have associations with the work of blacksmiths (due to the use of metal implements and tools), who are considered inferior people with whom relationships are carefully circumscribed (Larick 1986; Spear and Waller 1993). Even today, the majority of people who work in the small stone quarry that Jonas refers to are not Samburu but Turkana herders or Kikuyu agriculturalists.

Jonas was willing to do this work in order to further his education. Indeed, doing hard, physical work is for him a positive thing, not negative. It is part of his philosophy and is revealed in many of his comments about the need for Samburu to work hard to improve themselves, as in the following where he contrasts farmers from Kitui to the Samburu.

> Kitui is like Archer's Post [driest part of Samburu District]. The rain they receive is very little, but they grow a lot of food crops which is enough for them. They grow peas, beans, and many other crops. You see people working, because if [the growing] season ends they will be nowhere. From there you go to a place which is blessed by God, Nyeri. It's a place with a lot of rain throughout the year. Also Kisii, although it's small. If you go to Kisii, they have small farms, but almost all types of food are grown. When I come to our area I see that we have a lot of land, but we are just staying that way! Samburu are affected by laziness, lack of knowledge, and overvaluing what we have. I can't sell my cow [people say]. Because of land, we are still keeping cows.

While part of Jonas's work ethic may stem from his own personality, it was certainly shaped by his early experiences with education among the missionaries. It may be ironic that he developed a kind of Protestant ethic among Catholics, but it is no exaggeration to say that most of the missionaries were tireless workers who strove to establish themselves in places that were not only physically challenging but where they were not always welcomed by the local population. In fact, one of the priests who helped Jonas was later killed by local Turkana people.

Upon completing secondary school, Jonas applied for a job with the prison service and underwent a nine-month training course in Nairobi, conducted jointly with the military and police. The fact that this training was held jointly underscores the fact that work in the prisons was actually a paramilitary profession. After the training, Jonas served in the prison service for twenty years, moving to posts in many parts of the country. When he was briefly stationed in Maralal in the early 1970s, he heard that the County Council was allocating plots of land in towns. He applied and was allocated a plot in Poro town. Although he had hoped to get a plot in Maralal, the largest town in Samburu District, he accepted the Poro plot and began working on developing it in 1974. Later, he married a woman from Siambu and decided to establish his homestead there, rather than returning to Baragoi. When land adjudication began in 1978, he requested first to become a member of the group ranch and, later, to be given private land. Even before this time, he had been growing some crops around his home.

There are two aspects of his experience in the prison service that I will discuss further as they have some bearing on the land question in Siambu. The first element has to do with the significance that Jonas gives to law and individual rights. In discussing the conflict over land in Siambu, he repeatedly defended the position of those who sought private land by arguing that they did nothing wrong, they were merely exercising their rights under Kenyan law. He reports how the elders cursed the thirty-seven individuals, "To curse us, yet they know very well that we weren't at fault, we just after our rights." Interestingly, in this sentence he switched to English to emphasize the phrase *our rights* as if to acknowledge the English origins of these rights.

He makes many references to the importance of law when discussing the intervention by the Director of Lands who visited Siambu to resolve the issue.

The director of lands tricked people a bit, because he said *according to the law* in certain section if you are a member (of a group ranch) you *have a right* to get your share, even if it's an acre. The area was said to be 62000 acres. It should be divided to 334 people. So each and every person can get 60 acres if you are a member. (Emphasis added)

After listening to the statements from both groups, the director explained *what the law said.* He said, these 37 people *got their farms justly,* and if you come to divide this land, you should do so equally. (Emphasis added)

The director said that those who wanted individual farms instead of getting 100 acres each, everyone will get 60 acres. That is, *according to the law.* (Emphasis added)

Later, the surveyor started subdividing the land privately with the committee. After they completed subdividing 334 farms, they organized a meeting. They said that, *according to the law of lands,* you have to vote. The bag contains numbers. (Emphasis added)

Jonas's concern for the law and what it says goes beyond merely justifying actions that were unpopular in his community. I think he genuinely believes that the national laws are the most important and should be upheld even when they conflict with traditional practices or beliefs. Certainly, this is not very surprising for someone who spent most of his adult life supervising those who had broken the law and been sent to prison. He was part of the government apparatus and appears to have considerable confidence in it. Indeed, when anomalies in the land adjudication process were discussed (e.g., people being registered as members who were not residents of Siambu), he claimed that these errors were due to the weakness of the land committee, composed of elders, not of the land adjudication officers or the policy itself. He stressed that the committee had to be strong to withstand the temptation to be corrupted by those seeking membership in the group, and that a weak committee would do a poor job.

This comment highlights another theme that I see as part of Jonas's life philosophy: the importance of individual effort. This goes hand in hand with his emphasis on hard work and application of knowledge as pathways to success. When discussing his experiences working in the prisons, Jonas noted that there were two kinds of prisoners: the jailbird (he used that term in English) and those who could be rehabilitated. The jailbird was weak willed. He knew only crime and if let out of prison would find a way to come back: "If he is let out within a week the life outside doesn't agree with him. They [jailbirds] have no other work, only to counsel the first offenders to be even worse." Then there are the prisoners who can reform. If they listen to the wardens and take advantage of the opportunities in prison, they can make a life for themselves outside.

> You'll see those who put effort into learning these things can be very successful once they're out. . . . Some go there and come out as qualified carpenters, masons, farmers. Those are the ones who do well when they have somewhere to live, but those who don't have a place to live are the ones who do mistakes and are brought back. So we have those two categories.

Successful rehabilitation depends primarily on one's hard work and determination, one's individual character and willingness to learn. Jonas is not one to go in for environmental explanations of crime; he puts the emphasis on personal responsibility.

Certainly, his own life experiences underscore that hard work and determination yield success. While it does not appear that his father's family was impoverished, they were not extremely wealthy, either. As we have seen, he had to work his way through school, and then he worked for years in government service. He has also worked hard on developing his farm and plot in Siambu. Uncharacteristically for a Samburu, he views hard physical labor as virtuous and disdains what he perceives as the laziness and pride of some pastoralists. These are the same views often echoed by government workers from agricultural backgrounds.

In a similar vein, Jonas saw privatization of land not as an attempt by elite members of the community to grab land but rather as a means to mitigate the advantages held by wealthier pastoralists. At the same time, the opposition of wealthier families stemmed not from an urge to preserve land for future generations but to keep the poorer members of the community down.

> They [wealthier people who opposed privatization] were the ones who wanted to be leaders in order to fool people to stay like them. Because if they tell you, don't practice farming, so that the cattle can get enough grass, yet the cattle that you have are not enough for you, what will you eat? They like saying, let us just stay and look after cattle, but this is what is making people go and get jobs as watchmen, even as far as Mombasa, because of staying idle. What brought the Lowoiting [a neighboring group ranch] people back? Just the wheat leases. Nganyieke was the one who said Lowoiting should be ploughed so that those people who went to be watchmen could come back, and didn't people come?

Jonas prefers poorer pastoralists to use their land and feed themselves through their own efforts (along with wheat leases) rather than leaving Samburu District for work as watchmen in distant cities. Interestingly, while he admires hard work, he devalues work as a watchman. I suspect this is due to its low wages and lack of opportunities for advancement. Plus, although being a watchman involves risks it is not normally physically demanding. I have also observed that men working as watchmen are often unable to build up an asset base upon which to marry or retire. Compared to land ownership and the potential to feed one's family on farm produce, being a watchman appears to Jonas to be a poor alternative.

Economics aside, it was also clear that Jonas believed that certain families in Siambu opposed privatization because they wanted to deny lower-status families a chance to succeed and improve their relative position in the social hierarchy. Men from these families were the ones who led the group that destroyed Jonas's farm in 1987 by allowing their cattle to eat his maize and tear up the fence around the farm (see chapter 4). While they succeeded in ruining his crops that year, Jonas and the others who sought private land ultimately prevailed, in his view, since the land was eventually privatized and divided equally among all the households in Siambu.

Today, Jonas is relatively prosperous. His years of being a model farmer and early adopter of new ideas and technologies seem to be paying off. He recently acquired several exotic dairy cows, with assistance from the Ministry of Agriculture and Livestock Development. He was growing napier grass (typically found in the wetter parts of Kenya where dairy cows are stall fed) to supplement their diet. He told me he was getting good milk yields and was selling the surplus milk in town. He was also part of a self-help group that was running a maize-grinding business out of his building in Poro. For all of his success, his position in the community remained ambiguous. On the one hand, many people admired his hard work and acknowledged his success. On the other hand, quite a number were critical of him. They claimed that he was purely self-interested and that he used his relationships with government officers and agencies to his own advantage. To some extent, he was still seen as an outsider almost thirty years after coming to Siambu.

Case Two: Military, Education, and Employment—Lonyuki and Margaret

Lonyuki (sixty-seven) and Margaret (sixty) are a fascinating couple. As a warrior, Lonyuki was a chief under the colonial government and then served in the military in the 1950s. After a six-year stint, he returned to Samburu and served as one of the first elected as a councilor to the local government. He was also one of the first businessmen in Maralal, running one of the only licensed beer halls allowed in the town. Margaret was among the first Samburu girls to be formally educated. Growing up in Sirata Oirobi, about twenty kilometers south of Siambu, her family welcomed the first Anglican missionaries to Samburu District, and Margaret attended their school. She progressed through secondary education and, after being married to Lonyuki in the late 1950s and bearing four children, completed a certificate course in social work in Machakos (which is near the oft-mentioned Kitui in central Kenya). She traveled to Israel to complete her training and took up employment with the Kenya government where she worked for the next eighteen years. These experiences were clearly influential for both of them. Their marriage did not survive, though, and they separated in the 1970s. They remain in contact and, according to Margaret, get along quite well, especially now that they are older.

I have known Margaret for more than a decade. When I first met her, she was the district chairwoman of the Maendeleo ya Wanawake (Women's Development) Organization (MyWO), which is the largest women's organization in Kenya and, until 1992, was part of the ruling political party KANU. In her capacity as "women's leader," Margaret had been invited to a project-planning workshop by the project that I was working for at the time, the Integrated Food Security Programme (IFSP—a bilateral Kenyan-German project that was the precursor to SDDP). The weeklong workshop was held in a luxury hotel in the Shaba Game Reserve (just adjacent to Samburu District), and she and I, as the only female participants, shared a room, together with my four-month-old daughter. I was immediately struck by Margaret's easy manner, her openness and her sense of style. She wore beautiful clothes that were African in style (but definitely not Samburu) and had an elaborate and very attractive upswept hairdo. She told me about her travels to Israel, the Netherlands, and even Chicago. She had many stories to tell and was outspoken in her opinions on all subjects. Her education, experiences, and cosmopolitan flair immediately set her apart from other Samburu women I knew.

Over the years, we worked together on numerous occasions, and in the mid-1990s Margaret joined SDDP as a community development officer. She left a few years later to start her own organization that provides education and training to young, single mothers. Interestingly, she returned to her home town of Sirata Oirobi to start her school and, before raising enough funds to build her own offices and classrooms, used the vacant buildings of the first Anglican mission as her headquarters.

Certainly, Margaret's education made a tremendous difference in her life. Having a formal education enabled her to enter employment and to live independently. When her husband opposed her plans to travel to Israel for further studies, she went anyway, perhaps in the knowledge that more education would enhance her ability to get a good job and become financially independent. However, I suspect that a sense of adventure and curiosity about the outside world also motivated Margaret, as it did many men who joined the military or other types of employment. Her early exposure to Europeans (the missionaries in Sirata were British) rendered her less afraid of traveling and interacting with those who were different from her. Also important was the support she got from her own father. When arranging her marriage to Lonyuki, he insisted that Margaret be allowed to continue her education after marriage. When the marriage was falling apart, her father defended her against the Lotimi elders who tried to force her to stay with Lonyuki.

Although Margaret and Lonyuki separated, a divorce (which would have required return of the bridewealth) was never formalized, and Margaret was allowed to pursue her career and keep her children, who would normally stay with the husband's lineage in such cases. Of course, she also shouldered the primary burden of educating and supporting those children (six in all). Her work in government service included assignments in women's prisons as well as positions as a child welfare officer in the Department of Social Services. Like most government employees she was transferred from place to place and in this way saw most of the country. Unlike many Kenyan men who leave their families behind in their home areas while they work, she kept most of her children with her. At times, she left some of the children with her mother back in Sirata. After eighteen years, she left government service. She told me that, like other women, she had been employed on a contract basis and was not entitled to any pension regardless of how many years she worked.

I spoke to Margaret about the privatization of land in Siambu. In addition to Lonyuki, two of her sons got land during the subdivision. I was particularly interested in gleaning information about the women's perspective on the events in Siambu. I interviewed numerous women about the process, and most admitted that they knew little of what had happened. They were neither consulted nor involved directly in any of the decision making pertaining to land issues, but got some information through their male relatives, especially if their sons were warriors (who tend to discuss issues in their mothers' houses). Margaret confirmed what I had heard and added that women had little understanding of the implications of privatization, for example, in the case of land sales.

No, no. They had no idea about the selling of land, what are you going to lose. They think you just get money. Yeah. They have no idea what's the value of the land. Okay, they know it's good because they can, you know, keep our livestock there grazing and then they come home, that's all. But few of the women, now they know, you know, if we leave this land, we no longer have it, very few of them. Where will we go if this man sells this land? But they don't know where to go in case of disagreement between her and her husband, or with her sons.

> She pointed out that land in Siambu was valuable and coveted by many people because of its fertility. In addition to the risk of further land sales, she predicted that more people would fence their land, which would have negative implications for women.

> You know, Siambu people still move, although the land is divided, they are still living together, getting water and firewood. People are not so strict to the land, you know, as it is supposed to be. It's not fenced. Nobody's keeping an eye on who's cutting the firewood. People just go, but they know that that area belongs to so and so, but they just go and get firewood, water, building materials, you know, and nobody asks them. The time will come when you can never cross the border from one farm to another, and it's going to be very soon, and people will suffer because majority of the people who will suffer will be women, because where will they get firewood, water, you know?

Unlike most women I spoke to, Margaret had a much more detailed understanding of the events leading to privatization. She clearly understood the role of the General and the elders who opposed privatization. She also intimated that the murder of the watchman and the divisions between Kurpa and Siit subclans were significant in strengthening the opposition of the elders. Clearly, she was privy to information that most Samburu women did not have direct access to.

Beyond the land issue, Margaret's background and experiences have led her to embrace a strong platform of ideas about women's rights and position in Samburu society. This is demonstrated in her work against female genital cutting (FGC; also called female circumcision) and in favor of education for single mothers. During her time as chairwoman of Maendeleo ya Wanawake, she helped initiate a research and action program into FGC in Samburu. This program involved research into the reasons behind the continued commitment of Samburu men and women to FGC as well as the details of the operation itself. Based on the research results, an action program was designed that used the health consequences of FGC, such as hemorrhage at the time of the operation and problems during childbirth, as an entry point to discussions with women, men, girls, and boys about FGC. This campaign has continued and now emphasizes the modification of the FGC operation to something much less radical while trying to preserve the ceremonial aspects of this important rite of passage.

Since leaving MyWO, Margaret has continued to encourage women and men to abandon or modify FGC. Needless to say, to take on such a charged topic in public is to risk one's reputation, but Margaret remains unfazed. I think her confidence stems in part from her true belief that what she is doing is right but also from her feelings that she "knows best" what Samburu women need and has an obligation to work to educate them in this way. When discussing these topics, her tone often turns didactic. Although she understands the basis of Samburu beliefs, she has no doubt that many of them need to change and that it is her role to bring that change about. Indeed, I sometimes found this to be a problem when we worked together in SDDP. Our aim in the project was to facilitate discussion processes in communities, but Margaret had a habit of lecturing the community about what they needed to do rather than letting them come up with their own suggestions. While she may seem to think of herself as superior, it probably derives from her early and intense experience among Christian missionaries whose goal of conversion she has applied in her own way to the situation of Samburu women.

Margaret's recent work is dedicated to helping young, single mothers who are often cast out by their families when their pregnancies are discovered. Samburu culture places young girls in something of a catch-22 situation regarding premarital sex and pregnancy. There is no prohibition on premarital sex, and having a boyfriend is a sign of a girl's attractiveness and social success, but premarital pregnancy is anathema. This is particularly the case if the girl becomes pregnant before she is circumcised. In such cases, several steps are taken. Often, efforts are made to abort the fetus when the pregnancy is discovered. If this fails, a hasty marriage may be arranged with the father of the child. If she is not circumcised, this will be done as soon as possible. However, marriage may not be possible for numerous reasons, especially since premarital sexual partners are often from the same clan within which marriage is forbidden. When marriage cannot be arranged and a child is born, the girl may be abandoned by her family and forced to fend for herself. Even if she is allowed to stay on at her father's settlement, her chances for marriage are slim, and she will remain dependent on her father's goodwill. These are the girls that Margaret is trying to help by providing basic education and life skills to enable them to make a living on their own. She has made headway in building a school and dormitory facilities, but she is still struggling to find ways to sustain the operation. Whether or not her efforts succeed, she has chosen to intervene in the lives of one of the most powerless groups in Samburu society, and this is a reflection of her own life experiences and priorities.

Like Jonas, I first met Lonyuki when SDDP worked in Siambu in 1996. He was outspoken at meetings and came across as a leader of the area. I would occasionally see him in Maralal town where he invariably sports a dark pinstripe suit and a carved wooden walking stick. During the research on Siambu I discovered that he had been one of the individuals who sought private land as well as a land committee member, and so I sought him out to interview about his roles in the land adjudication process as well as his own life history. Lonyuki, who has two wives in addition to Margaret, had no formal education and does not appear to have been much influenced by Christian missionaries. Rather, his experience was primarily with government administration and the military. This may help explain why he seems to occupy an ambivalent position on questions of Samburu culture and change. He contrasts, for example, Samburu culture (*lwenet*) with civilization (using that term in English). But he is not exclusively in favor of one or the other. He views some aspects of Samburu culture as valuable and worth keeping while others are more expendable. For instance, he feels it is unnecessary for people to move to ceremonial settlements (*lorora*) for major age-grade ceremonies, primarily, he says, because it is inconvenient to move and because there is no communal area left in Siambu where the settlement can be built. On the other hand, he favors retaining rules relating to where and with whom warriors can eat. For them to eat in front of women or with children, he maintains, is demeaning and lacking in respect. However, they need not go all the way to the forest (as used to be the case). As long as they are out of sight of women and children, they can still eat near the homestead or in their own house.

In the case of land, Lonyuki firmly believes in the virtues of private land ownership. He was one of the first to be granted an individual farm during the adjudication process and says he initially opposed the General's call for the individuals to renounce their land claims. After subdivision, things have been good.

> Because if you prohibit someone from using your land, no one will stop you. If you refuse to let people cut wood on your land, no one will do it.

> If you refuse someone grazing rights on your land, no one will graze it. And if you forbid people to take water, no one will bother you. Although we Samburu have not made these prohibitions, not completely, but it is coming.

This is the familiar mantra of individual rights over land that one hears over and over again in Siambu. Like Jonas, Lonyuki was enamored of agricultural societies, especially those living in dry areas of the country. He cited the same example of Kitui mentioned by Jonas, pointing out how they do very well in their harsh environment and that the Samburu would do well to copy their example. He also predicted that privatization of land would continue, not only in the highland portion of Siambu, but throughout Samburu District. He told me he had plans to fence his land and that he would do so as soon as he was able.

In spite of his strong pro-private property stance, there are times when Lonyuki goes against his own advice. During the serious drought of 1999–2000, he allowed the General to graze cattle on his land.

> His cattle were here last year. All of them. Those cows that were in Nanyuki, about two thousand, all died. Other cows came here and went up to Malasso [the escarpment adjacent to Lonyuki's land]. These alone were about one thousand and three hundred. . . . the General stayed here because of friendship. Now, we left our cows to die because of friendship [laughing]. The many that were brought mixed with the few we had. (CL: Because of the drought?) Because the drought was serious and there wasn't anywhere to go. They depend on land that has grass. You can't tell your brother to move over—you have to stay together. But this coming together is a big mistake! (Lonyuki)

When times are tough, the dictates of culture appear to trump legal rights over land. In this statement Lonyuki reveals the ambiguity of owning private land in the midst of an extensive pastoral system and the need to balance individual preferences against ideals of friendship and obligation.

He also reveals ambivalent attitudes about another critical domain of culture—marriage. On the one hand, he argues that young people are destined to travel and intermarry with others.

> You can get a white girl, a Turkana girl, a Kalenjin girl, or one from Kitui. And this is when people have freedom. This is real civilization. Because

not everyone marries from their ethnic group. Second, my child might go to Machakos to look for a farm. He'll live there and he'll follow the culture of the Kamba people.

On the other hand, he was adamantly opposed to a couple of recent marriages between men and women of the Lotimi clan. He related stories about marriages in the past that violated rules of exogamy and the death and disaster that ensued. While acknowledging that the elders had been unable to prevent these recent marriages he cited the low attendance at the weddings as proof that people opposed them, and he predicted that such marriages were doomed.

We talked quite a bit about leadership since Lonyuki had been a councilor in the 1960s and has served on various committees since then. Indeed, rumor had it that he would run for councilor again in the upcoming election of 2002. In this discussion, his responses mirrored Jonas's emphasis on hard work and tangible results. He told me in some detail about what he had done as councilor, including forgoing his own salary to pay school fees for four boys, raising funds and managing the construction of the first primary school in Poro, negotiating a change in the gazetted forest boundary, and completing the first community cattle dip in the area. He was critical of leaders that followed him, saying that there had been virtually no development in the area since his time. A good leader was one who served the people, all the people, and who was impartial among different groups. This was certainly a reference to the Kurpa–Siit subclan rivalry, although when I asked him directly about this, he played down its significance.

Lonyuki's outlook on life and opinions about the course of social change reveal more uncertainty and mixed feelings than those of Jonas, or even Margaret for that matter. I think this stems partly from the fact that his experiences in the world beyond Samburu came later in life and were less thoroughgoing than those of the other two. By the same token, he has achieved levels of leadership in his community that Jonas never has. I don't mean to imply that he is uncontroversial, he certainly has his share of friends and foes, but his insider status is unquestioned, a factor that I think plays a part in being able to garner the requisite respectability required of a leader. His ambivalence about what is good and bad in Samburu culture may reflect the views of many Samburu who have some idea of the requirements of "civilization" but who are not ready to sacrifice elements of their culture that remain central to their sense of identity and belonging.

Case Three: Education and the Military—Lekeya

I remember Lekeya from the early SDDP meetings in Poro for two rather superficial reasons. One was his full beard—very unusual among Samburu men, who tend to have little facial hair. The other was his distinctive voice, which was very deep and resonant, and also unusually loud. I appreciated the fact that he spoke more slowly than most people, making it easier for me to follow his conversation. I wondered whether he was just speaking slowly for my benefit or whether he spoke that way all the time. He also had an air of worldliness about him, revealed by his Western dress and habit of smoking cigarettes instead of chewing tobacco, the latter being the norm for most Samburu. I immediately suspected that he had worked outside the district. As it turned out, his voice and communication skills were critical in his eighteen-year career in the Kenya army, much of which he spent as a radio operator in the communications department.

During my fieldwork, I learned more about Lekeya and visited him at his home to discuss issues related to the land question, agriculture, Samburu history, and his own life experiences. Unlike many Samburu men, even in Siambu, he was devoted to his agricultural work and, like Jonas, enjoyed experimenting with different crops. When I interviewed him, he was growing pyrethrum (a flower from which pesticide is extracted, a valuable cash crop in Kenya) and miraa (a semilegal plant that people chew for its stimulant effects, also a cash crop) in addition to food crops such as maize and potatoes.

His early education mirrors Jonas's experience in many ways. Also from the Baragoi area, he was sent to school through the coercion of the government-appointed chief and against the wishes of his father. His father adamantly opposed the idea of school, especially since his first son who went to school came back with a case of smallpox (or maybe chicken pox; this was not entirely clear) and lots of bedbug bites. When the chief informed his father that another son was required to attend school, his father attacked the chief and threw a spear at him. Fortunately, the spear missed, but Lekeya's father was arrested and held until the boy was produced to go to school.

From this dramatic beginning, Lekeya came to like school and worked his way through primary school. In contrast to Jonas, Lekeya did not have to work in the stone quarry but had the more respectable job of teaching one of the Catholic priests the Samburu language (perhaps his resonant and slow-paced speech were evident even then). In 1967, after completing seven years of school, he attended the technical school in neighboring Marsabit District for a year. However, he did not stick with this vocational training but opted instead to join the Kenyan army. He points out that the army was considered by Samburu warriors to be the most desirable kind of work.

> Samburus liked working in the army. At that time, a warrior who entered the army was considered a real man because that was the best job, there was no other. . . . A warrior wanted to be a warrior. Therefore, it was the same life in the army as being a warrior in Samburu; they both go to war.

Although he liked the army, he emphasized that it was hard work and that only relatively young men could stay in the army due to the physical demands. His main work in the army was as a driver and as a communication officer operating radio and telex signals. Highlighting the demands of army service, he recalled a time when he was the radio coordinator for a war games exercise and had to stay awake for almost three days, manning the radios and communicating among the different troops. It was a demanding and challenging task but obviously one that he enjoyed quite a bit.

Like others in the military, he traveled extensively in Kenya and learned about agriculture during his years of service. He admired the work of farming communities where people produced a lot of food on small plots of land.

> I saw people like the Luhya, the Kisii, even the Kikuyu. They don't have cows but they survive because of their small farms. A quarter of an acre, only, not like the twenty-three acres we have here, but they have one milk cow, a few goats, a couple of chickens, not counting the store full of food. They educate their children on a very small plot of something like pyrethrum or vegetables or a fruit tree. I admired that farming work and I saw the difference between them and pastoralists. Farmers have the life, because a cow doesn't have fat if it doesn't have food—if we don't have that food to eat, like beans and maize, we will just sell the cow and use all the money, and end up becoming laborers on others' farms.

He noted that it was becoming increasingly difficult for pastoralists to survive on livestock alone. Citing the increase in livestock diseases, human diseases, and drought, he argued that the Samburu need to combine farming with pastoralism in order to be food secure.

Thus, he had supported the move to privatize land at Siambu. However, he was not one of those who first sought individual farms. This was not because he opposed privatization, but because he lacked the opportunity to try to get land in Siambu. He was in the army when adjudication started and only later petitioned to be included in the land register along with one of his brothers and their father who had moved from Baragoi to Siambu a few years earlier. His request, while approved, was met with some resistance, because his family was from Baragoi and had not lived long in Siambu. His brother was among those who got an individual farm by filing an objection to the DLAO after the land committee rejected his request based on his lack of long-term residency in the area. Then, when equal subdivision was approved and the land register was reopened and nonresidents removed, the brothers and their father were threatened with removal. As it turns out, they were included in the final register and finally granted farms along with the other members.

In contrast to his brother, who continues to fight to regain his originally allocated farm, Lekeya is satisfied with his farm, seeing it as plenty large to support himself and his family. He is highly critical of his brother's continued refusal to give up his original land claim, and he blames the lawyers that his brother has hired.

> He is just hiring lawyers, unaware that they will never tire of being paid. That man is wasting a lot of money for nothing. He is cheated by some Kikuyu advisers whom I think, if they ever came here, would be killed, because this isn't their land! . . . All the other members agreed—why should he reject the community's decision? He should concentrate on his family's welfare, not fighting for nothing.

His opinions about his brother's ongoing land case reveal that Lekeya sees the need to balance individual rights with communal welfare and harmony. He firmly believes in the value and superiority of private land ownership, and he predicts that it will be extended even to the dry lowlands. He expects that new technologies like irrigation will enable people to farm land there that is currently unsuitable for cultivation. However, he stops short of privileging individual rights over those of the community. A decision by the community should be binding on its members. He fears that his brother's continued recalcitrance may lead to him being forced out of the community in the end.

We also discussed leadership, and Lekeya was highly critical of the current generation of leaders. He claimed that they were very ineffective and spent most of their time drinking and gossiping in bars in town rather than providing services to their people. He did not appear to aspire to leadership himself, though, preferring to concentrate his energies on his farm and his family. To this extent he resembles Jonas in his work ethic and emphasis on personal economic development as opposed to seeking a leadership position in the community. As in Jonas's case, this may also be due to his semioutsider status in the community. He did not grow up in Siambu and so may still be viewed as a relative newcomer. I also got the impression that his growing miraa may have compromised his reputation to a certain extent among some community members.

Conclusion

Experiences in formal education, the military, and employment influenced individuals in many ways. Beyond adopting the outward manifestations of modern Kenyan society, such as language, dress, and housing preferences, these individuals developed distinctive notions about the nature of progress and desirable lifestyles. They have internalized norms regarding the value of individual hard work, the superiority of crop cultivation over pastoralism, and the benefits of private property. While there is certainly a degree of individual variation, it appears that the duration of formal education (and, along with it, Christian missionary influence) is correlated with the strength of these attitudes. Thus, Jonas and Margaret, with the most formal education, are the strongest advocates for cultural change, while Lonyuki and Lekeya are more ambivalent about which aspects of Samburu culture should be maintained and which should change. However, the key point for the analysis of privatization in Siambu hinges on the fact that this group understood the concept of private property, perceived its advantages, and felt little or no compunction in seeking to acquire communal resources for themselves.

On a final note, it is worth considering what cost individuals have paid for maintaining these attitudes and beliefs that are often at odds with those of the majority of Samburu people. I have argued that they were impervious to leveling techniques applied by the elders trying to force them to back off their land claims, because their frame of reference had shifted to the community of modern Kenyans. This shift is revealed in their confidence that their ideas and beliefs about property and livelihood were actually superior to those of the typical Samburu. Thus, it was not that they necessarily wanted to leave Samburu to live among other Kenyans. Rather, they wanted to serve as examples of the Samburu future, to show the way, like missionaries. Their attachment to modern Kenya was psychological as well as physical, a kind of "imagined community," to use Anderson's (1983) term. Most of them spent many years working outside Samburu but chose to return to their homeland bringing with them the "good news" of progress. At least, this is what many of them think they were doing, even though their actions in pursuit of private land may appear more self-serving than exemplary. Put another way, they were used to being different from other Samburu, and they usually felt proud about these differences, not ashamed of them. Their sense of identity or self-confidence did not derive wholly from approval from the Samburu elders, and this made leveling ineffective.

CHAPTER 7

The Impact of Privatization of Land on Livelihoods

How did privatizing land affect the welfare and livelihoods of residents of Siambu? Are people better off after the subdivision of land into individual plots? Are they investing more in their land since their rights have become individualized? According to the theory of property rights, changing land tenure from communal to private provides greater incentives for individuals to invest in their land, since benefits of their investments accrue to them alone rather than to the entire community, as is the case with a communal land resource.[1] Increased investments in land, furthermore, should ultimately translate into improvements in efficiency and productivity and, presumably, in household welfare in terms of wealth and income.[2]

Indeed, these ideas about the superiority of private property stimulated the move toward individual freehold tenure in Kenya as a whole and were implicit in the decisions to grant individuals land during the adjudication process in Samburu. As described in chapter 4, DLAOs granted land to individuals on the grounds that they would be better able to develop the land than groups. They praised applicants who made improvements to their land, such as farming, fencing, or housing. Although improvements in productivity and welfare might be expected to follow privatization, there is little systematic data demonstrating the outcomes of privatizing pastoral land.[3]

Since Kenya government policies favor private property, and the land adjudication process in communal areas enables individuals to make claims for private ownership of land, it is important to understand the repercussions of privatizing pastoral land. Even though the pace of subdivision of group ranches in Samburu District has been slow, there are indications that the demand for privatization may be growing. This is revealed in the comments of younger men in Mbaringon, for example, many of whom claim to favor subdivision. As more and more Samburu boys and girls enter the educational system and get jobs, it is likely that these values will spread.

The question remains, however, whether privatization can deliver the benefits promised by its advocates. In the 1990s, many scholars studying pastoral systems from ecological perspectives concluded that extensive livestock production on communal land was the most appropriate use of semiarid lands in Africa (Behnke, Scoones, and Kerven 1993; Scoones 1994). They argued that the mobility and flexibility of pastoral systems enables them to make the best use of the patchy and fragile environment. When compared to conservative ranching models, pastoral systems were found to be more productive per unit area precisely due to the ability of pastoralists to move their herds to take advantage of seasonally available pastures (Sandford 1983). While pastoral systems are certainly far from perfect in their ability to meet the needs of rising populations, particularly when they are becoming more sedentary, it is unclear whether crop farming on private land would provide a more secure or lucrative livelihood. In addition to the ecological issues posed by the fragile environment and the corresponding vulnerability of crops to periodic droughts, there is the fact that Samburu people lack experience and knowledge about farming. Thus, it cannot be assumed that pastoralists such as the Samburu could make an automatic or easy transition to crop production, which requires a set of skills and understandings very different from those of livestock production.

Recent research in Kenya (Little et al. 2001; Boone et al. 2005) and Tanzania (McCabe 2003; Galvin et al. 2006) demonstrates that combining livestock production and agriculture are increasingly common among some pastoralists, with important implications for human livelihoods as well as conservation. McCabe's (2003) study of Maasai in northern Tanzania in the mid-1990s revealed that adoption of cultivation, in addition to livestock, led to improvements in household economy and nutritional status. In addition, simulation modeling of the same area suggested that the spread of agriculture did not appear to threaten the ecosystem integrity in the region, which includes the Ngorongoro conservation area, a premier site of wildlife conservation in Tanzania (Boone et al. 2002). Another application of the same modeling system, this time to subdivided group ranches in southern Kenya, cautioned that small parcel sizes reduce the numbers of livestock that can be sustained, potentially threatening livelihoods (Boone et al. 2005). Boone and his colleagues conclude that retaining access to larger areas of land, even in the face of subdivision, will facilitate livestock production. These studies suggest that livestock production and cultivation may be successfully combined, at least up to a point, but it is important to note that conditions vary considerably among different pastoralist areas, and conclusions from Maasai areas in northern Tanzania and southern Kenya are not necessarily applicable to northern Kenya. Thus, it is critical to study the ways in which agriculture and livestock production are combined and to build empirical evidence of the effects.

Examining the experience of Siambu after privatization sheds light on these issues. On the one hand, with its relatively higher rainfall and moderate temperatures, Siambu has one of the best environments for crop production in Samburu District. In addition, there was a small group of individuals who had been engaged in growing crops as early as the 1960s, providing at least a limited reservoir of knowledge relating to agriculture. On the other hand, the vast majority of people in Siambu only accepted privatization as a compromise to prevent the small group of individuals from taking all the land on the plateau. They did not adopt private property out of a desire to become farmers, and most of them had no experience with farming. Thus, while some factors favored the transition to farming, others mitigated against it.

The household survey discussed later aimed to assess household economic performance in Siambu postprivatization and to measure the contributions of livestock production, crop production (including land leasing), and other activities to household wealth and income. In addition, Siambu households were compared with households in Mbaringon where privatization has not occurred. This comparison provides perspective on the impact of privatization and helps assess the degree to which Siambu people have gained from privatization.

The evidence suggests that Siambu households have narrowed the gap in wealth (livestock) that existed between Siambu and Mbaringon prior to privatization. Indeed, Siambu survey households had higher levels of per capita wealth than those in Mbaringon in 2000–2001, the year the survey was conducted. This finding, however, must be considered in light of the serious drought prevailing in the district just prior to the survey, which may confound the results on wealth. Siambu households also have higher levels of per capita income compared to Mbaringon. Agriculture makes up a greater proportion of income on average in Siambu (10 percent) than in Mbaringon (0 percent)—even more when home consumption of crops and milk are included in calculating income. However, agriculture is less important than wage labor and trade to household cash incomes in both Siambu and Mbaringon. Furthermore, with cultivated acreages in Siambu averaging a little less than two acres, out of total parcel sizes of twenty-three acres, it is clear that Siambu families have not made a radical shift toward crop production over livestock. Livestock production and trade still contribute significantly to incomes in Siambu. In contrast to Maasai areas where privatization has led to massive sales of land, there have been few sales of land in Siambu, and there is no evidence that consolidation of land into a few hands is occurring there.

The results reported here suggest that while privatization has not transformed the Siambu community into farmers, it has provided new opportunities for investments in agriculture that form part of a portfolio of wealth and income-generating options. Given declining levels of livestock wealth in both Siambu and Mbaringon, families are responding by participating in a range of activities that yield income. Economic diversification is a coping strategy that characterizes both communal and private tenure systems. The fact that Siambu people still have access to enough land for extensive livestock production (the lowland group ranch and the adjacent government forest in addition to the plateau) means that they have not been forced to choose between crop production and livestock production, but are able to participate in both. To the extent that agriculture serves as one prong in their diversification strategy and to the degree that it yields surpluses, it may have cushioned the effects of recent droughts. This may partly explain why Siambu households are better off than their counterparts in Mbaringon.

Study Methodology

In order to assess the impact of privatization on the welfare of Siambu households, a survey was conducted with one hundred households in Siambu and, for comparison, one hundred households in Mbaringon group ranch, where land ownership remains communal.[4] The households were randomly selected from lists of households in each location.[5] The sample covers about 40 percent of households in each community; thus the results are representative of the situation as a whole. Table 1 shows the characteristics of the study population as a whole.

The household head and/or spouse were interviewed for each household in the sample. Demographic information was recorded for each household member, including gender, age, educational attainment, residency, and employment status. Data were also collected on livestock holdings, agricultural activities, assets and debts, livestock sales, nonlivestock income, annual and

TABLE 1. Characteristics of Sample Population

Location	Number of Households	Head of Household		Wives	Children								Dependents				Total	
					0–5		6–10		11–15		>15		Adult		Child			
		M	F		M	F	M	F	M	F	M	F	M	F	M	F	Pop	AAME
Siambu	100	90	10	111	56	56	65	55	42	36	68	41	8	15	15	9	677	565
Mbaringon	100	98	2	150	92	93	72	94	74	58	78	49	18	39	33	26	976	814
Total	200	188	12	261	148	149	137	149	116	94	146	90	26	54	48	35	1,653	1,379

Note: All household members were converted to active adult male equivalents (AAME). The conversion formula used was adult males = 1, children 0–5 = .52, 6–10 = .85, 11–15 = .96, adult females = .86.

weekly expenditures, twenty-four-hour food intake, military service, as well as leaders, stock associates, and patrons. These data enable conclusions to be drawn regarding the relative well-being of households in the two locations. Two-tailed Student's t-tests were used to establish the significance of differences between the two communities in key variables such as wealth and income. These are reported significant at the $p = .05$ level.

Comparability of Siambu and Mbaringon

In order to establish the validity of Mbaringon as a control case for Siambu, it is necessary to consider the comparability of the two communities, particularly at the start of land adjudication in Siambu in 1978. As noted earlier, both communities consist almost entirely of Samburu pastoralists for whom livestock form the basis of household food production. They share a similar history, and most cultural practices are virtually identical. By the 1970s, both communities were practicing seminomadic pastoralism, with households remaining more or less stationary while herds of livestock moved from place to place in search of pasture and water. While a few individuals were beginning to grow crops in Siambu, farming was not practiced in Mbaringon at this time. Mbaringon was known as a particularly good area for cattle due to its moderate temperatures, good pastures with little bush or tree cover, and salt springs.

In order to get an idea of household wealth at this time, which is measured in livestock holdings, survey households were asked to recall their livestock holdings in 1978.[6] While this is admittedly a long time for people to recall, pastoralists do have good memories of their herds in general, and that year was significant because it closely followed the circumcision of the new age-set, Lkiroro, in 1976, and it also corresponded with the first major outbreak of East Coast Fever (ECF) in the area. Thus, people did not have much difficulty in recalling their holdings at this time since they had been negatively affected by the outbreak.

In 1978, Mbaringon households had an average of 62 head of cattle and 71 head of small stock (sheep and goats). Siambu households averaged 43 head of cattle and 45 head of small stock in 1978. It is important to note that these data were gathered during the experimental economics games (see chapter 8), not as part of the main household survey. As a result, not all survey households responded. Sixty-six percent of Mbaringon survey households and 42 percent of Siambu survey households responded. However,

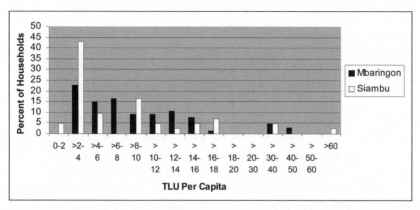

Fig. 3. Tropical livestock units (TLU) per capita in 1978 (Mbaringon, *n* = 66; Siambu, *n* = 42)

other nonsurvey households that participated in the games also responded to this question and their responses, though not included in the preceding figures, did confirm the trend demonstrated by these data. Therefore, I believe that these numbers are reasonably representative. Mbaringon households had greater livestock holdings on average. However, calculated in per capita terms, the mean livestock holdings in Siambu were 7.0 per person and 7.2 in Mbaringon—virtually identical. This is due to differences in average household size: 10 in Mbaringon and 7 in Siambu. Figure 3 shows the distribution of livestock holdings among Siambu and Mbaringon households in per capita terms. Siambu holdings are more skewed than those of Mbaringon: 43 percent of households owned between 2 and 4 TLU per person while there is one household that owned over 60 TLU per person. In Mbaringon, 23 percent of households owned between 2 and 4 TLU per capita, and the rest were relatively evenly spread between 4 and 14 TLU per capita. Although their mean per capita holdings are extremely close, these data suggest that there were more poor Siambu households in 1978 than was the case in Mbaringon.

Wealth Differences

The greater wealth apparent in Mbaringon in 1978 has not been maintained to date. Survey data reveal that Siambu households had significantly higher per capita livestock holdings than Mbaringon in 2000–2001. Care must be taken in interpreting these data, however. The differential effects of the 2000 drought on Siambu and Mbaringon may account for some of the difference. Furthermore, higher rates of polygyny in Mbaringon suggest that losses in wealth may be of recent origin, perhaps due to recent droughts.

Data were collected on livestock holdings for all households in the survey. While pastoralists tend to be reticent about the numbers of livestock they own, the survey was designed to elicit accurate figures. For example, rather than asking people to give the total number of livestock, they were asked to enumerate livestock according to age, sex, utility, and location. This detailed accounting corresponds with the way people normally think about their stock, according to utilities such as breeding versus nonbreeding, milking versus dry, at home versus at cattle camp, and marketable versus for home use.

Furthermore, the research assistants for this study were very familiar with the communities, being lifelong residents of their respective areas, and had good knowledge about household holdings. Finally, the drought of 2000 may have simplified the task of accounting for livestock since many households had suffered devastating losses that they remembered only too well. They were in a good position to know exactly what had been lost and what remained of their herds. Occasionally, herds were observed, but this was often impossible due to the animals being away for grazing during the day or being kept at distant cattle camps. The precautions taken in the study ensure reasonable veracity of the data, although there may still be a few cases of over- or underestimation. There is no reason to believe these would differ significantly across the two communities, however.

Considering livestock holdings at household level (table 2), Mbaringon is slightly better off with an average of 23.1 TLU compared to 19.5 for Siambu, although this difference is not significant. When considered on a per capita basis, however, the greater wealth apparent in Mbaringon evaporates. With an average of 3.92 TLU per person, Siambu individuals are significantly wealthier than Mbaringon individuals, who only have 2.57 TLU per person. Figure 4 shows the distribution of livestock holdings in Siambu and Mbaringon in per capita terms. Almost half of Mbaringon households (47 percent) own greater than 2 but less than 4 TLU per person. By contrast, only 31 percent of Siambu households are in this range. This is a reversal of the situation in 1978 when 43 percent of Siambu households were in this category compared to only 23 percent for Mbaringon (fig. 3). There are also

TABLE 2. Livestock Holdings (in TLU) in Siambu and Mbaringon, 2000–2001

Unit	Siambu	Mbaringon	t value	Significant	p value
Household TLU	19.50	23.10	−0.95	no	0.17
Per capita TLU	3.92	2.57	2.79	yes	0.003

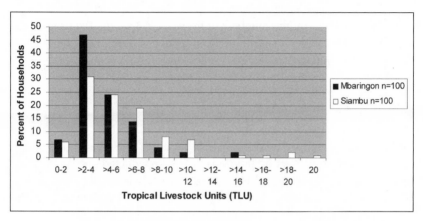

Fig. 4. Tropical livestock units (TLU) per capita in 2000–2001

more Siambu households in the higher ranges above 8 TLU per person. Neither community has per capita holdings above 20, however, which was not the case in 1978.

The Effects of Drought on Wealth

Several caveats are in order when considering these data. First, it should be noted that the household and per capita holdings for both communities are very low when considered as a basis for subsistence. Most estimates of the number of livestock required for subsistence relying entirely on livestock products conclude that 4 or 5 TLU per person are the minimum required for basic survival (Rutten 1992; Fratkin 1999). However, Rutten also presents an analysis based on human nutritional requirements that posits 9 TLU per capita as the minimum number of livestock adequate for subsistence (1992, 346). It is difficult to be definitive about how many TLU are required for subsistence, but with mean per capita holdings of 2 or 3 livestock equivalents, neither Siambu nor Mbaringon comes close to fulfilling their subsistence needs exclusively from livestock.

These low levels of livestock holdings, while part of a pattern of long-term impoverishment, also reflect the devastating impact of the recent drought of 1999–2000. The very large losses of livestock incurred during this drought mean that livestock holdings reported in the survey are particularly low. Data collected on the numbers of livestock lost during the drought reveal that while both communities lost animals, Mbaringon households tended to lose many more than those in Siambu. For example, Mbaringon households lost on average 24 head of cattle compared to only seven for Siambu households. For small stock, the average loss in Mbaringon was 23 head, while for Siambu it was only 13. Indeed, if we added the livestock lost in the 2000 drought to what remained after the drought, livestock holdings (at household level) in Mbaringon would be much greater than in Siambu (table 3). This means that had the survey been conducted one year earlier, before the drought, Mbaringon households might have been better off than their Siambu counterparts. The larger losses incurred by Mbaringon in the drought explain, at least in part, their current low levels of wealth.

A third consideration is the effect the drought has had on the relative value of cattle and small stock. Since many cattle died during the drought, the value of cattle postdrought is rising against the value of small stock. While 1 cow could have been exchanged for 6 or 7 goats a few years ago, it now takes 12 head of small stock to exchange for a cow. The scarcity of cattle, particularly breeding stock, has led to this increase in their value. While this is not a surprising development, it has an impact on the calculation of livestock equivalents in the two communities. Since the value of small stock is currently relatively low, households with higher percentages of small stock in their herds appear poorer than they would have before the drought and the changed relative value of the species. Again, this tends to make Mbaringon households appear poorer since they have higher percentages of small stock in their herds. Thirty-one percent of Mbaringon TLU are small

TABLE 3. Household TLU Taking into Account Drought Losses

Community	Average TLU per Household, 2000	Average Number of Cattle That Died in 2000 Drought	TLU, 2000 + Drought Losses
Mbaringon	23	24	47
Siambu	19	7	26

stock, while only 20 percent in Siambu are. As shown previously, Mbaringon households lost more cattle on average than Siambu households did, which served to increase the proportion of small stock in their herds. There is also a trend toward keeping more small stock, especially in Mbaringon, due to the favorable conditions for small stock obtaining there.[7] These higher proportions of small stock in Mbaringon herds make them appear poorer versus Siambu households at present, but in a couple of years, when cattle numbers have recovered, this effect will lessen as the relative values come back to normal. At present, then, Siambu people are better off in terms of per capita livestock holdings, but this difference appears to be at least partly due to the differential effects on drought in the two areas.

Polygyny and Wealth

Mbaringon households are significantly larger than those of Siambu. The average household in Mbaringon has ten members, while in Siambu the average number is seven. This difference is primarily due to the higher rate of polygyny in Mbaringon. Thirty-eight percent of Mbaringon sample households are polygynous, while only 23 percent are polygynous in Siambu. Also, there are more instances of men with three or four wives in Mbaringon (10 percent) than in Siambu (2 percent). In order to control for differences in consumption across age cohorts, all household members were converted to active adult male equivalents (AAME) using a formula developed by International Livestock Center for Africa (ILCA 1981) (see table 1). This conversion adjusted household sizes downward. Mbaringon's average household size reduced from 9.8 to 8.1, while Siambu household size fell from 6.7 to 5.6.

Among Samburu pastoralists, polygyny is often believed to correlate with wealth. That is, a man marries more than one wife primarily because he has livestock holdings that exceed the current capacity of household labor to care for. Since hired labor is fairly unusual, people rely on household labor to herd and care for livestock—the more livestock there are, the more labor is required. Thus, one might reasonably assume that a household with several wives must have a commensurately high number of livestock.

While this has been the norm historically, there are other reasons for men to marry more than one wife. Sometimes a second (or third) marriage is a strategy to deal with existing marital problems. Divorce is socially unacceptable and quite rare, but there is no stigma attached to setting up multiple households in distant locations. A man can marry a new wife and live primarily with her while the first wife and her children reside elsewhere. There is also an element of prestige associated with marriage. A large family is considered a positive asset to a man, and these days it seems it retains this image even without the wealth that one would expect to find alongside a polygynous family. Of course, periodic droughts and diseases can wipe out the wealth of a household, leaving them impoverished but still polygynous.

All of these considerations mean that we cannot automatically assume that polygyny equals wealth. In order to verify the relationship between wealth and polygyny, the number of polygynous households in each wealth category was calculated.[8] Table 4 shows that most polygynous households are in the richest two quintiles of sample households (Siambu, 52 percent; Mbaringon, 47 percent). By contrast, there are relatively few polygynous households in the lowest quintile (Siambu, 13 percent; Mbaringon, 10.5 percent). The correlation between polygyny and wealth was confirmed by regression analysis that revealed a positive correlation between wealth quintile and polygyny ($t = 2.46, p = .014$).

If polygyny correlates to wealth, then the higher rates of polygyny in Mbaringon should correspond to greater wealth. The fact that Mbaringon appears poorer than Siambu, in spite of higher rates of polygyny, suggests that the low livestock holdings in Mbaringon in 2000–2001 may be of recent origin, due to the recent drought, rather than an indication of long-standing declines.

Wealth Distribution

To further examine wealth in both communities, the population was divided into quintiles based on per capita livestock holdings. Table 5 shows the num-

TABLE 4. Polygynous Households by Wealth Category

Wealth Category	Percent of Polygynous Households			
	Siambu		Mbaringon	
	n	Percent	n	Percent
Richest quintile	7	30.43	8	26.32
Second quintile	5	21.74	7	21.05
Third quintile	4	17.39	9	23.68
Fourth quintile	4	17.39	7	18.42
Poorest quintile	3	13.04	3	10.53
Total	23	100.00	34	100.00

TABLE 5. Wealth Distribution Shown in Quintiles

	Richest Quintile		Second Quintile		Third Quintile		Fourth Quintile		Poorest Quintile	
	Siambu	Mbaringon	Siambu	Mbaringon	Siambu	Mbaringon	Siambu	Mbaringon	Siambu	Mbaringon
Number of households	25	17	19	19	18	20	19	20	19	24
Number of individuals	136	204	133	190	132	195	133	197	136	194
Mean per capita TLU	9.07	7.08	4.41	3.60	2.75	2.03	1.39	1.09	0.28	0.24
Minimum TLU	5.36	4.83	3.56	2.85	2.04	1.60	0.76	0.69	0.00	0.00
Maximum TLU	18.82	13.90	5.32	4.81	3.53	2.77	2.03	1.45	0.74	0.68
Percent total TLU owned	47.92	51.06	26.60	25.16	15.58	14.24	8.20	7.77	1.69	1.77

Note: Survey households were divided into five groups, or quintiles, according to wealth (measured in TLU). First, household TLU was converted to per capita TLU by dividing total household TLU by household AAME (active adult male equivalents). Then, households were ranked according to per capita TLU. Five quintiles were formed by dividing the total population by five and then successively counting off households in rank order to form each fifth.

ber of individuals and households in each wealth category and gives the mean, minimum, and maximum per capita livestock holdings for each. Looking at the number of households in each category again reveals the relationship between polygyny and wealth. In Mbaringon, wealthier households tend to be polygynous and therefore have more members. As a result, there are fewer households in the richest quintile (17), and the number increases to 24 households in the poorest quintile. Interestingly, the opposite pattern obtains in Siambu, with 25 households in the top quintile and 19 in the poorest quintile. Indeed, the average household size (in AAME) for Siambu households in the top quintile is 4.6 compared to 9.9 for Mbaringon. There are 2 households with only 1 member and 2 with 2 members in the top Siambu quintile. In these instances, the per capita figures may be misleading. For example, a household with 1 member and 9 TLU has a per capita TLU of 9 and is in the top quintile for wealth, although that household would probably not be considered wealthy by other Samburu.

Another interesting aspect of the wealth distribution is the percentage of total wealth owned by the top quintile. The bottom row of the table shows that the richest 20 percent of households in Siambu own about 48 percent of the total TLU, while the poorest 20 percent own less than 2 percent. This skew in wealth is also present in Mbaringon where the top 20 percent own 51 percent of total TLU, while the poorest 20 percent own only 2 percent. These findings suggest that stratification in wealth is significant in both communities.

The data on wealth distribution confirm that only the wealthiest households are in a position to subsist entirely off their herds (only 3 households in Mbaringon and 10 in Siambu have 9 or more TLU per capita). People in both communities must diversify their sources of food and income in order to survive. The possibility of diversifying into crop production was a major impetus to privatize land in Siambu and is even encouraged in Mbaringon by government and nongovernmental organizations (NGOs) as a way to supplement household food supplies. Wage labor has also proven to be an important source of income for households in both communities. The following sections will discuss the nature and importance of alternative income sources and agriculture to household welfare.

Summary

Since 1978, the gap in wealth between Siambu and Mbaringon has narrowed. In 2000, Siambu had significantly greater per capita livestock holdings than Mbaringon. These findings are mitigated, however, by the ways in which each community was affected by the drought of 1999–2000. In addition, the higher frequency of polygyny in Mbaringon, which is correlated with wealth, suggests that losses of wealth may be recent and due primarily to drought rather than to longer-term processes. Furthermore, the very small household size of some wealthy Siambu households may create an appearance of greater wealth than is warranted.

The following sections will explore to what extent participation in agriculture and other income-generating activities by Siambu households provides a cushion that may enable households to better withstand the effects of drought, thereby preserving their assets and explaining, at least in part, why the wealth gap between the two communities has narrowed over time. Investments in education are one strategy that positions individuals to enter the job market and to make more informed decisions regarding agricultural production. Thus, before turning to an analysis of incomes, the next section considers trends in educational attainment in Siambu and Mbaringon.

Educational Attainment

While households are larger in Mbaringon, their children have less education than those in Siambu. Fifty-nine percent of Siambu children between ages 5 and 17 have some education, and 27 percent of children between the ages of 10 and 13 have completed 4 years of primary school (table 6). In Mbaringon, 50 percent of children have some education, but only 15 percent of children aged between 10 and 13 have completed 4 years. The number of primary school graduates (completed 8 years of school) is also low in both communities. Out of 67 children aged between 14 and 17 years in Siambu, only 9 (13 percent) have completed primary school, compared to only 9 (9 percent) out of 101 in this cohort in Mbaringon. Low retention and completion rates are common in Samburu District, with dropout attributed to the demands of the livestock economy for child labor for herding, early marriages of girls, and circumcision for boys. It should be noted, however, that due to late start of education and interruptions, children completing 8 years of primary school may be over 17 years old and thus not show up in this calculation. Overall, Siambu has higher rates of education among children.

Are higher levels of education in Siambu a trend that is recent, perhaps due to increased settlement on individual farms, or does it have a longer history? Considering adult levels of educational attainment provides insight into

TABLE 6. Children's Educational Attainment

Cohort	Years Education Completed	Siambu								Mbaringon							
		Total Cohort[a]		Girls		Boys		Total		Total Cohort		Girls		Boys		Total	
		Girls	Boys	Comp[b] n	%[c]	Comp n	%	%[d]		Girls	Boys	Comp n	%	Comp n	%	Total n	%
5–17 years	> 0	122	141	60	49	94	67	59		216	200	85	39	121	60	60	50
10–13 years	≥ 4	39	42	10	26	12	29	27		71	71	9	13	13	13	18	15
14–17 years	≥ 8	28	39	6	21	3	8	13		48	53	5	10	4	8	8	9

[a]The total number of children (boys or girls) in the age cohort indicated in the first column (Cohort).
[b]The number of children (boys or girls) who have completed the number of years indicated in second column (Years education completed).
[c]The percentage represented by those who have completed the number of years compared to the total cohort.
[d]The total percentage of the cohort who have completed this level of education, combining girls and boys.
Note: For example, Siambu girls aged 10–13, out of a total of 39 girls in this age group, 10 have completed four or more years of schooling, representing 26 percent of this cohort.

the longevity of this trend. More adults in Siambu (44.4 percent) have attended school than in Mbaringon (29.4 percent), and 10 percent of Siambu adults have completed primary school, compared to only 7.8 percent in Mbaringon (table 7). Looking at educational attainment for men according to age confirms that Siambu has a longer history of education. Table 8 shows educational attainment by age cohorts roughly corresponding to the male age-grade divisions. Clearly, there is a positive trend in education in both communities with younger age groups having higher levels of education than their elders. In Siambu, however, the older age-sets have higher levels of education than in Mbaringon, particularly the Lkishili with an average of almost 2 years of education compared to only about a half year for Mbaringon. Out of 21 Lkishili from Siambu in the sample, 9 (42 percent) had 4 or more years of education, whereas in Mbaringon only 4 (13 percent) out of 32 Lkishili men in the sample had completed 4 years of education.

The Lkishili were the first age-set to have reasonable access to school in the 1950s and 1960s. Since education tends to inculcate attitudes favoring private property, the fact that more Lkishili were educated in Siambu may account for the relatively high number of men who requested private land there. Thus, while increasing participation in formal education appears to be a trend that pre-dates the privatization of land, it may partly explain why privatization was more actively sought in Siambu than in Mbaringon.

TABLE 7. Adult Educational Attainment

Years of School Completed	Siambu Adults		Mbaringon Adults	
	n	Percent	*n*	Percent
>0 years school	134	44.4	112	29.4
>4 years school	109	36.1	82	21.5
>8 years school	31	10.3	30	7.8
>12 years school	7	2.3	3	0.8
Total cohort	302		381	

TABLE 8. Average Years of Education Completed by Male Age Groups

Age Cohort (age-set name)	Siambu		Mbaringon	
	Years	*n*	Years	*n*
18–32 (Lmeoli)	4.4	67	3.2	82
33–47 (Lkiroro)	2.2	45	1.6	42
48–62 (Lkishili)	1.9	21	.6	32
63+ (Lkimaniki +)	0.1	12	0	13

In Siambu, more than 50 percent (52.2 percent) of men in the current warrior age-grade, Lmeoli, have completed 8 or more years of education. In Mbaringon, the corresponding figure is only 35 percent. Therefore, it appears that the trend toward higher levels of educational attainment continues in Siambu. Although individual families are investing in education by sending their children to school, the community of Siambu has been hard pressed to update and improve its aging primary school. In the early 1990s, a fund-raiser (*harambee*) was held to build a new school in Poro town. The original school was in serious disrepair, and its location immediately next to the dam was considered hazardous to the children. Funds were raised and a new building was begun. The building only reached the window level when funds mysteriously disappeared and the project stalled. Some members of the school committee were accused of having misused the funds, and the project was abandoned. In late 2001, plans were afoot to restart the project, and each household was asked to contribute KSh 500 ($6.25). When I left the field, contributions were still being collected, but there was no assurance that these funds would be better utilized than those originally collected for school construction.[9]

Meanwhile, the land around Siambu's other primary school, away from the town on the road to the escarpment, was being leased out for wheat farming and the funds used to expand the school. Currently, this school has enough classrooms, but the floors and walls are not plastered and there are very few desks, let alone other basic equipment.

The situation in Mbaringon is rather different as regards educational infrastructure. The primary school there was started by the Catholic mission in the 1980s and had slowly grown over the years. Community fund-raising in the late 1990s was supplemented by contributions from a development project and from St. Lawrence University, which brings students to the area twice a year for a field course that is part of their study abroad program. After twenty years, the university decided to express its gratitude to the Mbaringon community, who serve as hosts and teachers for the American students, by building two new classrooms and a staff room and renovating the existing classes. By the end of 2001, Mbaringon's primary school was one of the nicest in the district, physically. In spite of good physical infrastructure, enrollments are still somewhat below the capacity of the school in the upper grades and remain far below full enrollment for the school-age cohort. It appears, then, that while Siambu families are investing more in education, they are doing so individually, by sending their children to school (in Poro, Siambu, and Maralal) not by supporting the shared educational infrastructure. By contrast, while the physical infrastructure for education in Mbaringon is good due to efforts by some local leaders, community members, and others wishing to assist the community, families are not necessarily responding by sending their children to school, or keeping them in school.

The investments that Siambu families make in education should translate into better job prospects among educated men (and women) from Siambu compared to Mbaringon. With the skills and knowledge gained through formal education, they should be better able to compete in job markets requiring higher levels of literacy, numeracy, and other skills gained through education. The next section explores income sources and patterns of employment for Siambu and Mbaringon, and will show to what extent investments in education pay off in employment.

Income Differences

Mbaringon households have significantly higher total incomes than Siambu households.[10] An average household in Mbaringon brings in over KSh 80,000 per year, equivalent to about USD 1,000. In Siambu, average income is only KSh 57,318, or USD 716.00 (table 9, row A).[11] Considered in per capita terms, though, Siambu individuals earn more in a year at KSh 12,055 (USD 150) than do those in Mbaringon (KSh 10,357, USD 129) (table 9, row B). Thus, higher household size in Mbaringon dilutes the effect of higher overall income, but the per capita differences are not significant.

If the value of home consumption of crops and milk is added to income (table 9, rows C, D), Siambu's per capita incomes are significantly higher than Mbaringon's. Home consumption was calculated by assigning a value to home-produced, home-consumed crops and milk. Prevailing market prices of these commodities were used. In order to take into account variations in crop yields, an estimate of one crop failure in four years was assumed, and the crop yields reported in the survey (representing years with good yields)[12] were reduced by 25 percent. Since milk yields during the survey were uniformly low, these were not adjusted downward. Including home consumption, the average income in Siambu rises to KSh 95,658 and in Mbaringon to KSh 107,130. However, the per capita income difference is significant: Siambu per capita income almost doubles to KSh 19,382 while the increase

TABLE 9. Total Income, Per Capita Income, and Sources of Income

Row	Source of Income	Average Income in KSH		p-value	t-value	Significant
		Siambu n = 100	Mbaringon n = 100			
A	Total household income	57,318	80,979	0.003	-2.70	yes
B	Per capita income	12,055	10,357	0.14	1.05	no
C	Total income including value of home consumption	95,658	107,130	−0.97	0.16	no
D	Per capita income including value of home consumption	19,382	13,690	0.002	2.85	yes
E	Sales of own livestock	13,793	35,615	0.001	3.06	yes
F	Wage labor	19,544	28,092	0.09	1.30	no
G	Gifts	2,894	3,281	0.36	0.34	no
H	Agriculture (gross)	8,687	349	6.8 e-7	5.14	yes
I	Agriculture (net)	4,165	−655	0.0004	3.43	yes
J	Remittances	2,060	2,611	0.28	0.56	no
K	Trade	12,400	13,922	0.42	0.34	no
L	Value of home consumption	38,341	26,152	0.01	2.29	yes

for Mbaringon is only slightly over 60 percent, to KSh 13,690. This is an indication of the role of crop production on incomes in Siambu, which will be discussed further.

Examining income by source (table 9, rows E–L; figs. 5, 6, 7) reveals that both communities continue to rely on livestock sales for a significant portion of their income. However, wage labor and trade are also important, and, in Siambu, 10 percent of household income derives from agriculture. This makes sense given the fact that land in Siambu is more suited to agriculture and about 30 percent of sample households earn on average KSh 10,000 annually leasing land out for wheat farming. Agriculture is also practiced in Mbaringon, but, on average, it yields little income. Most households consume most of their harvest. These trends in agriculture will be discussed in more detail later.

Livestock Sales

Income from livestock sales makes up an average of 26 percent of income in Mbaringon and somewhat less, 17 percent, in Siambu. Due to the drought,

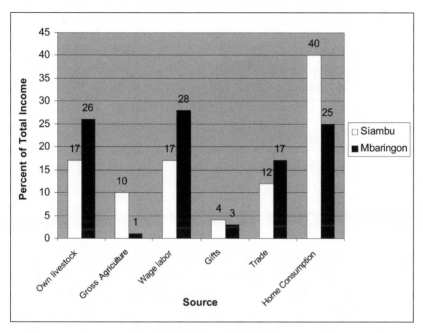

Fig. 5. Percentage of total income by source, Siambu and Mbaringon, 2000. *Own livestock* means sales of the household's own livestock. *Gross agriculture* denotes the gross proceeds from sales of agricultural produce, not deducting costs of production. *Gifts* include gifts and remittances. *Trade* includes livestock trade and other activities such as selling firewood, charcoal, or running a shop or restaurant. *Home consumption* is the value of home-produced and home-consumed crops and milk.

sales of livestock were higher than they would normally be. In particular, people sold more breeding stock, including females, in 1999 and 2000 than they ordinarily would, due to the drought. Mbaringon and Siambu households both sold two cattle, on average, but Mbaringon households earned almost twice as much from cattle sales: KSh 20,000 versus KSh 11,000. This is due to higher prices fetched for their animals, which tended to be older at the time of sale. Both communities sold more than twice as many male as female stock, consistent with their herd structures, which are predominantly female, since milk production for home consumption is still the major objective of livestock production.[13]

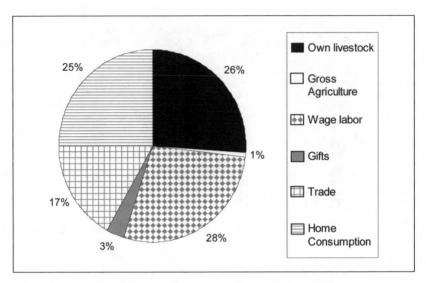

Fig. 6. Income by source, Mbaringon ($n = 100$)

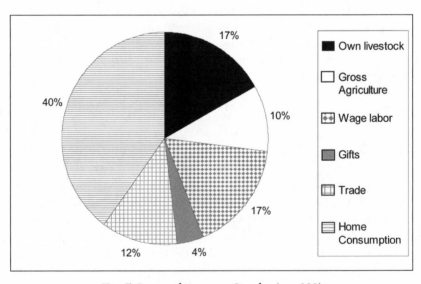

Fig. 7. Income by source, Siambu ($n = 100$)

Mbaringon households sold, on average, twenty-two head of small stock, earning KSh 17,000, while Siambu households only sold four head, earning on average KSh 2,700 from small stock. These levels of sales are mostly due to the pressures of the drought but may also reflect the greater proportion of small stock present in Mbaringon herds and the increasing commercialization of small stock production among some households. The higher prices received for cattle and greater sales of small stock result in higher incomes from livestock sales in Mbaringon.

It is clear from these data that Siambu households have not boosted their livestock production after privatization. Not only do they sell about the same numbers of cattle as Mbaringon households, but they have not attempted to upgrade the productivity of their livestock by investing in improved breeds. Given the fact that they own their land and that the land has reasonably good rainfall, Siambu has some potential for improved dairy production using exotic breeds. Indeed, the Ministry of Agriculture and Rural Development (MARD) has promoted the idea of improved dairy cows in the area. To date, however, only two individuals have invested in dairy cattle, and one was given the animals by the ministry as a subsidy to demonstrate the viability of improved dairy production. When asked whether or not they had improved breeds of livestock, only three survey households (3 percent) in Siambu answered in the affirmative compared to eighteen (18 percent) in Mbaringon.

The low level of investment in productivity improvements in Siambu, which also extends to agriculture where there is little use of inputs such as fertilizers, pesticides, or tractors, may stem from the failure of land owners to access credit that could enable such investments. One rationale for privatizing land was that it could be used as collateral for bank loans. Use of credit among Siambu households was rare, and it was not used for investments in agricultural productivity. Ten households (10 percent of surveyed households) reported having outstanding credits. These loans were used for purchases of food, house construction, marriage expenses, and to start livestock trade. Furthermore, land was generally not used as collateral. According to records of the Land Control Board (LCB) from 1991 through 2001, only five individuals from Siambu used their land to obtain credit.[14] This limited use of land as collateral for credit is consistent with evidence from other studies. Bruce and Migot-Adholla et al. (1994) conclude that land owners seldom use land for collateral due to fear of foreclosure in case of default. At the same time, lenders are wary of accepting titles as collateral because of the difficulties in foreclosing and selling land that occur in cases of default. In the absence of credit and given the generally low levels of wealth and income in Siambu, it is not very surprising that privatization alone has not resulted in greater investment in agricultural productivity.

Wage Labor and Trade

Mbaringon households earn more income from wage labor than Siambu households. On average, Mbaringon households earn KSh 28,092 from wage labor annually, while for Siambu households the figure is KSh 19,544. Sixty-six percent of Mbaringon households report earning some income from wage labor, compared to 40 percent for Siambu.[15] As shown in table 10, Mbaringon households participate in a range of activities, but the most common are watchman, casual labor, and civil service. The fact that many men have been employed as watchmen supports the observation that there is a strategy among young men from this area of leaving home before marriage, working in Nairobi and other big towns, and investing the money in livestock in preparation for marriage. Later, they return home, get married, and settle down, perhaps never seeking employment again. This strategy was particularly common among the Lkishili and Lkiroro age-sets, which explains the fact that many men who are not currently employed report having been employed in the past. Of course, individuals may also seek employment on a temporary basis during droughts or other disasters, returning home at the

TABLE 10. Households Participating in Wage Labor by Type of Job

| Job | Percent of Households Participating | |
	Siambu	Mbaringon
Agricultural labor	7	3
Carpenter	2	4
Herding	0	9
Mission	1	2
Watchman	1	14
Casual labor	11	15
Teacher	2	3
Civil service	18	17
Development agency	0	5
Other professional	1	4
Total	43	76

end of the crisis period. Thus, both long-term and short-term strategies are at play.

The strategy of seeking employment during the warrior period in order to build up assets before marriage appears from anecdotal evidence to be less successful now than in the past. Although many young men still leave to pursue work outside the district, they often do not remit much money back home, nor do they purchase many livestock. Indeed, a number of them stay away for extended periods, some even permanently. The rising cost of living in Nairobi and other Kenyan cities, plus the lure of living in such locales, appear to be undermining the strategy of building assets in the pastoral sector to pave the way for "retirement" there. This may not be an entirely negative development to the extent that it constitutes an exit strategy from pastoralism, which, as we have seen, cannot support the growing population. However, there is a difficulty when men leave behind wives and children with no means of support who are then particularly vulnerable, since they are forced to rely on relatives or friends for assistance.

A number of informants are employed as civil servants in the government.[16] These individuals earn relatively high salaries (from about KSh 50,000 to KSh 100,000 annually) and have a greater level of job security than those in other forms of employment. They also tend to rely almost exclusively on their salaries, showing less diversification of income sources than other groups. This is demonstrated by the fact that, on average for both Siambu and Mbaringon, civil servants' income from employment accounts for 88 percent of their total cash income (not including home consumption). This is much higher than the overall average share of income from wage labor of 17 percent for Siambu and 26 percent for Mbaringon. Having secured relatively lucrative positions, civil servants do not pursue other options to a great extent.

The fact that almost equal numbers of individuals are employed as civil servants in Mbaringon as in Siambu may be interpreted in two ways. On the one hand, it suggests that the greater investments Siambu households are making in education have yet to pay off since people from Mbaringon are also employed in the civil service in the same numbers. On the other hand, when considered as a proportion of all those employed in Siambu, civil servants comprise 43 percent of the total. In Mbaringon, only 22 percent of the total number employed are in the civil service. In this sense, then, education and skills may be paying off in that civil service employment is more common in Siambu than in Mbaringon.

Income Diversification by Wealth Category

More insight into the strategies employed by various segments of the population is gained by considering the patterns of diversification of income across wealth categories. As explained previously, the population in each sample community was stratified into quintiles according to wealth. Figure 8 shows the average percentage contribution of different income sources for the richest (Q1) and the poorest (Q5) quintiles. It is apparent that different strategies are pursued by different wealth groups. Households in the wealthiest quintile earn most of their income from selling their own livestock and from home consumption of crops and milk that they produce. Livestock sales are particularly important in Mbaringon, making up almost 45 percent of this group's income. Second in importance is home consumption, constituting 35 percent of income. Siambu households in the top quintile, by contrast, rely heavily on home consumption from both crops and milk (45 percent) and less on livestock sales (17 percent). Sales of crops provide 10 percent of their income, while these sales are nil for Mbaringon households in this quintile. Trade and wage labor are less significant income sources for the households in the top quintile, in both Mbaringon and Siambu.

The wealthiest households in Mbaringon rely quite heavily on livestock sales for their income. In this regard, they look like traditional pastoralists, except that they are more integrated into markets, with some of them concentrating especially on producing large numbers of small stock for sale. In contrast, wealthier households in Siambu have diversified out of livestock more than those in Mbaringon. This pattern of diversification supports the earlier contention that the appearance of greater livestock wealth in Siambu is primarily an artifact of the recent drought, but it also demonstrates the importance of crop production, both for home consumption and sale, to Siambu incomes.

The poorest families in the fifth quintile depend heavily on wage labor and small-scale trade and petty commodity production (grouped together as "Trade"). Many of them engage in relatively low-paying jobs, such as watchmen, casual laborers, and farm workers. There are also some in civil service jobs, earning reasonably good salaries. Such households may be poor in terms of livestock wealth, but they have high incomes. For the poor households of Mbaringon, wage labor contributes 40 percent of their income, and trade constitutes 37 percent. Households in the lowest quintile in Siambu only earn 32 percent of their income from wage labor and less than 20 per-

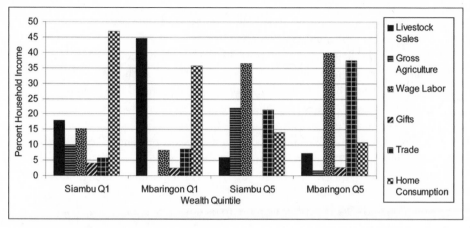

Fig. 8. Percentage of household income by source, richest (Q1) and poorest (Q5) wealth quintiles

cent from trade. Again, the difference lies partly in the contribution of agriculture to income in Siambu. Almost 20 percent of income for the poorest quintile in Siambu is from agriculture, while this is negligible for Mbaringon. Home consumption makes up about 12 and 10 percent of income for this quintile for Siambu and Mbaringon, respectively. Thus, it is important but not nearly as significant as for the households in the top quintile.

Many poor households, lacking livestock and other opportunities, resort to mining the available natural resources to earn income. They cut and sell firewood in nearby towns of Kisima (Mbaringon) and Poro (Siambu). They burn charcoal, cut timber poles, collect honey, and brew beer and gin, for which there is a ready market in both communities. These activities are labor-intensive but are an option for poor families who lack capital to start other businesses, such as livestock trading, shops, or hotels (Little et al. 2001).

Livestock sales are a minor part of the income of households in the lowest quintile in both Mbaringon and Siambu. This makes sense given the general poverty of this group. In Mbaringon, there is a community of hunter-gatherers.[17] These people are believed to be of Maasai descent (though their origins are debated by scholars; see Spear and Waller 1993), traditionally hunters and gatherers owning few or no livestock. Most of them are still poor in livestock and specialize in gathering wild honey from the forest adjacent to Mbaringon group ranch. These families are involved in collection and sale of other forest products, such as firewood, timber, and charcoal. Their inclusion in the sample may account for the fact that livestock sales are less important among the poorest quintile in Mbaringon.

Gifts, including remittances from employed relatives and friends, do not make up a major part of income for any wealth group. They may in fact be more significant than reflected here, since people tend not to keep track of all the gifts they receive, particularly small gifts of food that commonly circulate within settlements.

To sum up, diversification of income sources is present in both Siambu and Mbaringon. The two communities differ in the relative importance of different activities. Livestock sales are the most important source of income for wealthier households in Mbaringon, with agriculture (both home consumption and sale) contributing more to income in Siambu. Wage labor and trade are significant sources of income, especially for poorer households that lack livestock.

The Role of Agriculture

Agriculture has contributed positively to incomes in Siambu, but the supposition that privatization would transform pastoralists into farmers has not proven accurate. In Mbaringon, relatively high subsidies to agricultural activities have encouraged more people to become involved, but the low returns of farming demonstrate the risky nature of the activity in this area, which is only marginally suited to crop production. The following sections will discuss the organization of agriculture and other new land uses, such as leasing and selling land in Siambu, in some detail. This is warranted since agriculture has become an important part of the local economy and contributes significantly to household consumption and income. Following the discussion of Siambu, more brief remarks will be made about agriculture in Mbaringon, the aim being to compare and contrast the experiences in the two communities.

The Organization of Agriculture

People in Siambu began cultivation on a small scale in the 1960s, as discussed in chapter 4. These early attempts were often viewed with derision by the rest of the community, who did not see any value in the activity. Immediately after the decision was made in 1986 to divide Siambu into equal-sized parcels among all the group ranch members, the community punished several individuals believed to have been overzealous about farming. Today, attitudes have changed. During the survey there was no one who viewed farming as useless or a waste of time. On the contrary, virtually all individuals interviewed pointed out the advantages of farming as a way to get food and money. Some individuals even perceived a moral superiority in farming—which certainly clashes with the general view of Samburu pastoralists that digging in the earth is undignified.

These positive attitudes about the benefits of farming were in sharp contrast to the situation on the ground during the survey. That is, there was a widespread crop failure during the year 2000 due to the prevailing drought. Indeed, only two households reported harvesting anything in 2000. When asked to report on their latest harvest, most informants had to go back to 1998, since even 1999 was a very bad year for most households. This highlights the fact that, even though Siambu has relatively good potential for farming, it is still a risky area periodically affected by drought.

The pro-farming attitude of Siambu people is belied by their small farm sizes. Although 77 percent of the survey households participate in agriculture, as opposed to only 49 percent for Mbaringon, the average farm size in Siambu is just under 2 acres (1.9 acres). Only five households cultivate more than 5 acres, and the largest farm size recorded in the survey was 8 acres. These figures were corroborated by the Ministry of Agriculture and Rural Development's recent farm census in Siambu, which found average farm size of 1.6 acres and a total of 77 farmers (Republic of Kenya 2001). Thus, although each household has access to about 23 acres of land, they are only cultivating a small portion of it.

If the ministry's farm census data are correct, then it appears that my household survey covered virtually all of the households that actively cultivate, meaning that only about 40 percent of all households in Siambu are involved in farming. This is partly attributable to geographic features. Some families live on steeply sloping areas on the edges of the escarpment where farming is quite difficult. It also stems from the fact that not all people are equally interested in farming. After all, as we saw in chapters 4 and 5, the majority of people were originally against individual land tenure, and they only agreed to it as a compromise solution to end the serious conflict that had developed over land. Remembering this, it is not that surprising that many households do not farm, in spite of the positive rhetoric about agriculture.

Another factor to consider is that, out of the thirty survey households that lease land out for wheat farming, seven do no cultivation of their own. They are involved in agriculture as landlords, not as cultivators. This may be a sensible strategy, since the average annual income from wheat leases (KSh 10,909) slightly exceeds that of crop sales (KSh 10,844). Of course, those growing crops also gain through home consumption of the produce, on average valued at KSh 6,034. On the other hand, the opportunity cost of household labor in farming activities was not included in calculations of farm costs. If included, these additional labor costs would likely offset the benefits of home consumption, making leasing equally as profitable as cultivation.[18]

Another hindering factor could be the costs involved in cultivation. The average cost of inputs among survey households in Siambu was KSh 4,201. However, there was a huge range— from zero spent on inputs up to KSh 69,600. Participation in agriculture among poor households is actually relatively high. Eighteen out of nineteen households (95 percent) in the lowest wealth quintile participate in agriculture, and they spend an average of KSh 3,935 on agricultural inputs. Thus, it appears that being poor does not prevent people from participating in agriculture. It should not be overlooked that some households that are poor in livestock wealth may have considerable incomes from other sources. Even among those households that rank poorest both in terms of livestock wealth and income (quintiles 4 and 5 in both), eight out of ten (80 percent) participate in agriculture, and those which sell crops earn an average of KSh 5,110 from these sales. However, poverty may come into play when considering farm size. Most poor households have small farms of one acre, while the biggest farms are owned by the wealthiest households. Thus, although poor households are able to participate in agriculture, they may be limited in their ability to increase farm size.

Both men and women participate in farming. According to informants, between 70 and 80 percent of men are involved in all stages of farming, from clearing through to harvesting. Women's participation rates are very similar, with slightly higher percentages in weeding (81 percent) and harvesting (83 percent) than those of men in the same activities. Data on participation rates point to very little division of labor along gender lines in farm labor. This may be a reflection of the gendered responsibilities for agricultural plots. In many households, men and women have separate plots (Holtzman 1996). Thus, men spend more time on their own plots, while women concentrate on theirs. Not all households adhere to this pattern, however. In these cases, plots are worked jointly by men and women (Holtzman 1996). A time allocation study for farm labor was not conducted for this study, but anecdotal evidence suggests that men may have overestimated their participation somewhat, particularly in what are normally considered female tasks, such as weeding and harvesting. However, there is clearly a big range in terms of labor participation rates, and some men are very involved in farming. I observed a number of men busy working in their fields with no women in sight. They were clearly the most involved in farming in their households. This arrangement has advantages, since women have a heavy burden of domestic work while men have more leisure time, as a rule. Children and other relatives also help out on farms, though their participation is far below that of husbands and wives.

Hired labor is not very common in Siambu and is mostly used for the arduous task of weeding (22 percent of households). However, hiring labor can become a major cost when it is used on larger farms. Since the larger farms are owned by wealthier households, they are better able to afford hiring labor. In fact, during the survey some informants expressed surprise when they realized how much they had spent on labor and how it cut into their profits. Since most people do not keep records of their farming activities, they tend to be unaware of the breakdown of costs and benefits of their farming operations.

Crops and Yields

Survey households were asked to report on inputs and yields for their last successful harvest. For most households, this meant recalling back to 1997 or 1998, since harvests for 1999 (during the onset of the drought) and 2000 (when drought effects were easing and the survey was conducted) were negligible. The data on inputs and yields, therefore, cover several years but represent relatively good harvests.

The major crop grown in Siambu is maize. Out of 77 households involved in farming, 72 reported growing maize, while 33 grew beans. Beans are often intercropped with maize. Small amounts of vegetables, such as potatoes, kale (*sukuma wiki*), tomatoes, cabbage, onions, and carrots, are also grown. Crops are grown both for home consumption and for sale. People also report giving away various quantities of produce to friends and neighbors as gifts. The average yield per acre of maize in Siambu was 5.4 bags of 90 kilograms each. The average yield of beans per acre was 2.7 bags of 90 kilograms. The expected yield for farms on Lorroki plateau, according to Ministry of Agriculture and Rural Development, is 4 bags of maize per acre, and 12 bags is the target yield, based on the potential of the land, ideal farming practices, good seeds, and so forth. For beans, the expected yield is 0.64 bags per acre and the target yield is 3.2 bags per acre (Food Situation Report, Ref: SBU/CROP/VOL V/32/83, September 4, 2001).

The productivity of farms is, thus, on the higher side of what is expected on Lorroki plateau. This is not surprising considering that Siambu is one of the most suitable areas for farming in the district. However, compared to the target, or potential, yield of 12 bags of maize per acre, Siambu yields of 5 bags are low. Yields of beans for Siambu exceed the expected yield of 0.64 bags and approach the target yield of 3.2 bags.

Informants give many reasons to explain the relatively low yields of maize. Their main complaint is about damage done to crops by wildlife. Even though elephants and zebras have been more or less eradicated from the area, bush pigs, porcupines, and baboons remain a problem.[19] According to informants, bush pigs can destroy an entire field in a day. Besides crop destruction, lack of enough rainfall is also cited as a problem along with crop diseases and poor varieties of seeds.[20] The main explanation for low yields, offered by government staff, is poor farming practices because of lack of knowledge about proper agricultural methods. There has been very little extension work going on over the last several years due to reductions in government budgets, so little has been done to alleviate this knowledge gap. This aspect should not be discounted, considering the limited experience of Samburu people with agriculture, historically. Unlike other pastoralists, such as the Turkana or Pokot, who have considerable experience with agriculture, this is not the case for the Samburu. Becoming a farmer is not a simple process and may be particularly challenging in the fragile and erratic environment characteristic of Samburu District.

Crop Sales and Home Consumption

Farming households in Siambu sell and consume their produce. Out of 77 survey households participating in crop production, 44 reported crop sales. The average annual income from crop sales was KSh 10,844 (USD 135), ranging from a low of KSh 100 (about USD 1) to a high of KSh 80,500 (about USD 1,000). The median income from crop sales, what most people earned, was KSh 5,000 (USD 62.50). As we saw earlier, income from crops constitutes, on average, 10 percent of household incomes. For most households, sales of crops supplement household income but are not the major income source. However, for 23 households in Siambu, agriculture income makes up more than 50 percent of their total cash income, and for 6 households, it constitutes more than 90 percent. These are poorer households with few or no cattle and no income from other sources. A few of them are making reasonably good incomes from agriculture (KSh 20,000–30,000), but others are in the red, with net negative income from agriculture, although they still benefit from home consumption. These cases demonstrate that agriculture may provide an alternative livelihood for livestock-poor households in Siambu, a point made by numerous informants. It would be interesting to see how these households invest surpluses ultimately generated by agriculture, whether into livestock or farming, or both.

Aside from selling their crops, Siambu households consume much of what they produce. Data on home consumption reveal that, on average, households are able to consume their own maize for twenty-six weeks, about six months. They normally have about half of the maize ground into flour from which they make the staples *ugali* (stiff maize porridge) and *uji* (maize porridge). The whole maize is used in the dish *githeri,* which is a combination of boiled maize and beans. The average quantities of maize and maize flour consumed at home are 267 kilograms. Beans do not last as long, and fewer families grow them. Those who harvested beans consumed an average of 35 kilograms over a ten-week period. Kale is an important supplement to the diet and is highly nutritious. It is difficult to quantify amounts of kale harvested since it grows for a long period and is harvested by picking leaves daily. On average, households that grew it reported consuming kale for about six months. An average household might consume about 20 to 30 leaves of kale a day, but the amount varies widely. Potatoes and cabbage were also consumed by the households that grew them, but were far less common than maize and beans.

In order to get an idea of the significance of home consumption, the average amounts of various crops consumed were valued using the current market prices per unit (table 11). The total value of home consumption averaged KSh 6,034 (USD 75). Maize contributed about half this total, with beans next in importance, followed by potatoes and cabbage. Kale, while important in the diet, has a relatively low value. Beans are relatively expensive, reflecting their high protein content and relative scarcity in the market. It is worth noting here that considering the high cash value of beans and the good yields of beans that characterize Siambu, it might be advisable for farmers to invest more in this crop, both for sale and for home consumption. Home consumption supplements, but does not replace, purchased food in Siambu. Average weekly expenditures on food for Siambu households are KSh 625. Thus, household consumption represents the value of about ten weeks of purchased food commodities.

Leasing Out Land for Wheat

About a third (30) of survey households lease their land out for wheat growing, earning an average of almost KSh 11,000 annually, as noted earlier. Table 12 shows that households from all wealth and income categories lease out land. Although it appears that poorer households are more likely to lease out land, regression analysis on land leasing by wealth and income shows no significant correlation between either factor and leasing. On average, households lease out 16 acres of land for wheat farming. Most households also farm some of their land but, as mentioned earlier, seven households do no farming of their own.

Two issues of concern regarding leasing are the sustainability of this form of mechanized agriculture and the use of proceeds from wheat farming. Wheat farming in Siambu is a capital-intensive, mechanized operation. Large tractors and harvesters are used that leave deep ruts in the fields, especially when the ground is muddy. Most of the land in Siambu is relatively flat, so the dangers of soil erosion appear low. On hillside areas, however, as in neighboring group ranches also being farmed, this is a risk. Some efforts are made at plowing on contours, presumably to protect against erosion. Fertility is another concern. After twenty years of continuous cropping, it seems probable that the fertility of the land has declined. On the other hand, the yields of

TABLE 11. Average Cash Value of Home Consumption, Siambu

Crop	Price per unit (KSH)	Total Value (KSH)
Maize (kg)	11	1,419
Maize flour (kg)	11	1,518
Beans (kg)	58	2,030
Potatoes (kg)	7	616
Kale (piece)	0.33	91.08
Cabbage (head)	36	360
Total		6,034.08

wheat appear to be fairly good. According to the farm manager, 800 acres were farmed in Siambu in 2001, and the yield was 18 bags per acre, which matches the target yield calculated by the Ministry of Agriculture and Rural Development (personal communication, November 16, 2001). The main concern expressed by the wheat farmer himself is the falling profitability of wheat farming in the country. He complains that since the liberalization of the grain market several years ago American wheat is being dumped, duty free, into Kenya via Egypt, a member of the COMESA free trade area. He claims that Kenyan farmers cannot compete with the imports that sell for USD 100 per ton while his production costs are USD 240 per ton. If the government does not act to rectify the situation and enable farmers to compete, he says he is considering leaving Samburu altogether (field notes, May 22, 2001).[21]

How people use the money they get from leasing out land is another issue of concern to Siambu residents. A number of informants claimed that when men are paid for wheat (and it is invariably men since they are the title deed holders) they go immediately to the local bar, or even to bars in Maralal, and come home having spent the money. One man even said that he had ceased leasing his land because it brought no benefits. Judging by his character, he might have been one of those men who used up all his money in the bar and perhaps thought better of it later. Systematic evidence is not available on the use of wheat lease proceeds, but it seems likely that there is a grain of truth to the lament about men misusing the money. It has been shown that women tend to spend money on household needs, while men tend to spend it on themselves (Kennedy and Peters 1992). Since men have first access to the wheat money, they have the opportunity to waste it. In contrast, food crops are often, though not always, marketed by women, so the proceeds are more likely to be spent on household needs.

TABLE 12. Households Leasing Out Land in Siambu by Wealth and Income Quintiles

Quintile	Wealth		Income	
	n	Percent	*n*	Percent
Richest	8	27	8	26.5
Second	4	13	5	17
Third	6	20	6	20
Fourth	4	13	8	26.5
Poorest	8	27	3	10
Total	30	100	30	100

Land Sales

Having title to land gives one the right to sell that land. Interestingly, although all informants emphasized the fact that they were happy about owning their land because it gave them greater autonomy and control over what they did with it, they were almost universally negative about the phenomenon of selling land. They perceive sales as dangerous because of the risk that a man would sell off all his land and then have nowhere to live and nothing to leave his children. The fact that men, as title holders, are able to sell land without the consent of their families was also emphasized, and, as with the money from wheat leases, there was the feeling that men often wasted the money they received from land sales.

The area chief has been making efforts to limit land sales. Like other people, the chief feels that owning land is a positive thing. He mentioned some advantages during a car ride to Maralal.

> The advantage of having your own land is the control one has over one's own affairs. No one can prevent you from doing what you want. In communal areas, you may not be able to build a mabati [iron-roofed] house, because someone might take away that land and you be allocated land elsewhere (in case of subdivision). (Field notes, October 19, 2000)

While acknowledging the benefits of greater individual autonomy resulting from privatization, he nevertheless insists that this autonomy must be limited to prevent people from selling land. In this connection, he has declared that anyone wanting to sell land in Siambu must first pass through the local chief's committee for approval before presenting the case to the district Land Control Board (LCB), which has jurisdiction over all land transactions in the district. He has written to the LCB to this effect also declaring that no land in the area be sold for less than KSh 20,000 per acre. He argues that such actions are necessary to prevent people being taken advantage of by unscrupulous buyers who would otherwise buy land for low prices. These moves by the chief are quite recent, happening at the end of the year 2000, and it is too early to see whether they will have any effect on land sales. However, discussions with others who have been involved with buying and selling land and the operations of the LCB suggest that it will be difficult to prevent sales. Indeed, reviewing the decisions of the LCB over the last ten years confirms this view, since virtually all proposed sales were approved. The criterion of "willing buyer, willing seller" appears to be the basis for LCB decisions.

There are some indications, though, that the government is concerned about the danger of title deed holders (mostly men) selling land without the consent of their families. A 1996 circular from the Office of the President sent to all District Commissioners, the chairmen of LCBs, instructed them to personally chair all LCB meetings and to ensure that family members were present during the hearings and that they agreed to any proposed sales or transfers. Also, in 1997, the Samburu LCB claimed that it would henceforth require a letter from the area chief approving land sales (LCB Minutes, July 30, 1997).[22] While these moves signal an interest in safeguarding the rights of family members, there is no evidence that these rules have been followed by the LCB in Samburu District. The LCB's minutes do not indicate that the views of family members have been elicited nor whether they are present at the meetings. Letters from chiefs approving sales did not always accompany applications, either. Indeed, in a few cases, application forms themselves were missing—the only evidence of the sale being the minutes recording that it had been approved.

One example that was related by a couple of informants lends support to the fact that families are sometimes involved in land transactions, though it is probably the exception rather than the rule. This case involved a man who owns a relatively large parcel of land adjacent to Siambu, in Poro A. Over the years, he has sold off bits of the land until relatively little remains. On one occasion, he was trying to sell some of the land without the knowledge of his family. He actually took a woman to the LCB meeting claiming she was his wife. When his real wife found out, she went to the DC herself and explained what her husband was trying to do. In this case, the DC refused to allow the sale, because it was not agreed to by the family members.

It took courage for this woman to oppose the sale of land and to undermine her husband in front of the DC. One informant, a close relative of the wife commented on the case.

> To tell you the truth—because the only example is that woman to come to the DC; she's a hero. And other women, they want also to come and do the same thing, but they have fear. Because men are tough. And other women, still, if they believe that their husband is selling a piece of land, maybe they can get a bit of money. I don't know, because our women are

still not in decision making. Even within the family. Very few women are tough and can make decisions in the family or in the community [where] they live. But when it comes to the land, that's a man's issue. And women need to be educated on this.

The gender bias in allocating land to men puts women in a weak position for claiming their rights. People are often unaware of the processes and procedures relating to land adjudication, more so women who are marginal to community decision-making processes, as we saw in chapter 3. Therefore, in order to challenge or prevent a sale of land, the woman requires adequate information about her husband's intentions as well as about the procedures governing land transactions. Armed with that information, she may be able to halt an unwanted sale, but she will also have to face the consequences of her actions: the wrath of her husband.

How significant are land sales in Siambu? Is the concern about them justified by their extent? All survey households were asked whether they had bought or sold land. Ten households (10 percent) reported selling land, while only two reported purchasing land. Row A of table 13 summarizes the survey data on land sales in Siambu. Ten households sold land, and the average amount sold was six acres, about a quarter of their parcel. They received about KSh 10,000 per acre, or KSh 60,000 total for a sale. In all, 59 acres were sold by these households.

To get a more comprehensive picture of land transactions in Siambu (Poro B), and in the district as a whole, the minutes of the LCB were reviewed for the period 1991 through 2001, summarized in row B of table 13. The LCB approved 82 sales of land over this period, out of which 26 (32 percent) involved land in Poro B. Virtually all applications for sales from Poro B were approved—only once the LCB deferred decisions on applications because of lack of information. The average number of acres sold was 9; the average price per acre was KSh 10,543, the median was KSh 10,000, and prices

TABLE 13. Land Sales in Siambu

Row	Data Source	Number of Sales	Average Acres Sold	Average Price per Acre	Total Acres Sold
A	Household Survey	10	6	10,666	59
B	Land Control Board Records	26	9	10,543	239

ranged from a low of KSh 5,000 to a high of KSh 18,000. The total number of acres sold was 239. Most sales were to Samburu people, some from Siambu. Very few sales were to non-Samburu. Most of the sales reported by survey households were recorded in the LCB minutes, although a few had not passed through the LCB and are therefore not legally binding.

Critics of privatization of pastoral lands have noted the risk that after subdivision the poorer members of the community will sell their land to the better-off people, inaugurating a process of land consolidation that will ultimately force the poor off the land. In his study of subdivision of group ranches in Kajiado District, Rutten documents that within two and half years of subdivision in a sample of five group ranches, 2.7 percent of the land had been sold. In one ranch, 86 percent of its members had been involved in some kind of land transaction within the same period (e.g., sale, subdivision, gift, or mortgage) (Rutten 1992, 385–88). The rapidity of sales in Kajiado was striking, and much of this land was purchased by non-Maasai, particularly Kikuyu (1992, 390). However, Rutten found no significant correlation between wealth and land sales.

> Sellers of land can be found among the young, old, literate, illiterate, rich and poor alike. The involvement of all of these groups seems to reflect the broad range of viable logic behind the selling of land; acquisition of capital for investment in productive assets, expensive consumer goods or for sheer subsistence. (392)

Even though land was being widely sold in this area of Kajiado, there was no clear evidence, at least not by 1992, that the poor were selling land disproportionately. Rutten appears to have expected this to be the case, and he points out in a footnote that anecdotal evidence suggested that the poor were more likely to sell, but that his data were not sufficient to demonstrate a significant correlation (1992: 391).

To discover whether there was any tendency for the poor, or the wealthy for that matter, to sell land disproportionately in Siambu, analysis was conducted on wealth and income data for all the sellers found in the LCB minutes who were from survey households. The results, shown in table 14, indicate that households in the poorest quintiles for both wealth and income sell land most frequently.[23] However, they tend to sell less land per transaction than better-off households. Since all households own about the same amount of land, this is a real difference. Thus, the total acres sold by the richest wealth quintile (42 acres) and the poorest wealth quintile (50 acres) are close. The top income quintile sold twice as much land (63 acres) as the poorest income quintile (30 acres). Interestingly, households in the richest quintiles for wealth and income received the lowest prices per acre. This may be due to the fact that they were selling more acres at a time and provided buyers with a quantity discount.

The sale of 239 acres of land over the last ten years constitutes roughly 3 percent of the total land held in individual plots in Siambu; about the same percentage as was sold in Kajiado within only two and a half years after subdivision. Looking at land sales over time reveals a declining trend (table 15). More land was sold in the early years after title deeds were issued in 1992. Thus, 79 acres were sold in 1994, and 80 acres were sold in 1995. The number of acres sold sharply declines to only 12 in 1996 and 24 in 1997. There were very few sales in the 1998–2001 period. It seems, then, that those who wanted to sell land did so promptly after subdivision was finalized. It may also be possible that the communal pressure against land sales is having some effect on discouraging sales.

These data do not indicate widespread land sales or a great risk of many

TABLE 14. Siambu Land Sales by Wealth and Income Categories (*n* = 13)

Household Category	Sales		Average	Total	Average Price/Acre	
Wealth Quintiles	n	Percent	Acres/Sale	Acres Sold	(KSH)	Total (KSH)
Richest Quintile	2	15	21	42	7,545	316,000
Second Quintile	1	8	8	8	10,000	80,000
Third Quintile	2	15	10	20	11,500	230,000
Fourth Quintile	1	8	10	10	10,000	100,000
Poorest Quintile	7	54	7	50	10,456	478,000
Totals	13	100		130		1,204,000

	Sales		Average	Total	Average Price/Acre	
Income Quintiles	n	Percent	Acres/Sale	Acres Sold	(KSH)	Total (KSH)
Richest Quintile	3	23	17	63	8,363	488,000
Second Quintile	0	0	—	0	—	0
Third Quintile	3	23	8	23	10,000	230,000
Fourth Quintile	2	15	7	14	12,500	160,000
Poorest Quintile	5	39	5	30	10,600	326,000
Totals	13	100		130		1,204,000

people becoming landless. Most people sell modest amounts of land, and only a few individuals have sold all their land. Furthermore, most land has been sold to other community members or other Samburu people. There is no evidence that land is being sold to outsiders. One explanation for the low levels of land sales may have to do with the small plot sizes. Since people only have about 23 acres, there is not much margin for selling land and still being able to use the remainder for any productive purpose. This situation contrasts with that in other areas of Lorroki where individuals with relatively large parcels are selling land off in chunks of 20 to 100 acres at a time. The LCB minutes documented this pattern of sales for areas such as Poro A and Suguta Marmar A. It might also be the case that the very struggle over land that occurred in Siambu has reinforced its value for the people there and made them more reluctant to sell. Furthermore, the possibility of leasing out land for wheat farming may reduce the incentive to sell, because leasing provides a good annual return without sacrificing ownership rights.[24]

Inheritance of Land

Privatization of land has made it into a commodity that can be farmed, leased, and even sold. This new status of land also raises the question of inheritance. Since Samburu people lack a concept of private ownership of land, inheriting land is unheard of, and therefore no cultural norms exist for how this should be done. I tried to gather information about how Siambu people are handling the issue of inheritance, but since privatization occurred relatively recently there is still little experience among community members about how land will be passed from one generation to another.

TABLE 15. Siambu Land Sales by Year

Year	No. Sales	Total Acres Sold
1994	7	79
1995	7	80
1996	2	12
1997	3	24
1998	1	?
1999	1	3
2000	2	33
2001	3	8
Total	26	239

Note: Acreage was not specified for the 1998 land sale

Most people believed that inheritance of land would follow similar lines as inheritance of cattle. That is, when the father died, his land would go to his sons. However, this is not as simple as it seems. Normally, when a man dies his remaining cattle go to his oldest surviving son. In fact, by the time men die (assuming a fairly long life), they have few cattle left. Most of their livestock have been allocated to their wives, who then pass it on to their sons. Or, men have already transferred wealth to their sons over the years. Thus, at death, a man has already divested most of his assets. What remains is passed to the oldest son.

The situation is different with land. For one thing, a man does not allocate land to his wife (or wives) in the same way as he does livestock. It is true that women may cultivate the land and even have an identifiable plot that is theirs for this purpose, but I did not get the impression that this imputed any sense of ownership, at least not in terms of transfer of the asset to sons, as is the case for livestock. Bruce and Migot-Adholla note that even when other family members are allocated rights in land, the household head retains a "suprafamilial" right over land transfers (1994, 21). This would appear to be even more likely in Siambu where customary land rights, in terms of individual or household use, do not exist as they do in farming societies. Instead, these rights have been established by the governmental system of registration and titling. Since land ownership is unitary and specified in the title deed, it is difficult to see how multiple claims to ownership could be accommodated within the legal framework. While the LCB is making some moves toward considering rights of family members in its deliberations on land sales, this practice is a concession to social pressure and does not actually confer any legal rights on those not named on the title deed.

There is another difficulty posed in trying to translate the practice of primogeniture in livestock (at least pertaining to the father's remaining livestock at death) to the case of land. At the time of subdivision of land in Siambu, many sons received their own parcels of land. However, since minors were not included in the subdivision, the current warrior age-set was left out of the process. In many families, this means that the oldest sons have their own parcels already while younger sons do not. Thus, if the father's land is passed on to the oldest sons at his death, the younger sons will continue to lack land while the oldest will have two shares. This does not happen with livestock, since younger sons receive livestock both from their father and mother before their deaths. When discussing the problem of inheritance, many informants claimed that younger sons would inherit land, since they had not received any at the time of subdivision. Such a practice would entail diverging from the traditional practice of inheritance by oldest sons.

It remains to be seen what pattern land inheritance will take in Siambu. There were very few cases of inheritance which had occurred, but one story was instructive. An old woman related to me how her husband's land was left to the second, younger, wife, not to her or her sons. This apparently happened when she was living with one of her sons elsewhere, while the second wife was living with the husband. When he died, the younger wife, supported by some relatives, claimed the land. My informant, the first wife, was bitter about this and was emphatic that her sons would challenge the younger wife's claim.

Although all details of the story are not clear, it illustrates the kind of confusion that might occur over land inheritance when there are no recognized rules or traditions to follow. It could be that this man wanted to leave the land to the younger wife in order for her to hold it for her minor sons. In this sense, it would follow the pattern some people claim to prefer: allowing younger sons to inherit land. On the other hand, the first wife also had younger sons without land and clearly felt that her rights had been violated.

Inheritance of land is likely to become more problematic in the near future as the older men die. I have shown that simply translating rules for inheritance of livestock to land is not straightforward, particularly since the argument about the rights of younger sons to inherit land is clearly contradictory to the practice with livestock. It will be interesting to see how new rules of inheritance are deliberated and decided upon. Since one of the things Siambu people like about private ownership is the freedom it gives them to control their affairs, to what extent will they work to develop shared norms and rules for inheritance? Or will individuals be left alone to decide the fate of their land? Another possibility is that the younger sons may work to establish new rules in their favor, spurring yet another conflict over land in Siambu.

Agriculture in Mbaringon: High Subsidies, Low Returns

The potential for agriculture in Mbaringon is lower than in Siambu due to lower and more erratic rainfall patterns and less favorable soils. In spite of these factors, a few individuals have been experimenting with agriculture for the last decade or so. On occasion, these innovative individuals have reaped good harvests, prompting others to become more interested in the activity. The real boost to crop production in Mbaringon came in 1998 when a local

NGO began to subsidize agriculture by providing loans of seeds, fencing materials, and tractor-plowing services. If an individual cleared a field of one acre and collected enough fencing posts (cut from the forest), the NGO would supply barbed wire for fencing, bean seeds for planting, and the services of a tractor to plow the farm. In 1998, 104 farmers were supported in this way in Mbaringon, and small farms began to appear all over the area. The fact that the average number of years that survey households have been involved in farming is three confirms the critical role played by these subsidies in prompting people to try farming. Indeed, out of the 49 households that participate in agriculture, 31 (63 percent) had received subsidies from the NGO over the last three years.

While the NGO does not have any data on the yields of these farms, data from the household survey shows that average yields of beans were two 90-kilogram bags per acre.[25] For maize, which some farmers also grew, the average yield was three bags per acre. These yields are lower than those in Siambu and on the low side of the expected yields for the area. Personnel from the project confirm that yields were low and that, as a result, most people were unable to pay back their loans (Adamson Lanyasunya, personal communication, December 3, 2001). However, the project policy is to work in a community for three years only. Thus, support to Mbaringon farmers ceased in 2000. The NGO did request that the Ministry of Agriculture and Rural Development assist farmers in this area by providing seeds if they were available, and, indeed, fifty-nine individuals in Mbaringon were given 6 kilograms of bean seed for the short rains of November 2001 (Agriculture officer, personal communication, November 16, 2001). This is enough to plant about a quarter of an acre. My observations suggest that about a third of existing fields have been planted. Since the rains have been relatively good and the growing season for these beans is less than three months, they may be able to harvest something. The question remains to what extent those who have attempted farming in the area will continue to do so after the end of subsidies.

Interestingly, while the NGO intended to promote agriculture in the area, their efforts actually led to a backlash against farming and the enclosure of land. This was prompted in 1999 when tractors hired by the NGO suddenly appeared in Mbaringon and began plowing in a rather haphazard manner. Cattle tracks were plowed under in some places, and some fields were plowed very close together. The elders soon called a meeting and complained about the profligate plowing. They decided to impose a limit on farm sizes, which was unheard of before. They declared that individuals could enclose no more than an acre and that the land had to be used for cultivation, not just for growing grass. To date, this directive stands, and no one has tried to enclose an area much bigger. Of course, if this rule is enforced, it caps farm sizes at one acre, thereby limiting any possible benefits to be had from crop production.

Most households that farm in Mbaringon consume the harvest. Out of forty-nine households that practiced farming, only fourteen reported selling crops. This accounts for the fact that many households have negative net incomes from farming—they spend money on inputs but do not recover this through sales. Among those who sold crops, the average income was KSh 2,395, ranging from a low of KSh 240 to a high of KSh 9,000. In terms of home consumption, the average value was KSh 4,567, with about three-quarters of this value deriving from beans. Mbaringon households only consumed their harvest for seven to eight weeks compared to twenty-six weeks for Siambu. Furthermore, home consumption in Mbaringon only replaces about seven weeks of purchased food supplies, compared to ten weeks for Siambu.

Since the survey only considered one harvest, it is not possible to project a trend from these data. However, observations of farming in Mbaringon over the last ten years and discussions with informants underscore the risky nature of the activity.[26] People who have attempted to grow crops many times report more crop failures than successful harvests. In addition to lack of rainfall, wildlife are a threat. Elephants and zebras are still common in Mbaringon, and the farms lie directly in the path of elephants that traverse the area while moving from the forest to the salt springs at Kisima. Livestock are also a problem and may enter fields that are not well fenced. Lack of knowledge about agriculture is a greater problem here than in Siambu, where people have longer experience with farming. This may explain why hired labor is actually more common in Mbaringon than in Siambu. Those households that can afford to hire labor prefer doing so to investing their own labor in farming. Hired labor may provide income-earning opportunities for some people, but it also reduces the profitability of agriculture.

In short, farming in Mbaringon is a risky endeavor. When supported by subsidies, more households became involved, but this raises the possibility that they will drop out now that subsidies have ended. In good years, home consumption of produce may supplement household food supplies, but the good years are few and far between, making significant investments in crop production a questionable endeavor.

Two Patterns of Diversification

This discussion of data on income sources reveals two patterns of diversification that differentiate Mbaringon and Siambu: households in Mbaringon have tended to diversify into wage labor and trade, while those in Siambu have additionally concentrated on crop farming. Siambu households have also invested more heavily in educating their children, and this appears to be paying off in that a higher percentage of employed people in Siambu have civil service jobs than in Mbaringon. In this section, these two patterns will be discussed with reference to a new model for understanding diversification strategies among East African pastoralists (Little et al. 2001). While this model provides a useful framework for discussing diversification, the Siambu and Mbaringon cases also contribute new insights into diversification processes.

There is a growing literature on diversification strategies among pastoralists stemming from the consensus among experts in the field that pastoralists cannot and do not any longer subsist entirely from livestock products (Ensminger 1992; USAID 2002; McCabe 2003; Fratkin and Roth 2005). In a recent review of the literature, Little et al. propose a model for analyzing diversification strategies among pastoralists in the East Africa region. Their framework identifies a number of key variables to explain the varying patterns of diversification observed among different groups of East African pastoralists. Among wealthy pastoralists, they contend, "diversification is a strategy of accumulation or investment; for the impoverished it is a matter of survival" (2001, 405). They consider three sets of variables as important in determining diversification decisions among pastoralists. First are conditional variables: elements of the environment and exogenous forces that impinge on pastoral production. These may be thought of as push factors—when not conducive to pastoral livestock production, they tend to push people to diversify into other livelihoods. Included in this category are external income transfers (e.g., food aid), human population density, per capita livestock holdings and distribution, and open rangeland per capita. Second, opportunity variables are the pull factors because they determine what possibilities exist to diversify. Here, they consider climate, distance to cities and market towns, available services and infrastructure, and education. Finally, local response variables influence which population groups will take advantage of the available opportunities. Wealth, gender, age, and other social factors are included as local response variables (2001, 406).

In the communities under discussion here, this framework may assist to some degree in spelling out the patterns of diversification observed. In terms of conditional variables, both communities are subject to many of the same trends. Per capita livestock holdings are low and falling as populations rise; human population density is relatively high compared to the drier lowland areas of Samburu District, meaning that open rangeland per capita is relatively low. Food aid is sometimes present, as in the drought of 1999–2000, but it is not always available and is inadequate for household needs. All of these factors tend to undermine successful pastoral livestock production and to push people to diversify their livelihoods.

In terms of opportunity variables, Siambu and Mbaringon have some similarities and some differences. Both communities are relatively close to a market center, Poro and Kisima, respectively, and are equidistant from the district headquarters, Maralal. They also have about the same level of services and infrastructure. We have seen that they differ to some extent in educational attainment, and these differences are reflected in the proportion of employment in the civil service. Climatic differences between Siambu and Mbaringon are salient, since the higher and somewhat more reliable rainfall in Siambu coupled with better soils means that there is a higher potential for crop farming there than in Mbaringon. This partly explains the higher rates of participation in agriculture in Siambu.

Land tenure, while not discussed by Little et al., is another factor that could be included as an opportunity variable in this model. The impact of the change to private land holding in Siambu on diversification strategies is, however, equivocal. On the one hand, the observation that 76 percent of households that participate in farming began cultivation after privatization lends support to the notion that the change itself encouraged greater participation in agriculture. This was due to the certainty of monopolizing any gains reaped from the activity, as well as the fact that the advent of private land holding removed the earlier problem of external interference in or sanctioning of farming activities.[27] In addition, private land tenure enabled individuals to benefit from their land in entirely new ways, such as leasing it out for wheat farming or selling it. As discussed earlier, almost 30 percent of survey households have leased land for wheat farming, while 10 percent have sold some land. The proceeds from these activities constitute an important addition to household income, although there are fears among community members that men misuse the proceeds of leases and sales. In short, agriculture has assumed an important role in household food production and incomes in Siambu. To this extent, it is a distinctive strategy of diversification in this area.

On the other hand, almost 50 percent of households in Mbaringon also participate in agriculture without private land tenure, though, as noted earlier, 60 percent of those participating may be doing so primarily due to subsidies to crop production. Furthermore, while many households in Siambu practice some farming, farm sizes remain small (average 1.9 acres) in comparison to total parcel sizes (23 acres). Livestock continue to contribute more to household food production and income than agriculture. Thus, in spite of the enabling conditions for farming provided by climatic conditions and land tenure arrangements, people have not been transformed into farmers. Farming is an important supplement to food and incomes in Siambu but has not replaced livestock production.

While agriculture represents a distinctive strategy for diversification in Siambu, Mbaringon households have tended to diversify into wage labor and trade. The high number of men employed as watchmen, primarily in Nairobi, reflects the fact that this is a virtual niche market for Samburu men who are sought after for these jobs. Indeed, most men who seek work as a watchman rely on contacts among their friends and relatives already working there in order to find potential employers.[28] The fact that men from Mbaringon have been pursuing this strategy for over twenty years means that they have a relatively well-developed network of contacts and opportunities, facilitating younger generations of men to secure jobs. Small-scale trade in products such as firewood, charcoal, timber, and honey is enabled by Mbaringon's position between the forest and the growing town of Kisima, where demand for these products is rising. Siambu is also adjacent to a forest and a town, and trade in these items is also evident there, but it appears that the greater growth of Kisima, perhaps because of its position on the main road to Maralal, generates higher demand for these items.

Little et al. also discuss the importance of local response variables, such as gender, age, and wealth, in shaping diversification strategies. The preceding analysis revealed different patterns of diversification according to wealth category, although the differences between the two communities hinged, again, on the importance of agriculture versus wage labor in Siambu and

Mbaringon, respectively. The contention that middle wealth groups do not diversify as much as the poor and wealthy (2001, 406) is not supported by these data, however. Middle wealth groups in both communities earn more than half their income from nonlivestock activities, and with per capita livestock holding of about two, they are certainly reliant on income for their survival.

In terms of the gendered nature of various income-generating activities, the data on Mbaringon and Siambu support the notion that men dominate livestock sales, while women are engaged in other activities. In both Mbaringon and Siambu, women are more involved in selling natural resource products, such as timber and firewood, and in brewing alcohol than in selling milk (an activity highlighted by Little et al.). Sales of hides and skins from their own animals also constitute an important source of income for women. The relatively low amount of milk sales is certainly partly due to the prevailing drought during the survey but also reflects the relative lack of surplus milk even in good periods. The fact that milk is perishable and must be marketed rapidly makes it less desirable as a commodity for sale than forest products (2001, 420–21).

The model developed by Little et al. is useful in specifying the dynamics of various push and pull factors that influence decisions on diversification. The Mbaringon and Siambu cases confirm the appropriateness of many of the variables delineated in the model and suggest that land tenure should also be taken into account in areas where it is changing, since it opens up new opportunities for land use. The threats to the environment posed by activities such as charcoal burning and firewood and timber extraction are serious. Other options with fewer negative effects need to be explored. The business of brewing alcohol is another double-edged sword.[29] While poorer women may earn a good income from brewing, the deleterious effects of widespread insobriety are evident in both Mbaringon and Siambu. Household assets are often depleted to buy drink, and intrahousehold conflict grows as a result of the combination of drunkenness and impoverishment.

Conclusion

This chapter began by asking the question, are Siambu households better off after privatization of land? The analysis of data on per capita wealth shows that, currently, they are significantly better off than Mbaringon households. This is particularly interesting considering that they were somewhat worse off than those in Mbaringon before land adjudication began in 1978. However, these results are mitigated by the fact that some of the improvement of the situation of Siambu households may be due to the effects of the recent drought and, therefore, may not be sustained over the long run. If home consumption of crops and milk is included in income, Siambu is also better off than Mbaringon in per capita terms.

Privatizing land in Siambu has not in and of itself brought about a transformation of the community into one of commercial farmers, but it has created new opportunities for diversification into cultivation of crops, leasing out, and selling land. These opportunities have been incorporated into the diversification portfolio of Siambu households and do contribute notably to household food consumption and income. The shift to private land may provide these families with an additional hedge against the ever-present risks inherent in the pastoral environment and enable them to preserve livestock (and other) forms of wealth. It is also notable that even though Siambu households are not investing much in improved livestock or capital-intensive agricultural inputs, they are investing in education by sending more children to school. These investments in human capital appear to be paying off in that a greater proportion of employed people in Siambu have better-paying civil service jobs than in Mbaringon. At the same time, individual family decisions to send children to school are not translating into financial support for educational institutions in Siambu, which consequently suffer from decaying buildings and lack of furniture and equipment. Mbaringon's recent improvements in infrastructure stem largely from external subsidies, and it remains to be seen whether better school facilities will encourage higher enrollments.

Privatization entails risks as well as benefits, particularly the possibility of selling the land and thereby losing access to it forever. Thus far, the vast majority of households in Siambu have not fallen victim to this danger, and they appear to be aware of its existence. The trend is toward fewer land sales, and most land is sold within the community. There is no indication that consolidation of holdings is occurring or that people are selling whole parcels and becoming landless. The small size of parcels coupled with norms against selling land may account for the limited number of land transactions. More problematic perhaps will be developing rules for how land is inherited, since the model of livestock inheritance does not transfer easily to land.

The privatization of land in Siambu fits neither the optimistic scenario of property rights theorists nor the gloomy forecasts of those who favor communal ownership in pastoral areas. To a certain extent, privatization has resulted in gains for many households, but these derive neither from abandoning livestock production for commercial farming nor even from significant investments in agriculture or improved livestock. On the contrary, it is in its role as supplement to the livestock economy that cultivation has proven valuable by providing additional food and cash that enable households to better preserve their livestock wealth and thereby survive crises. Fears that pastoral land will be sold off and pastoralists rendered landless have not been realized in Siambu. Perhaps the very struggle over the land that occurred has raised awareness of its value and convinced people to hold on to it. Of course, for most households that still rely on extensive livestock production, land use has changed relatively little in spite of privatization. Achieving household food security and reducing vulnerability to crises is a challenge facing people all over Samburu District. The different patterns of diversification present in Mbaringon and Siambu demonstrate the variety of means that individuals are using to confront this challenge.

CHAPTER 8

Privatization and Behavior:
Evidence from Experimental Games

The previous chapters have shown how privatization came about in Siambu. I have argued that the switch from communal to individual ownership of land was not the result of an ideological shift in favor of privatization among most community members. Instead, it was the outcome of a conflict over competing and contradictory interests: those of the Group of Thirty-seven, who favored privatization as a means to better their situation and gain entry into modern Kenyan society, and those of the elders of the blanket, who defended common property to preserve their wealth and positions of authority.

Data presented in the previous chapter on land use and agricultural production show that management of land has changed since privatization. Land has become a commodity that can be farmed, leased out, and sold. At the same time, most land remains unfenced, and livestock still move relatively freely in the uncultivated areas. Thus, land use is a hybrid of private and common ownership. A common rhetoric about the positive values of private property has developed in the decade following privatization (chapter 5). Private property is seen as promoting progress and development—setting the Siambu community apart from its neighbors who still live on group ranches.

This chapter addresses the question of whether changes in land use, coupled with the rhetoric about individual control, autonomy, and development, manifest themselves in changes in behavior among Siambu people. Do they, in fact, behave more individualistically than Samburu people who still own land in common? By adopting norms that favor individual ownership and rights have they abandoned customary norms about sharing, fairness, and cooperation? Are they less trusting of each other now that each individual has greater control over his own decision making? By the same token, since individuals claim a greater autonomy over their land and livelihood, do they continue to respect the authority of the elders? Put another way, having lost authority over the commons have elders lost authority more generally as well? All of these questions seek to understand to what extent a change in one institution, in this case property rights over land, results in changes in norms and behavior across the board.

Experimental Economics: An Approach to Examining Behavior Change

There are a number of methods for exploring individual behavior. Quantitative data on certain behaviors are available and may be employed as proxy indicators of general tendencies. For example, enrollments in school, use of health facilities, wage labor rates, or speaking a metropolitan language might be marshaled as evidence that people in a community are modernizing, or at least participating more in modern society. Sociologists and anthropologists often survey attitudes and values of their research informants to try to gauge their likely behavior. Indeed, I have argued in earlier chapters that experiences in formal education, employment, and the military created the type of attitudes and generated economic resources that led individuals to seek private land in Samburu District. However, attitude surveys, in isolation, may be weak indicators of behavior since they only reveal what informants say they would do in a given situation, not what they actually do. An anthropologist interested in looking at behavior (or behavior change) would supplement these forms of information with qualitative data, essentially anecdotes, as evidence of behavioral trends. By closely examining particular situations and how individuals act, and react, conclusions are drawn about behavior and possibly generalized across a population.[1]

While this approach provides an ethnographically rich and contextualized account, its very specificity makes it difficult to generalize, within or beyond a community. To draw more general conclusions about behavior, we require methods that enable us to control for local differences, as far as possible, in order to detect underlying patterns of behavior. Experimental economics is a method that uses bargaining games to do just that. The overall purpose of experimental economics is to test the assumptions of economic theory regarding human behavior. By controlling the context and the choices available to participants, the games generate behavior that can then be analyzed statistically, replicated, and compared within and across populations (Camerer and Fehr 2004).

One of the most important findings of experimental economics has been the fact that behavior in games diverges sharply from the "rational egoist" assumption that underlies neoclassical economic theory (Camerer 2003; Henrich et al. 2004). Ensminger notes that "it appears that even in highly developed societies, individuals place some value upon sharing and cooperation even when they are given every opportunity not to" (2000, 159). She goes on to note that results of cross-cultural experiments have found that members of small-scale societies in developing countries are no more fair, trusting, or cooperative than people in the developed world. Ensminger argues, in contrast to a moral economy perspective, that it may be elements of the institutional environment that account for levels of trust, fairness, and cooperation rather than generalized levels of these factors in a given society (169–70).

If institutions influence the levels of trust, fairness, and cooperation that we observe in society, then we might expect an institutional change to be reflected in behaviors that reveal these norms. Specifically, we might expect the change in property rights in Siambu to alter those levels among community members, and for these changes to be revealed in behavior of individuals in experimental games. I hypothesized that Siambu people would play more selfishly and display lower levels of trust in games that measured these variables. This hypothesis was based on my observation of the high value they assigned to individual freedom and control over land. Another hypothesis was that they would be less cooperative as a result of private land ownership. A decline in cooperation was a logical consequence of breaking up large homesteads and increasing agricultural activities where labor sharing across households was not much in evidence. Finally, I expected them to show less respect for elders' authority than people in Mbaringon, because elders had lost their authority to make decisions regarding land use. An experimental game was designed to test the strength of elders' authority.

This chapter reports on experiments conducted to test these hypotheses about behavior in Siambu, using Mbaringon as a comparative case. Behavior of individuals from the two communities in the games provides clues about how behavior may have changed since privatization. However, these results must also be considered within the broader ethnographic context in order to assess their importance. That is, there should be some consistency between behavior in games and behavior observed in real life. The next section discusses the methods used in conducting the games in Siambu and Mbaringon, while subsequent sections discuss each game in turn.

Methods

The methods used in these experiments drew heavily from the protocols used in the MacArthur Foundation–funded cross-cultural project in which games were played in fifteen small-scale societies across the globe (Henrich et al. 2001, 2004; Ensminger 2000). In the United States and other developed countries, games are usually carried out with university students in laboratory settings. This provides a high level of control over experimental conditions. Obviously, conditions in rural Kenya are different. Vigorous attempts were made to guarantee that participants in the games remained anonymous to each other (i.e., the players did not know who they were playing with in any particular game). However, since these are small communities where virtually everyone knows everyone else, the participants knew, in general, with whom they were playing, even though the identity of their particular partner remained unknown. On the other hand, compared to university students in the United States, the sample of people who played the games was more representative of the population as a whole (Ensminger 2000). I initially restricted players to adults from survey households, in order to have demographic and other information about the players to use in the analysis. However, particularly in Siambu, it was necessary to allow nonsurvey households to participate in the games due to a shortage of players.[2] In these cases, short surveys were conducted at the game site to gather basic information on the players.

Another interesting pattern of behavior that influenced participation occurred in both communities. On the first day of the games, many men turned up to play. However, on subsequent days, the number of men in attendance fell while the number of women rose. It seemed that men had attended initially to check out the games and, being satisfied that there was nothing amiss, sent their wives and female relatives in great numbers thereafter. To cope with this gender imbalance it was necessary to let some men play more than one game, while some women were not able to play. When men played more than one game, I placed them in a role that did not require a decision in the second game (i.e., as a recipient in the Dictator or Punishment Game). In this way, their experience in the first game did not influence the outcome in the second game since they were not in a decision-making role. No one played the same game twice.

In order to minimize contamination in the population (i.e., from people discussing the games and possibly colluding), games were played in rapid succession in each community. In Siambu, games were played in one site on Monday, Tuesday, and Wednesday and at another site on Thursday and Friday. The following week, they were played at Mbaringon at one site Monday and Tuesday and another site Wednesday through Friday. Five different games were played in each community, for a total of 280 individual games. Since a different game was played each day, discussions that occurred overnight were less relevant to the following day's game.

The week before the games, I held public meetings in each community to explain that they would have a chance to play some fun games for real money. I did not reveal the underlying purpose of the games (to measure behavior and to compare across the communities) or any specific procedures, but rather told people that this was part of a larger exercise being done in various communities around the world. People seemed to accept this logic, and the prospect of earning a little money provided additional incentive for them to turn up on game day.

The procedure for each game was essentially the same. People would gather in the morning at the primary school where the games were played, and the directions for the game were read to them.[3] Scripts of the games had been translated (English–Samburu) and back-translated (Samburu–English) by different research assistants to ensure clarity of language, something that turns out to be rather important in the games. After reading the instructions, a number of examples were done with the group to ensure that they understood the logic of the game and the roles of the various players. We were careful to point out that all players remained anonymous to each other and that only I would know how much any player had offered. These are important elements of the game situation, since the goal is to enable people to play as freely as possible without worrying about their play being known to others (to eliminate reputation effects). We then paid each participant a show-up fee of KSh 40. This ensured that no one would leave empty-handed, even if they ended up with no money from the game. The stakes for the games were KSh 100 (USD 1.25), equivalent to one day's casual labor wage. In the Public Goods Game, each player was given KSh 50 (USD 0.63), but due to the doubling of their contributions, they stood to earn more than in any other game (discussed later).

At this point, I would move to the playing room with one research assistant, while the other research assistants would stay with the participants and send each player to the other room one at a time. They monitored people while they waited to make sure that no one discussed the game or strategy while they waited. Thereafter, players were chosen at random, by drawing their names from a hat, and sent in to play.[4] When they came into the playing room, the instructions were repeated and several practice examples were played with them to confirm their understanding of the game and implications of different choices. Most games were easily understood by the players. The only game where I felt some of the older participants had a bit of difficulty was in the Punishment Game (discussed later) where the mathematics were more complicated. In such cases, I took extra time to explain the game and review additional examples. I did not find it necessary to eliminate any player due to misunderstanding of the games. After playing, people either went home with their takings or waited in a separate room for their payoff, depending on the type of game. I now discuss each game in turn.

Dictator Game

The Dictator Game is designed to measure fairness. Each pair of players (who remain anonymous to each other) is given an endowment of KSh 100. Player One is then given the opportunity to divide the money between himself and Player Two. He may opt to keep all the money (the economically rational strategy), or he may give any fraction of the money (in ten shilling increments) to the other player. Whatever Player One does not give to Player Two is his to keep. Player Two's only role is to accept the offer given by Player One. Positive offers from Player One indicate a concern for fairness over self-interest. I played this game with 30 pairs of players in Siambu and 32 pairs in Mbaringon.

As noted earlier, I had hypothesized that Siambu people would behave in a more individualistic, self-interested way than those from Mbaringon. However, their offers in the Dictator Game were actually higher, averaging 30 percent of the stake, compared to only 24.6 percent for Mbaringon. This difference is not statistically significant at the .05 level, though.[5] The overall mean offer of 27.3 percent is slightly higher than the range of developed country experiments where means range from 10 to 25 percent (Camerer and Fehr 2004, 72). However, fewer players kept the whole pot for themselves (7.5 percent combining Siambu and Mbaringon) than is common in developed world experiments where up to 30 or 40 percent of players elect to give nothing to Player Two (Camerer and Fehr 2004).

Looking at the distribution of offers (fig. 9) reveals some interesting as-

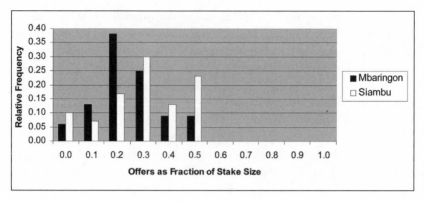

Fig. 9. Distribution of offers in the Dictator Game (Mbaringon, n = 32; Siambu, n = 30)

pects of how the game was played in Siambu and Mbaringon. Twenty-three percent of the players in Siambu split the stake 50–50 with Player Two, compared to only 9 percent in Mbaringon. In contrast, 38 percent of players in Mbaringon gave 20 percent, making this the modal offer there. Only 19 percent of players in Siambu offered 20 percent; the modal offer in Siambu was 30 percent. Overall, the distribution is quite similar to what Ensminger found among the Orma, another group of Kenyan pastoralists (2004, 373). The spread of offers over the range from 0 to 50 implies that there is no consensus on a single norm of fairness, unlike in U.S. studies where modal offers of 0 and 50 indicate the two competing norms of pure self-interest and fairness (374). While this is a reasonable interpretation of these data, I was puzzled by the Mbaringon people's fondness for giving 20 percent. Not only did they have a mode of 20 on the Dictator Game, but this mode turned up again in the Punishment Game and the Trust Game where Player One faces a similar set of circumstances. I will return to this issue after discussing the other games.

Since the mean offers between the two groups are not significantly different, it appears that privatization has not had an impact on fairness, or at least not one that is detectable in the games. People in Siambu are just as fair-minded as those in Mbaringon. On the other hand, it is possible that Siambu people associated this game with the land issue there, and this so-called cueing effect may have had some effect on the results.[6] It is plausible that since the participants in the game knew I was studying the land issue, they connected the game, in their minds, to that particular issue and opted for the same kind of solution that had worked in that case—equal division of resources. Then again, only 23 percent of players in Siambu chose a 50–50 split, so I do not want to overstate the possible influence of the land question on their play in the Dictator Game.

While I had initially hypothesized that privatization of land in Siambu would make individuals more selfish, the results of the cross-cultural experiments (which I only learned of after I returned from the field) suggest another interpretation of this institutional change (Henrich et al. 2001). They found that the degree of market integration was highly correlated with offers in Ultimatum and Trust Games. Both of these games are similar to the Dictator Game in that Player One decides on how to split a pot of money with Player Two. In the Ultimatum Game, however, Player Two has the option of rejecting Player One's offer, in which case both players get nothing. In the Trust Game the amount Player One allocates to Player Two is increased by the experimenter and then Player Two has the option of returning money to Player One. The cross-cultural project found that societies with higher levels of market integration tended to give higher offers in these games (Henrich et al. 2004, 31–32). Recent research by this group, also including subsequent experiments I conducted in Samburu, replicated these results with the Dictator Game, demonstrating again a positive association between market integration and higher offers (personal communication, Jean Ensminger, January 2007).

It may be that greater interaction with the institutions associated with markets actually instills norms of fairness. As discussed in chapter 7, both Mbaringon and Siambu are integrated into markets: they trade livestock and other commodities and participate in wage labor. The offers in both communities are on the high side compared to less market-integrated societies studied in the cross-cultural project and therefore tend to confirm the hypothesis about market integration. Privatization of land in Siambu has brought people there into greater contact with markets for land and government institutions more generally, helping explain why their offers were high—contrary to my hypothesis.

Punishment Game

The Punishment Game is similar to the Dictator Game: pairs of anonymous players are allocated a hundred shillings, and the first player gets to decide how the money is divided between them. In this game, a third player (also anonymous) is given a chance to punish Player One if he feels his offer to Player Two was inappropriate. Player Three is given an endowment of fifty shillings. If he wants to punish Player One, he must pay to do so: for each shilling he pays, three shillings are deducted from Player One's takings. This game is designed to test the extent to which people are willing to pay to uphold social norms, in this case norms of fairness (Camerer and Fehr 2004). When Player Three spends his money to sanction Player One, he signals his willingness to engage in costly enforcement of social norms. Fehr and Fischbacher (2004) found that offers of 50 were never punished and that punishment increased as Player One's offers decreased. An offer of 0 was punished, on average, with 9 punishment points, resulting in a reduction of Player One's taking of 27 points. Figure 10 shows the distribution of offers by Player One in the Punishment Game. In Siambu, mean offers rose from 30 percent in the Dictator Game to 34.8 percent in the Punishment Game. Presumably, this reflects Player One's knowledge that offers perceived as unfair will be punished by Player Three. The mean offer in Mbaringon barely increased, however, from 24.6 percent in the Dictator Game to 25.2 percent in the Punishment Game. Again, the modal offer in Mbaringon was 20 percent. The difference in means of offers between Siambu and Mbaringon is significant (Mann-Whitney test: $z = 2.6$, $p = .0089$).

Before discussing the punishment behavior in this game, it is important to explain an innovation made to the format used by Fehr and Fischbacher. In discussing this game with my research assistants, they pointed out that punishment in Samburu society normally involves compensating the aggrieved party. Thus, they felt that people would be much more likely to punish Player One if they knew that the money deducted from his takings would go to Player Two (the aggrieved party) rather than back to the experimenter. Since we wanted to observe punishment behavior, this alteration to the game made sense and was implemented. By making the game resemble customary practice, we hoped to elicit the same kind of behavior we might observe in real life. The trade-off to making this alteration in the game is that the results are not entirely comparable with results of games played without it.

The pattern of punishment behavior in the games, especially in Siambu, resembles Fehr and Fischbacher's findings. Offers of 50 were never punished in Siambu, but one was punished in Mbaringon. There were no 0 offers in either community. Punishment tended to increase as offer size decreased, particularly in Siambu, where offers of 40 were punished on average

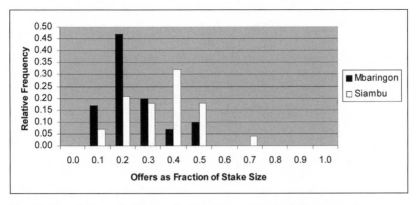

Fig. 10. Distribution of offers in the Punishment Game (Mbaringon, $n = 30$; Siambu, $n = 28$)

with 1.5 points while offers of 10 were punished with 11 points. In contrast, offers of 10, 20, and 30 were punished with about the same number of points in Mbaringon. On average, Player Three spent 8 percent of his or her endowment to sanction Player One. Similar patterns of punishment behavior have been found in recent experiments conducted by the cross-cultural group, including additional experiments with the Samburu, further confirming the broad tendency of players to punish offers that diverge from equal sharing (Henrich et al. 2006).

The strategy of those doing the sanctioning is further revealed if we consider the outcome of their behavior on what Players One and Two ultimately took home at the end of the game. In Siambu, the effect of punishment behavior was to virtually equalize the takings of Player One and Player Two. Player One took home, on average, 52.7 percent of the stake, while Player Two got 47.2 percent. In Mbaringon, sanctioning was less effective in equalizing the takings of Player One and Two: Player One received 63.5 percent of the stake, and Player Two took home 36.5 percent on average. There could be two reasons for this difference. It might be that punishers in Mbaringon did not understand their role, or how the sanctioning and compensation worked. Alternatively, it is possible that people in Mbaringon are more tolerant of lower offers. They did sanction lower offers, but not to the same extent as in Siambu.

If the players in Mbaringon did not understand the mechanics of the game, then the problem rests with the experimenter. As noted earlier, I had some reservations about how well older participants understood this game, but this did not differ between the two sites, and I did not feel that it was grounds for eliminating players in either place. To check for any effect of age on punishment behavior, I removed all Player Threes who were fifty-five years or older. In both Mbaringon and Siambu, the mean for punishment did not change substantially when these players were removed. In Mbaringon the mean changed from 7.9 to 8.0 percent, while in Siambu it rose slightly from 8.9 to 9.3 percent. It seems unlikely that age affected punishment behavior in the two communities.

The fact that lower offers were punished less severely in Mbaringon, however, is consistent with the fact that more low offers were made, especially offers of 20, in Mbaringon. That is, many Player Ones offered 20, seemingly confident that they would not be punished. There was also a distinctive pattern of punishment for offers of 20 in Mbaringon. Either the offer was not punished at all, and Player One was allowed to keep eighty shillings while Player Two got 20, or the offer was punished with 10 punishment points, reducing Player One's takings to 50 and raising Player Two's takings to 50 as well. This pattern suggests that two norms could be at work: one norm of fairness that dictates a 50–50 split, and another norm that accepts an offer of 20 as fair.

The behavior of the only player who sanctioned an offer of 50 is instructive. When this player decided to sanction the offer of 50, I was surprised, and, after he had played, I asked him his reason for punishing Player One. He responded that Player One was being irresponsible. By giving away half of the money to a stranger, he was not putting his family's needs first. This kind of behavior should be punished, he argued. In his mind, keeping more for oneself (and one's family) was the appropriate strategy for this game.

In general, these results demonstrate that people in both communities are willing to engage in costly sanctioning behavior to uphold social norms of fairness. Siambu players heavily sanctioned low offers and strove to equalize the takings of Player One, consistent with their play in the Dictator Game. Fair-minded behavior is rewarded, while low offers, signaling selfish behavior, are punished. Furthermore, there is evidence that a 50–50 split is generally considered the fair outcome in these games in Siambu. The situation is less clear in Mbaringon, but the toleration of low offers demonstrated in this game is also consistent with the peak of offers at 20 in both Dictator and Punishment Games. A different norm of fairness might be operating here.

Trust Game

As the name suggests, the Trust Game examines trusting behavior. It also considers trustworthiness. For this game, Player One (the investor) was given one hundred shillings and the choice to invest any part or all of this entire amount by giving it to Player Two (the trustee). Whatever amount the investor gives to the trustee is tripled by the experimenter and given to the trustee. Then, the trustee may choose to return any fraction of the whole amount to the investor.[7] Thus, the more the investor trusts the trustee (to provide a good return on his investment) the more will be invested. A trustworthy trustee will return the initial investment made by the investor.

Taken together, investors' offers in Siambu and Mbaringon averaged 33 percent, which is lower than among the Orma (44 percent) or among U.S. participants (>50 percent) (Ensminger 2000). Interestingly, while I had hypothesized that Siambu players would be less trusting than those in Mbaringon, the opposite appears to be the case. Siambu investors made significantly higher offers (37.3 percent) to trustees than did those from Mbaringon (29 percent) (Mann-Whitney test, $z = 2.8$, $p = .004$). These results are, again, consistent with the findings of the cross-cultural project where trusting behavior is more pervasive in societies with higher levels of market integration.

Similarly, returns from trustees in Siambu tended to be higher than in Mbaringon. Returns are calculated as the percentage of the investor's offer that the trustee returns. Siambu players returned, on average, 64 percent, while Mbaringon players only returned 55 percent (see figs. 11, 12). Trust was more highly reciprocated in Siambu than in Mbaringon. The overall average return, combining Siambu and Mbaringon, was 59 percent: slightly higher than among the Orma, where only 54 percent of the investor's offer was returned on average (Ensminger 2000, 166). While these results give an impression of greater trustworthiness among Siambu players, this might be an inaccurate reading of the results. Because offers in Mbaringon tended to be lower, many players did not return the full offer.

They appeared to be considering the overall payoffs. If they returned 100 percent of a low offer, say 20, then the investor would end up with 100 shillings while the trustee would only get 40. In contrast, if they returned zero, the investor still got 80 shillings and the trustee received 60. Thus, the investor still came out ahead even when trust was not reciprocated on low offers. However, for offers of 50 (the highest given), reciprocating trust yielded

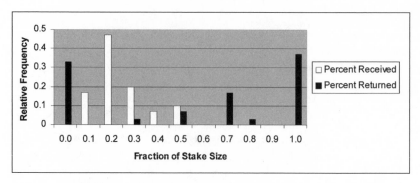

Fig. 11. Distribution of offers received by Player Two (as a fraction of Player One's endowment) and returns from Player Two (as a fraction of Player One's offer) in the Trust Game in Mbaringon ($n = 30$)

equal takings for both players. It appears that trustees were striving to equal-ize the takings, and they were more successful in doing so in Siambu. For ex-ample, in seven cases (23 percent) in Siambu, takings of investors and trustees were the same, while in twelve cases (40 percent) trustees came out ahead. In Mbaringon, by contrast, only three pairs (10 percent) had equal takings, and trustees only came out ahead in three cases (10 percent). Mbaringon trustees actually returned 100 percent of the investor's offer more often than in Siambu, but this was balanced by their returns of 0 for low offers.

Trustees' concern about takings might have been lessened had they been given an initial endowment equal to that of investors (see note 7, this chap-ter). In that case, the game might be more effective in examining trustwor-thiness. These results do demonstrate, however, that trusting behavior is re-warded in both Siambu and Mbaringon.

Public Goods Game

The Public Goods Game provides an opportunity for four players to con-tribute part of their endowment to a "community project." Each player is given 50 shillings and can contribute any amount (in 10-shilling increments) to the project. The contributions of the four players are then combined and doubled by the experimenter. The total amount is divided equally among the players. The game involves the danger of free riding by players who con-

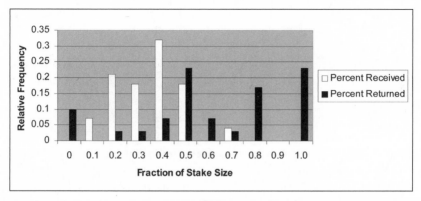

Fig. 12. Distribution of offers received by Player Two (as a fraction of Player One's endowment) and returns from Player Two (as a fraction of Player One's offer) in the Trust Game in Siambu (*n* = 30)

tribute nothing but share in the takings. The game is different from the others discussed here in that the four players see each other during the game. However, they are not allowed to talk to each other, and they do not know the offers of the other players (each one puts their offer in a separate envelope out of view of the others). Even though communication is not allowed, being able to see the other participants in the group provides considerable information to the players, especially in small communities where most people know each other.

Interestingly, the average offer of players in Mbaringon (57 percent) exceeded that of players in Siambu (48 percent). However, this difference is not statistically significant (Mann-Whitney test, z = 1.24, p = .21). Particularly striking, however, is the fact that 31 percent of players in Mbaringon contributed their whole endowment to the community project, while only 6 percent did so in Siambu. These findings indicate that the mutual trust required for successful cooperation is possible in Mbaringon when the players know with whom they are playing. On the other hand, Siambu players appeared unsure of the prospects for good outcomes to cooperation.

Regression results in the Public Goods Game indicate that players with more education make lower offers. In general, regressions conducted on individual-level variables were not significant in any of the games. Two exceptions were education in the Public Goods Game and location in the Trust Game. The education result (t = 2.03, p = .04) indicates that higher levels of

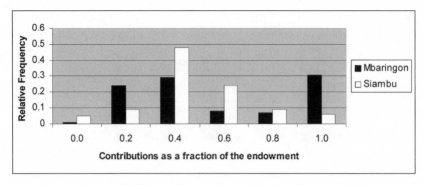

Fig. 13. Distribution of offers in four-person Public Goods Game (Mbaringon, n = 84; Siambu, n = 80; endowment = 50 Kenyan shillings with doubling of contributions by experimenter)

education in Siambu actually work against provision of public goods, like schools. As discussed earlier, the Siambu community has had difficulty cooperating in building the new school. In this connection, Ensminger (2004) points out the cuing effect of the Public Goods Game. The game resembles the Kenyan fund-raising institution of *harambee* that I also discussed in chapter 4, and it is likely that when people play the game, they behave as if they were participating in a *harambee*. Ensminger surmises that Orma offers in the game were higher than in the Trust Game due to this association with *harambee*, where there are sanctions against free riding. Interestingly, the mean offer in Mbaringon (57 percent) is exactly the same as the Orma mean for this game.

The fact that Siambu offers were lower may be a reflection of the weakness of *harambee* in Siambu. Sanctions failed to rein in the corruption that marred the earlier school-building attempt, which has led to disillusionment among many with the whole process. Further, I would argue that individuals with more formal education tend to be more skeptical of such community projects for a couple of reasons. First, they may be savvier about the prospects for misuse of funds than people with less education. Second, they are less likely to obey the pressure applied by chiefs to contribute to *harambees*. While some *harambees* are well-intentioned and successful, money is also raised for dubious purposes or for projects that will not directly benefit the individuals who are asked to contribute. Chiefs are often instructed to raise a certain contribution for any event the district administration needs to host. After a while, people become tired of the incessant rounds of fund-raising. Individuals with more education may be more aware of their right to refuse voluntary contributions, while people lacking formal education tend to have less understanding of their rights and may view the demands of the chief for contributions as legal requirements. As shown in chapter 4, levels of education are higher in Siambu than in Mbaringon. These differences appear to affect the level of offers in the Public Goods Game.

Another element of the Siambu ethnographic context is salient in considering these results. This is the fact that when land was privatized, households were forced to move to their new parcels. While efforts were made to keep families together, there was inevitably some separation. Even if parcels were geographically contiguous, large homesteads were broken up as each household moved onto their parcel. Settlement structures reflect this change: virtually all Siambu homesteads are composed of a single household, not an extended family as is customary. This physical separation of households has had deleterious effects on the kind of day-to-day cooperation normally involved in pastoral livestock production and domestic work. When neighbors are far away, it is less likely that women, in particular, will be able to share daily tasks. Indeed, I did not witness the informal gatherings of women in Siambu that are typical in Mbaringon where women come together frequently to share child care, gather firewood, or fetch water. In addition, it was more difficult to assemble men for meetings in Siambu than in Mbaringon (or many other communities where I had worked previously). While there was often a small group of men in the town center, fewer men turned out for public meetings unless the issue to be discussed was very urgent. Thus, it appears that privatization of land may have had a negative effect on cooperation and public-spiritedness in Siambu, and this is born out in the results of the Public Goods Game.

Elders' Authority and the Dictator Game

When land was privatized in Siambu, elders lost their legal authority over that land. They could no longer make binding decisions about how individuals would use the land as they do on communal or group ranch land by, for example, closing off certain areas for grazing and imposing fines on violators. I have noted that land use remains a hybrid of individual and common use in spite of privatization. However, to the extent that land is used communally, it is based on mutual agreement among the land owners, not on the authority of elders. Legally, any individual owner can assert the right to keep live-stock off his land. A few have done so by fencing their parcels. Furthermore, individual rights to grow crops are recognized and even protected by the elders. Ironically, elders now favor individual rights over communal uses, whereas in the past they favored communal interests over individual ones. Even if elders' authority over land has not been completely lost, it has been seriously compromised and transformed. Does this relative loss of authority extend to other realms of daily life? Is respect for elders' authority less in Siambu than in areas that remain under communal land tenure, like Mbaringon?

To help answer this question, I designed a version of the Dictator Game that attempted to measure adherence to elders' authority. The game is played just the same as the normal Dictator Game. However, before it is played, I convened a meeting of local elders and explained the Dictator Game to them. When I was sure they understood the game, I asked them to agree on what offer they felt was most appropriate (*keishakino*) for Player One to make. In this way, they set a norm for the offer. In both communities, the elders agreed that a 50–50 split was the best offer to make. When giving instructions to the players, I told them that the elders had decided that 50–50 was the best offer to make. However, they remained free to make any offer they chose. To further ensure their anonymity, this game was played double-blind, so that even I (the game administrator) would not know who made which offer. To do this, each player made his or her offer in a separate room from the playing room, placing the offer in an unmarked envelope and depositing the envelope in a box. After all the offers were made, the box was retrieved and the offers were recorded and distributed randomly to the recipients.

The mean offer in Mbaringon was 26.3 percent, slightly higher than in the first Dictator Game (24.6 percent). There were no zero offers in Mbaringon. Indeed, while there is still a mode at 20, the whole distribution is shifted to the right of where it was in the Dictator Game (figs. 9, 14). The opposite effect is visible in Siambu. The mean offer dropped significantly from 30 percent to 20.6 percent, and there is a mode at 10 percent.[8] Whereas about 23 percent of players had given 50 percent in the first Dictator Game, this dropped to only 7 percent in the game with the norm. The difference in means between Mbaringon and Siambu in this version of the Dictator Game was nearly significant: Mann-Whitney gave $z = 1.83$, $p = .06$.

These results suggest that players in Siambu did not adhere to the norm

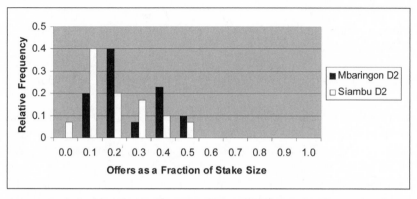

Fig. 14. Distribution of offers in the double-blind Dictator Game with norm set by elders (Mbaringon, n = 30; Siambu, n = 30)

set by the elders. On the contrary, the drop in offers indicates the opposite: players flouted the authority of elders by giving particularly low offers. There is the risk that this drop was an effect of the double-blind treatment in this experiment. However, if that were the case, we would expect a similar drop in Mbaringon, which did not occur.[9] Furthermore, the mean of all offers, combining Siambu and Mbaringon, was 23.5 percent, not significantly different from the combined mean in the first Dictator Game, 27.3 percent (Mann-Whitney, z = 1.75, p = .07). While Siambu players clearly diverged from the norm established by the elders, the rise in offers of 40 and the absence of 0 offers in Mbaringon suggest some effort to respect the norm, although the mean for offers only rose slightly.

These results are supported by some of the observations made previously. The fact that the Siambu community has found it difficult to cooperate on community projects and that it is difficult to call men together for public meetings may also signal a decline in respect for elders' authority. During my fieldwork I also observed two cases of intraclan marriage in Siambu. Marriage within the larger section, Lmasula, is allowed, but marriage within the clan (Lotimi) is unheard of. In these two cases, members of the warrior age-group challenged their elders, arguing that there was no meaningful reason to deny these individuals the right to marry. They made arguments from modern science (i.e., the two were not genetically closely related) in order to support their case. Most elders privately opposed the marriages but could not stop them. There appeared to be a general feeling that there was no way to stop them, even if they were wrong. These examples indicate a reduction of elders' authority in Siambu, a finding that is confirmed by the game results.

What Is Fair?

In all of the games in which Player One decided how to split the endowment given to both Player One and Player Two (Dictator, Punishment, Dictator with Norm), there was a strong peak of offers at 20 in Mbaringon. I wondered what made players so fond of this offer. Was it mere chance, or was something more systematic at work? Several other pieces of information gleaned during the games encouraged me to examine this issue more deeply. First, a few players in the Dictator Game told me that they gave 20 because this was fair. They pointed out that their main priority was themselves and their family responsibilities and that giving away too much was not the right thing to do. Then, when discussing the Dictator Game with the elders in Mbaringon, some of them took the position that 20 was a reasonable offer. Again, they argued that family needs should take precedence over sharing the money with a stranger. However, others pointed out that since the money had been given to both players, it was only fair to split it evenly. Similarly, the player who sanctioned an offer of 50 in the Punishment Game also justified his action on the grounds that family concerns should be paramount over sharing with others outside the immediate family. Thus, the discussion appeared to hinge on the issue of ownership. Who really owned the money in the game?

Further investigation revealed that concepts of fairness depend crucially on the notion of ownership. After the games, I had discussions with a number of people in which I posed several hypothetical situations involving sharing. These examples were common occurrences in daily life. For example, I asked women, if they had a kilogram of sugar at home and someone came by asking for sugar, how much would they give them? Or, if they were butchering a goat to eat and someone came by, how much meat would they give? Say they were hunting (which is unusual but not entirely unheard of these days) and killed a gazelle and were butchering it and someone came by, how much meat would they give them? Or, they were walking with a friend in the forest and came upon a dead gazelle, how would they split the meat?

The answers to these questions were very uniform across informants, regardless of age, gender, and wealth. In cases where the individual clearly owned the resource, the amount he or she would give away was about 20 percent. So, in the sugar example, women said they would give the person a glass of sugar, which is about 200 grams, 20 percent of a kilogram. They might give more or less depending on their relationship to the person, but a glass was the norm. Similarly, when butchering an animal that belonged to them, either because it was in their herd or because they had hunted it, they would give a hind leg to the passerby (there is even a saying to this effect). A hind leg is about a quarter of the beast. However, if ownership was clearly joint, as in the case when two friends discover a dead gazelle in the forest, then a 50–50 split was considered fair. Since neither friend had more right to the dead animal than the other, they would split it equally.

When ownership was clear, norms of fairness were also clear. In all these examples, informants from both Mbaringon and Siambu gave answers almost immediately. Very little thought was required, because the norms were known. Only in the case of sugar did women hedge slightly, explaining that they might give a little more to close friends or relatives. Otherwise, there was no doubt or hesitation in their replies.

Considering the offers made in the games in light of these norms, I think that the question of ownership remained ambiguous enough to enable multiple interpretations. Even though the wording of the instructions is clear—the money is given to both players—the fact that Player One gains physical possession of the money and is given the right to decide on the split creates a situation of virtual ownership by Player One. After all, if ownership was really shared, then why would Player Two have no right to participate in the decision on how to divide the money? Thus, a player could reason that he actually owned this money and, in that case, an offer of 20 was perfectly fair. If he gave more weight to the instructions about joint ownership, then the 50–50 split would have been the appropriate offer. Confusion about ownership may also account for the spread of offers in both communities.

Two conclusions follow from this analysis. First, the Dictator Game might be a more accurate measure of fairness if the ownership issue is rendered unambiguous. One way to test this (in Samburu) would be to play the game using one of the hypothetical situations, like finding the dead gazelle in the forest, and see if offers were more consistent. Second, if concepts of fairness vary across cultures and are situationally dependent, even experiments may not be an accurate basis for comparisons. Specifically, Mbaringon people may have appeared to be less fair-minded in these games than players in the United States or elsewhere, but they may have been making

equally fair offers according to their norms of fairness and their understanding of ownership in the game. It is not the case that they lack consensus on
what is fair, as Ensminger proposed, but that there are at least two norms of
fairness that depend on how ownership is construed. While this insight may
enable us to alter the game to make it more accurate in Samburu, this may
come at a cost of less comparability across cultures.

Conclusion

In general, the use of experimental economics is geared toward gaining understanding of universal processes: whether humans behave in narrowly self-
interested ways, how to explain the propensity for cooperation, examining
the role of market institutions on behavior. Here, my emphasis has been
somewhat different. Instead of looking at how the Samburu case contributes
to our knowledge of human behavior in general, I have concentrated on how
games can enhance understanding of a localized process of institutional
change. The intention was to combine the rigor of the experimental method
with ethnographic data to draw conclusions regarding the extent to which
behavior has changed following privatization of land. Essentially, the experiments were another method with which to approach the problem, a method
that could provide more generalizable results than qualitative ethnography
alone.

The games have yielded some insights into behavioral change in Siambu.
Contrary to my original hypotheses that Siambu players would be less fair-
minded and more selfish due to the nature of social relations under privatization, they actually made higher offers than Mbaringon players, significantly higher in the Trust Game. These results suggest that privatization has
not had a negative impact on fair-minded or trusting behavior. These findings are, furthermore, consistent with the results from the cross-cultural
project that found offers positively correlated with degree of market integration. While both Mbaringon and Siambu are integrated in markets, the fact
that land has become a commodity in Siambu adds an important dimension
to their experience of markets and associated institutions. The intensive involvement of the Siambu community in the land adjudication process may
also have been significant in this regard.

In contrast, lower levels of cooperation observed in the Public Goods
Game appear to be linked to land tenure change. Privatization has created
conditions that make cooperation more difficult. Households are dispersed,

making it harder for women, especially, to congregate to share in domestic work. Men are also less available for public meetings, which may be a result of the same dispersal and also the greater demands on their time from increased cultivation activities. Paradoxically, the higher level of education in Siambu has a negative effect on contributions to public goods, since individuals with more education are less likely to participate.

Game results and ethnographic observations suggest that elders' authority in Siambu is on the decline. People did not respect the norm set by elders in the Dictator Game, even though it accords with the commonly shared norms of fairness in the community. Indeed, their low offers can be interpreted as a repudiation of elders' authority. The cases of intraclan marriage are further examples of the disregard for the opinion of the elders. While it would be premature to conclude that elders have lost all authority, the trend toward individual decision making goes beyond the rhetoric of control and autonomy and is exhibited in behavior in the games and in real life.

A possible explanation for this finding is that as individuals become more integrated into institutions of the modern state, they are less beholden to traditional authorities. This was certainly the case among those who originally sought land in Siambu. As shown in previous chapters, these men were willing and able to violate community norms because they were seeking entry into the community of modern Kenyans. Integration into an alternative set of institutions does not mean that norms cease to matter, however. In the Dictator and Trust Games, without the prompting of elders, Siambu players demonstrated concern for fairness and a propensity for trusting behavior. Henrich et al. suggest that "extensive market interactions may accustom individuals to the idea that interactions with strangers may be mutually beneficial" (2004, 46). If so, higher offers in Siambu may reflect the need for individuals to signal their propensity for fairness and trustworthiness in institutions that extend beyond the ethnic group. These behaviors may become habitual so that even in the game situation with minimal risk of detection, players continue to exhibit prosocial characteristics. The greater extent of market integration in Siambu compared to Mbaringon may well explain why Siambu players offer more in Dictator and Trust Games, while Mbaringon players show more preference for traditional norms of fairness (the 20 percent offer) and adhere more closely to elders' authority.

CHAPTER 9

Conclusion

Analysis of changing property rights in Siambu has a number of implications for thinking about institutional change. First, it demonstrates that bargaining power is central to the change process and that power is gained and lost in a dynamic process over time. Privatization did not happen automatically, nor was it the result of an overall ideological shift in favor of private ownership. Those who came to favor private ownership did so primarily due to their life experiences and interaction with a different set of institutions. However, new preferences alone were insufficient to change the norm. In order to mount their challenge, these individuals needed to increase their bargaining power vis-à-vis the elders. Both sides worked to build up their bargaining power, making the final outcome uncertain until the end. Shifts in bargaining power, not power per se, were critical in defining the course of the conflict.

Second, this study confirms the value of using multiple methods, including those eliciting qualitative and quantitative data. Working on the ground with those actually involved in the change process enriches our understanding of how and why things happened the way they did. I found it especially useful to be able to discuss written documentation about events with the same individuals who took the actions reported in the documents. On the other hand, quantitative data on livestock and agriculture were valuable in trying to assess the complex impacts of privatization for household well-being. These data are often missing in studies of subdivision of group ranches (Rutten 1992; Kimani and Pickard 1998), which draw conclusions based on assumptions or simulation models about production that are not fully substantiated with actual household-level data. Many of these conclusions portend the demise of pastoralism in areas where land is privatized. They may be correct in identifying the constraints that privatization puts on extensive use of the range, but they are unable to discuss what people are actually doing in these situations. This study shows that it is not only people in Siambu who are diversifying out of pure pastoralism into other activities—this is also happening in Mbaringon where land is still owned jointly. Further, the fact that Siambu people are currently better off in terms of livestock than those in Mbaringon indicates that privatization per se does not necessarily lead to greater impoverishment. On the contrary, cultivation appears to provide an important supplement to household income and consumption. However, if fencing increases dramatically in Siambu, this will have negative effects for livestock production, at the minimum forcing people to graze more in illegal places, such as the forest, or in less-desirable areas, such as the escarpment. Privatization has complex effects, and we need to study these with adequate data on a wide range of variables.

Finally, both qualitative and quantitative approaches were used in examining the behavioral consequences of privatization. Experimental games are a promising way to isolate certain types of behavior and generate data that are comparable across field sites—in this case two communities in close proximity. It is also useful to compare these results with those of the cross-cultural project that includes a far more diverse sample. The games confirmed some of my hypotheses about behavior but not others. Even when hypotheses were not confirmed, however, these results stimulated me to take a deeper look at certain phenomena that were interesting in themselves, such as what the norms of fairness are in different contexts. The games provide a means to consider the distribution of particular behaviors and, in that way, triangulate with ethnographic observations. By using the games in combination with ethnographic and demographic data that economists and political scientists rarely have access to, anthropologists can contribute to larger debates in the social sciences regarding the nature and meaning of human behavior.

While this book has primarily relied on close examination of local cases, I have tried to spell out the connections between events in Siambu (and Mbaringon) and macrolevel phenomena. For example, I showed how academic ideas about the nature of common property were rather directly translated into government land policy in the 1970s. I have also considered the impact of experiences with modern institutions, such as formal education, employment, and military service, on the attitudes and values of individuals. The ways in which district-level government officers interpreted and acted on government policy were important in shaping the conflict over land in Siambu.

Certainly, the forces of capitalism and modernity had an important impact on the motivations of actors in Siambu. For those individuals who sought private land ownership, the values of modern Kenyan society played a formative role in defining the reference group from which they sought approval. Access to education and the knowledge and skills obtained through contact with the state apparatus provided them with human and economic capital that they used to challenge common property. The developing market in land that informed Kenyan policy relating to land adjudication in pastoral areas lowered the costs to them of violating the norm. Finally, the changing relative price of land, which came about as a result of an emerging market in land leases, made private ownership even more economically valuable. In contrast, the elders of the blanket had everything to lose and little to gain through privatization. Their wealth, authority, and power derived from and depended upon the status quo institutions that they, accordingly, sought to preserve.

While it is possible to trace the influence of external conditions and forces on the motives and opportunities of the actors, they were not determinative. If they had been, then the Group of Thirty-seven would have prevailed in Siambu as individual land seekers did elsewhere in the district, including in Mbaringon. Particular characteristics of the situation and how the conflict proceeded led to a compromise solution. Each side in Siambu began the conflict with a certain endowment of resources and power. Over the course of the conflict, these endowments shifted. The elders enhanced their power by threatening retaliation and building powerful coalitions. The emergence of a few charismatic leaders was important, because they were able to articulate to the rest of the community how high the stakes were and to mobilize collective action against the privatizers. When leveling tactics failed, these leaders intensified their efforts to build bargaining power by forming alliances. They managed to overcome the tendency to accept state policy, which had hindered opposition to individual land allocations in Mbaringon. While they challenged state policy, they did so through the organs of the state itself, effectively bypassing local state actors and seeking redress at the national level.

By contrast, the Group of Thirty-seven relied on the backing of the state officials at the local level and failed to organize collective action beyond their small group. They were unable to mobilize collective action, since their land claims constituted private gains, not collective goods. If they had realized the extent of opposition they would face, they might have behaved differently.

However, the powerful alliance struck between the elders and the General proved too much for them to overcome. The final compromise solution was an outcome of relatively equal power relations but also the predilections of one individual. And, in a somewhat surprising twist, the elders later appropriated the language of the modernizers to reinforce their own position and to shore up community solidarity. An outcome that equalized access to land became yet another resource to be mobilized to establish a new power asymmetry.

Policy Implications

How can the experience of privatization of land inform policies toward pastoralists? As I have noted throughout the book, there has been a sea change in thinking about the value of pastoralism over the last ten to fifteen years, as numerous studies have demonstrated the rationale and utility of pastoral production systems, successfully challenging earlier assumptions that pastoralism is environmentally destructive and unsustainable. Among scholars of pastoralism, this new thinking has been largely accepted and is the basis for current advocacy efforts to support mobile pastoralism and secure pastoralists' access to resources, particularly land. Ironically, as the scholarly community has become more convinced of the utility of pastoralism, pastoralists themselves continue to change, including, as documented here, diversifying out of pastoralism into wage labor, trade, and, in some cases, cultivation. What then should policymakers and those who work with pastoralists make of these seemingly contradictory trends?

This study has shown that privatization in Siambu was a complex, historically contingent process influenced by many factors, both exogenous and endogenous to the community. Although the Siambu community, on average, is somewhat better off than the Mbaringon community at the time of this survey, this result should not be misinterpreted to mean that privatization of land among pastoralists in general would have positive economic outcomes. Much depends on the process of privatization and how gains are distributed. In fact, the subdivision into more or less equal parcels of land in the Siambu case appears to be unique among cases of privatization of pastoral land and may be an important reason why the outcomes have been generally positive. Furthermore, the fact that Siambu households retain access to land for herding, both within the privatized area and beyond it in Porokwai group ranch and the neighboring forest, has been an important factor in preserving

livestock production. In that sense, the Siambu experience echoes the recommendations of advocates for pastoralism for flexibility and access to key
resources.

Mobile livestock production remains important to most Siambu households and has not been destroyed by privatization. Cultivation of crops has
been facilitated by privatization and has added to the diversification of livelihoods in Siambu. Thus, it is through greater flexibility and diversification, not
less, that Siambu households appear to be succeeding. If parcels were fenced
and access to livestock were denied, and if other land for herding became un-
available, Siambu households would likely suffer negative consequences.
While at the present time these scenarios do not appear likely, it remains to
be seen how land inheritance will impact the integrity of parcels, land use
practices, and access to land by various social groups.

The message for those interested in pastoral areas is that there is a need
to pay attention to the multiple outcomes of privatization. For the reasons
discussed in this book, some individuals will continue to pursue private land
ownership, for reasons that are not primarily based on the ecological or economic viability of private holdings. It is important to understand the specific
effects of these processes and to share this knowledge with communities
where privatization is being proposed. At the same time, we need to acknowledge that pastoral systems, even those that are extensive and have
communal land ownership, are changing. In Kenya, most pastoralists cannot
and do not survive only off their herds. They are seeking alternatives, and
more needs to be done to make these alternatives viable.

The focus of this research has been on microlevel power differentials
within communities, a better understanding of which I believe could improve the practice of development work with pastoralists. The current development mantra is "participation," and there are a host of methods available
for trying to stimulate participation by community members. Yet, achieving
genuine participation remains a challenge. One of the reasons for this is the
tendency to view communities as undifferentiated wholes and, as a consequence, to underestimate the extent to which attitudes, values, and interests
vary among community members. Pastoralist communities are perhaps even
more susceptible to this type of interpretation because they are known as being egalitarian and making decisions through consensus (as discussed earlier
in chapter 5). Thus, participation usually ends up being consultation with elder men who are then given responsibility to "mobilize" the rest of the community. At the same time, many elders understand the power of develop-

ment agents and do their best to please them in order not to jeopardize the anticipated flow of benefits. Among Samburu, for example, they will allow women to come to meetings and even let them speak, in order not to alienate the agency. But, when the agency is not there, things go on as usual. Missing the complexity and differentiation of interests and concerns among community members may mean that development activities only serve the interests of a small group within the community or may overlook important problems that are never voiced since processes are controlled by a particular segment of the population.

These challenges are beyond the scope of this book, but perhaps the Siambu experience can provide some clues for addressing this problem. If development workers desire more genuine participation from a broader cross section of the community, then they need to have a deeper understanding of internal power dynamics in the communities they work with. This implies that they need to spend more time talking to people, and they need to build rapport, not only with elders but with all social groups. They need to get an idea of what the crucial issues are in the community they are working with and whose interests are at stake. They also need to take their own positions of power more seriously and realize how easy it is for them to dictate the course of events without meaning to.

The experience of land adjudication in Samburu also illustrates the signal importance of information. Lack of information about and understanding of the process seriously constrained the ability of communities to object to privatization. Conversely, spreading information about the events in Siambu was an effective way to build opposition. Similarly, communities require more and better information about development projects. As with land adjudication, most community members do not understand the overall objectives of projects, how their community fits into the larger scheme of project or program plans, or how decisions are made in projects. This puts them in a very weak position to take advantage of potential benefits of a project. The fact that many projects fail to share this kind of information enables a few people to remain in full control of the project and tends to negate the possibilities for true participation by community members. Some individuals may consciously limit information flow, but I think that many are genuinely unaware of the problem.

Improving the lives of pastoralists is the stated goal of development policies and projects working in pastoral areas, as well as a concern of many students and scholars of pastoralism. During every drought we are reminded by the media that pastoralism is on the brink of collapse, yet pastoralists continue to survive and demonstrate great resilience in the face of many challenges. Their livelihood systems and cultures are, as I have illustrated in this study, complex and dynamic. Examining the course of institutional change that underpins this dynamism can enhance our ability to understand how groups and individuals respond to a shifting matrix of possibilities, how their actions shape the trajectory of change, and the consequences of change for well being and social relations.

Notes

CHAPTER 1

1. Chong (2000) has developed a formal theory that examines the interactions of individuals' dispositions (norms, values, beliefs, etc.) with instrumental interests that emerge at particular decision points. My approach is similar to Chong's in attempting to understand the emergence of dispositions as well as strategic action that occurs when individuals are confronted by specific choices.

CHAPTER 2

1. The term *iloikop* has also been used by Maasai to refer to groups of Maasai speakers who practice agriculture. As Galaty (1993) points out, the Samburu do not practice agriculture and so this label appears inaccurate in their case. It also seems logical that *lokop* may refer to people "of the land" since the term for "land" is *nkop* and "being of" could be rendered *loo*.

CHAPTER 3

1. I have changed the names of individuals in order to protect their privacy.

2. See Bates (1989) for an explanation of the agrarian roots of the independence struggle. Kitching (1980), Cowen (1980, 1981), Swainson (1980), and Leys (1974, 1978) all examine the early development of accumulation strategies among African Kenyans and how these influenced the independence struggle and the postindependence institutional arrangements that favored private property and capital accumulation.

3. See discussion of common pool resources (CPRs) in chapter 1. Pastoralist communities provide examples of how management rules evolve over time, enabling effective use of their common resources. Pastoralists often limit access to key resource areas such as dry season pasture and permanent water sources. Individual herding strategies also act to spread the risks of production over the landscape to minimize losses from localized drought and disease outbreaks. Colonial-era grazing schemes and subsequent group ranch development have interfered with and in some cases altered these strategies often to the detriment of the environment. On CPRs see Ens-

minger and Rutten (1991), Behnke, Scoones, and Kerven (1993), Bromley and Feeny (1992), McCabe (1990), Ostrom (1990), Ostrom, Walker, and Gardner (1993), and Scoones (1994).

4. Hodgson (2001, 204) notes the same influence of "tragedy of the commons" thinking on policies toward the Maasai in Tanzania.

5. Rutten (1992) and Hedlund (1979) detail early experiments with privatization among Kaputiei Maasai in the early 1960s, predating the formulation of the group ranch concept. Fears of increasing encroachment on their land by agricultural Kikuyu convinced most Kaputiei Maasai to accept group ranches as a defensive mechanism against privatization and the attendant loss of land to outsiders.

6. The District Land Arbitration Board consisted of twenty-five members selected by the administration from community members (again, almost exclusively elder males) who were assigned the task of deliberating on land cases.

7. This calculation does not include hectares of Ngutuk Ongiron or Girgir group ranches, which were not available in the records. There is a big range in sizes and memberships of group ranches, but this average figure gives some indication of the inequities that resulted from large individual ranches being allocated alongside group ranches. The acreages that would be received by group ranch members upon subdivision would be far smaller than those of the individual ranches.

CHAPTER 4

1. Hodgson (2001) discusses how educated Tanzania Maasai continue to dominate contemporary development activities, now by acting as self-proclaimed representatives of their people and appealing for support through the rubric of "indigenous peoples."

2. Nadasdy (2002) analyzes similar difficulties posed by conflicting concepts of property as they impinge on agreements about land ownership between the Canadian government and indigenous people of First Nations.

3. See Escobar (1995) and Rist (1997) for extended discussions of the rise of discourses of development and their impact on developing countries.

4. Ensminger (1997), for example, discusses the persistence of customary systems of land tenure in spite of the presence of land titling systems. See also Shipton (1988), Berry (1988), and Fleuret (1988).

5. Hodgson (2001) discusses this same tendency among Maasai elders who employed colonial authority to strengthen their own positions vis-à-vis the warriors.

6. Samburu faithfulness to government is a characteristic noted by the colonialists and may be a reason they are praised as good soldiers and watchmen. It's only quite recently, in the late 1990s, that an increasing disillusionment with government is expressed in frustration over the inability or unwillingness of the government to stop Turkana cattle raiding. There is also irritation over suspected rigging of elections, which led a section of voters to go over to the opposition in the 1997 election, even though they had little understanding of what the opposition was. It was a protest against the excesses of the dominant political party, KANU.

7. The legality of the nullification of the adjudication process is questionable. Indeed, one of the individual land owners continues to fight in the courts for the right

to his original allocation. Nowhere in the documents I reviewed in Maralal or Nairobi could I find a particular section of the land law cited as basis for nullifying an adjudication process. Furthermore, according to a lawyer familiar with such cases, once individual claims have been registered, as they were in Siambu, they cannot be revoked after the sixty-day period for appeals to the minister has expired (Isaac Lenaula, personal communication, November 11, 2001). Clearly, the pressure brought to bear on government officials led to the nullification, regardless of presence or absence of the appropriate legal provision. If the High Court finds in favor of the individual, this may have dire implications for Siambu since all the title deeds may be brought into dispute. Certainly, such an outcome will reopen many old wounds and threaten the harmony that equal subdivision restored.

8. Bruce and Migot-Adholla (1994) and Juma and Ojwang (1996) discuss the implications of privatization of land.

CHAPTER 5

1. There are a number of theories of institutional change in the literature of New Institutional Economics, law, and economics. Many of these theories have an evolutionary component, arguing that institutions develop and change toward increasing efficiency, coordination around focal points, or as an outcome of market competition (see Knight 1992 for a fuller discussion of these types and Ellickson 2001; Kanazawa and Still 2001; Voss 2001; and Eggertsson 2001 for specific examples).

2. For the Samburu, see Spencer (1965) and Holtzman (1996). For the Maasai, see Rigby (1992).

3. In a different context, Chong (2000) discusses how some Southerners in the United States were able to evade new norms against racial discrimination by leaving the institutions in which the new norms were enforced.

4. While many owners have picked up their title deeds from the Land Registry in Nyahururu, many others have yet to do so. This may be due to the relatively high costs incurred in traveling to Nyahururu, over 100 miles away from Siambu, and the fee required to obtain the deed itself. Other reasons for not collecting the title deed may stem from feelings that land rights are secure even without the physical deed in hand. This is likely true, since it is the registration of the land and not the piece of paper the deed is printed on that constitutes ownership in a legal sense (Isaac Lenaola, personal communication). On the other hand, some individuals may not have collected the deed due to lack of understanding of the importance of the document— those who continue to use the land more or less communally may not feel a need to defend their ownership of a particular parcel.

CHAPTER 6

1. Straight (1997) notes the importance of Western dress in Samburu conceptions of development and its association with Christian mission influence. Comaroff and Comaroff (1997, 218–322) discuss the introduction of Western clothing and architecture as key aspects of mission activity and analyze how their adoption by Africans was in no way automatic or straightforward but rather part of processes of cultural construction.

CHAPTER 7

1. Demsetz (1967), Barzel (1989), Cheung (1970), and Libecap (1989) provide theories of property rights primarily from an economic perspective. See Ensminger for discussions of changing property rights in Kenya in general (1997) and among another Kenyan pastoralist society, the Orma (Ensminger 1992; Ensminger and Rutten 1991); and Acheson (2000) for analysis of a contrasting case of overexploitation of privately owned land in the United States.

2. A volume edited by Bruce and Migot-Adholla (1994) reports findings of eight studies in Africa that provide empirical evidence both confirming and disputing the assumption that land registration and titling leads to increases in agricultural productivity. For Kenya, factors other than titling prove important in explaining agricultural performance.

3. Rutten (1992) and Peters (1994) discuss processes of privatization of pastoral land among the Maasai of Kenya and the Tswana of Botswana respectively. However, these studies lack detailed quantification of economic performance before or after privatization. The studies reported in Bruce and Migot-Adholla (1994) are all in crop-producing areas.

4. For the purposes of the survey, a household was defined as the head of household (usually male, but occasionally a widow or single mother) and all the dependents of that individual. Dependents included the wife or wives (for polygynous households), their children (only children who were dependent were included; married daughters relying on their husbands or sons who were supporting themselves were not included, even if they were coresident), and other dependents (such as grandchildren or other relatives who were dependent on the household head). Hired laborers were not included, but children who were living with the family for extended periods, usually to provide herding labor, were included because many of these children remain in the household for their entire youth and may inherit part of the family livestock.

5. The lists used were the group ranch registers for Mbaringon and Siambu (Porokwai). The lists were reviewed to remove dependents (males under eighteen or still dependent on their parents) who were registered members. Since all land owners in Siambu were automatically members of Porokwai, the group ranch register was used there as well. The group ranch register was much easier to access than individual title deeds (a significant fee is required to view the register of title deeds, and one would need to know which title deeds in advance, whereas the register has all the names of individuals who received land during the subdivision).

6. Wealth was measured in livestock holdings. Although investments in other forms of property, such as shops and rental buildings, are increasing, they are still relatively rare compared to the almost universal ownership of livestock. In order to correct for the differences in size and value between different classes of livestock (cows, sheep and goats, camels), a standard measure was used, the tropical livestock unit (TLU). For the 1978 holdings, I used the pre-drought exchange rates to calculate TLU: 1 TLU = 1 cow, 8 sheep or goats, and 0.40 camel. However, the 2000 holdings were calculated using the actual prevailing rate: 1 TLU = 1 cow, 13 sheep or goats,

0.40 camel. To calculate per capita holdings, I used the average household size from the 2000 survey for both 2000 holdings and 1978 holdings.

7. Advantages of small stock over cattle are several. The higher reproduction rate of small stock means flock sizes increase rapidly, enabling a swifter recovery from drought or other disaster. They may also survive drought better than cattle, as was the case in the 1999–2000 drought. Small stock are easier to sell and can be readily sold for immediate cash needs. They are also well suited to the types of pasture now available around Mbaringon and in Laikipia District where many Samburu have moved over the last decade.

8. Survey households were divided into five groups, or quintiles, according to wealth (measured in TLU). First, household TLU was converted to per capita TLU by dividing total household TLU by household AAME (active adult male equivalents). Then, households were ranked according to per capita TLU. Five quintiles were formed by dividing the total population by five and then successively counting off households until that number was reached. As a result, each quintile comprises approximately the same number of individuals but not the same number of households.

9. This school was finally completed in 2005 with funds donated by the Catholic mission that built the school. It appears that minimal community contribution was required.

10. Income includes sales of own livestock, wage labor, trade, sales of crops, and gifts.

11. The exchange rate at the time of the survey was USD 1 = KSh 80.

12. Households were asked to report on the last harvest they had. Most households reported on the 1998 harvest, but some went back to 1997, and a few had good harvests in 1999 and 2000. In all cases, however, these represent reasonably good yields for those farmers, and therefore all were reduced by 25 percent to take into account years of crop failures.

13. Herd structures are predominantly female. For Siambu, out of average cattle holdings of 16 head, 11 are female (68 percent). Mbaringon households have on average 15 cattle, 10 of which are female (66 percent). Very few mature males are kept. On average, Siambu households have no steers and 1 bull, while there is an average of 1 steer and no bulls in Mbaringon. That means that the male stock are immatures being kept until they are old enough to sell or to be used as breeding bulls. The maximum number of bulls in Mbaringon households was 5, compared to 3 in Siambu. The maximum number of steers was 10 in each community. Mbaringon households have more small stock than Siambu households do, with an average of 55 sheep and 23 goats, compared to 24 sheep and 12 goats in Siambu. Again, small stock flocks are predominantly female (for sheep: Mbaringon, 83 percent; Siambu, 70 percent; for goats: Mbaringon, 82 percent; Siambu, 75 percent). It appears that virtually all excess males are sold.

14. The Land Control Board has jurisdiction over all land transactions. When land is used as collateral for a loan, the bank (or other financial institution) puts a charge on the land, and this is recorded with the LCB. Out of a total of 44 charges in the LCB minutes from 1991 through 2001, only 5 were from Siambu.

15. The actual number of households reporting wage labor is lower than the total percentage of households reporting employment in table 10 because some households have more than one source of wage labor income.

16. In the survey, civil service employment included police and military service.

17. While their ethnic identity is distinct from Samburu, they are very integrated in the Samburu community in Mbaringon. There is intermarriage between the two groups, and they are physically and linguistically indistinguishable. See Spear and Waller (1993) for discussion of ethnic boundaries and attitudes among Maa-speaking groups.

18. If we value household labor at the market rate of KSh 100 per day, then it would only take sixty days of labor to offset the average value of home consumption. It seems likely that people spend at least this amount of time working on their farms in a year.

19. Large wildlife are rare in this area, probably due to the efforts of farmers to discourage them from consuming crops. The wheat farmer employs watchmen to guard fields from both human and wildlife predators. A device called a thunder-flash, something like a flare that also makes a booming noise, is used to scare off elephants.

20. People in Siambu were very upset when the seeds provided as a subsidy by an NGO in 1999 and 2000 were meant for drier areas and, being unsuitable for their area, resulted in low yields.

21. Indeed, the wheat farmer did leave Siambu in 2005, though I was not able to interview him regarding his reasons. Since then, several individuals, including members of the Siambu community, have continued to lease land to grow wheat albeit on a somewhat smaller scale.

22. Bruce and Migot-Adholla (1994, 124) express reservations about the practice of including family members in the LCBs, noting that this will deter a free market in land and reduce efficiency of land allocations.

23. Due to the small sample size (13) regression analysis was not performed on the correlation of wealth and income on land sales.

24. Bruce and Migot-Adholla (1994, 17) point out that given lack of other opportunities for employment or old age insurance, land rentals are viewed more positively than sales by small holders.

25. Most households reported harvests for 1999, very few for 1998, only one for 2000. Some households went back to 1994 or 1995 to find a harvest.

26. The author has personally been involved in trying to farm in Mbaringon over the last decade and has experienced only two or three decent harvests over that period. Many years have been complete failures, even for beans.

27. Bruce and Migot-Adholla (1994) argue that land registration and titling in agricultural areas do not improve security or output. However, this is due to the fact that customary land tenure systems in farming areas do provide enough security. I would argue that in pastoral areas where customary systems do not provide security for crop production (to the contrary, they often punish this activity), land titling has improved security, and this partly explains why more people are farming in Siambu than before.

28. Holtzman (1996, 258) also notes the frequency of employment of men from

this area as watchmen and discusses the importance of networks of friends and acquaintances in securing jobs as watchmen.

29. See Holtzman (2001) for a discussion of the gendered household economics of brewing.

CHAPTER 8

1. In his recent work on Bali, Barth advocates such an approach to understanding behavior (1993).

2. The total number of participants in games was 350 per community. With 100 survey households, this meant we required 3.5 adult players per household.

3. An exception to this was with the Public Goods Game where directions were read to each group after they came into the playing room.

4. In the first games, I stratified the players by wealth. However, I found that random selection also resulted in a mix of wealth (and other variables) among the players and decided it was unnecessary to continue to deliberately stratify the sample.

5. I used the nonparametric Mann-Whitney test to compare the mean offers in Siambu and Mbaringon. I chose a nonparametric test because of the nonnormal distribution of offers in the games. The results of the Mann-Whitney test for the Dictator Game were $z = 1.64$, $p = .10$.

6. Researchers in the cross-cultural project mentioned earlier are currently studying cueing effects by purposely designing game situations that simulate real-world situations and comparing the results with noncontextualized game situations.

7. I played this game according to protocols mentioned in Ensminger (2000). Another version of the game (Berg, Dickhaut, and McCabe 1995) gives Player Two an equal endowment to Player One.

8. The drop in offers from Dictator to Dictator with norm was significant in Siambu: the Mann-Whitney test yielded $z = 2.49$, $p = .01$.

9. The double-blind treatment aims at controlling for experimenter effects. Thus, the fact that offers dropped significantly in Siambu could be due to experimenter effects there, aside from any effect of the elders' setting a norm for the game. Since I am somewhat less well known in Siambu than in Mbaringon (where I have lived for over ten years), it is possible people made higher offers in the first Dictator Game out of concern for what I would think of them. On the other hand, the fact that I am very well known in Mbaringon could also be a reason for people worrying about how I perceived their offers. It is difficult to speculate on the direction of experimenter effects. My general feeling was that people were not overly concerned about my knowing their offers.

Bibliography

Acheson, J. 1994. Welcome to Nobel Country: A Review of Institutional Economics. In *Anthropology and Institutional Economics,* ed J. Acheson, 3–42. Lanham, MD: University Press of America.

Acheson, J. 2000. Clearcutting Maine: Implications for the Theory of Common Property Resources. *Human Ecology* 28 (2): 145–69.

Agrawal, A. 2003. Sustainable Governance of Common Pool Resources: Contexts, Methods, and Politics. *Annual Review of Anthropology* 32:243–62.

Anderson, B. 1983. *Imagined Communities.* London: Verso.

Anderson, D., and V. Broch-Due. 1999. *The Poor Are Not Us: Poverty and Pastoralism in Eastern Africa.* Oxford: James Currey.

Bailey, F. G. 1969. *Stratagems and Spoils: A Social Anthropology of Politics.* New York: Basil Blackwell.

Barth, F. 1981. *Process and Form in Social Life: Selected Essays of Fredrik Barth.* Vol. 1. London: Routledge and Kegan Paul.

Barth, F. 1993. *Balinese Worlds.* Chicago: University of Chicago Press.

Barzel, Y. 1989. *The Economic Analysis of Property Rights.* Cambridge: Cambridge University Press.

Bates, R. 1981. *Markets and States in Tropical Africa: The Political Basis of Agricultural Policies.* Berkeley: University of California Press.

Bates, R. 1989. *Beyond the Miracle of the Market: The Political Economy of Agrarian Development in Kenya.* Cambridge: Cambridge University Press.

Behnke, R., I. Scoones, and C. Kerven, eds. 1993. *Range Ecology at Disequilibrium: New Models of Natural Variability and Pastoral Adaptation in African Savannas.* London: Overseas Development Institute.

Berg, J., J. Dickhaut, and K. McCabe. 1995. Trust, Reciprocity, and Social History. *Games and Economic Behavior* 10:122–42.

Berry, S. 1988. Concentration without Privatization? Some Consequences of Changing Patterns of Rural Land Control in Africa. In *Land and Society in Contemporary Africa,* ed. R. E. Downs and S. P. Reyna. Hanover: University Press of New England.

Boone, R. B., S. B. BurnSilver, P. K. Thornton, J. S. Worden, and K. A. Galvin. 2005. Quantifying Declines in Livestock Due to Land Subdivision. *Rangeland Ecology and Management* 58 (5): 523–32.

Boone, R. B., M. B. Coughenour, K. A. Galvin, and J. E. Ellis. 2002. Addressing Management Questions for Ngorongoro Conservation Area using the Savanna Modeling System. *African Journal of Ecology* 40:138–50.

Bourdieu, P. 1990. *The Logic of Practice.* Stanford: Stanford University Press.

Brockington, D. 2001. Women's Income and the Livelihood Strategies of Dispossessed Pastoralists near the Mkomazi Game Reserve, Tanzania. *Human Ecology* 29 (3): 307–38.

Bromley, D., and D. Feeny, eds. 1992. *Making the Commons Work: Theory, Practice, and Policy.* San Francisco: ICS Press.

Bruce, John W., and S. Migot-Adholla, eds. 1994. *Searching for Land Tenure Security in Africa.* World Bank: Kendall/Hunt.

Camerer, C. 2003. *Behavioral Game Theory: Experiments in Strategic Interaction.* Princeton: Princeton University Press.

Camerer, C., and E. Fehr. 2004. Measuring Social Norms and Preferences using Experimental Games: A Guide for Social Scientists. In *Foundations of Human Sociality: Economic Experiments and Ethnographic Evidence from Fifteen Small-Scale Societies,* ed. J. Henrich, R. Boyd, S. Bowles, C. Camerer, E. Fehr, and H. Gintis. Oxford: Oxford University Press.

Cheung, S. N. S. 1970. The Structure of a Contract and the Theory of a Non-Exclusive Resource. *Journal of Law and Economics* 13 (1): 45–70.

Chong, D. 1991. *Collective Action and the Civil Rights Movement.* Chicago: University of Chicago Press.

Chong, D. 2000. *Rational Lives: Norms and Values in Politics and Society.* Chicago: University of Chicago Press.

Coleman, J. S. 1990. *Foundations of Social Theory.* Cambridge: Harvard University Press.

Comaroff, John L., and Jean Comaroff. 1997. *Of Revelation and Revolution: The Dialectics of Modernity on a Southern African Frontier.* Vol. 2. Chicago: University of Chicago Press.

Cowen, M. 1980. The Agrarian Problem: Notes on the Nairobi Discussion. *Review of African Political Economy* 20:57–73.

Cowen, M. 1981. Commodity Production in Kenya's Central Province. In *Rural Development in Tropical Africa,* ed. J. Heyer, 121–42. New York: St. Martin's Press.

Dahl, G., and A. Hjort. 1976. *Having Herds: Pastoral Herd Growth and Household Economy.* Stockholm: University of Stockholm Press.

Delville, Philippe L. 2000. Harmonizing Formal Law and Customary Land Rights in French-Speaking West Africa. In *Evolving Land Rights, Policy, and Tenure in Africa,* ed. C. Toulmin and J. Quan. London: DFID/IIED/NRI.

Demsetz, H. 1967. Toward a Theory of Property Rights. *American Economic Review* 57 (2): 347–59.

Edgerton, R. B. 1992. *Sick Societies: Challenging the Myth of Primitive Harmony.* New York: Free Press.

Eggertsson, T. 1997. Introduction. In *Empirical Studies in Institutional Change,* ed. L. Alston, T. Eggertsson, and D. North. Cambridge: Cambridge University Press.

Eggertsson, T. 2001. Norms in Economics, With Special Reference to Economic Development. In *Social Norms,* ed. M. Hechter and K. Opp. New York: Russell Sage.

Ellickson, R. C. 2001. The Market for Social Norms. *American Law and Economics Review* 3 (1): 1–49.

Ensminger, J. 1992. *Making a Market: The Institutional Transformation of an African Society.* Cambridge: Cambridge University Press.

Ensminger, J. 1997. Changing Property Rights: Reconciling Formal and Informal Rights to Land in Africa. In *The Frontiers of the New Institutional Economics,* ed. J. Drobak and J. Nye. New York: Academic Press.

Ensminger, J. 2000. Experimental Economics in the Bush: Why Institutions Matter. In *Institutions, Contracts, and Organizations,* ed. C. Menard. Northampton, MA: Edward Elgar.

Ensminger, J. 2004. Market Integration and Fairness: Evidence from Ultimatum, Dictator, and Public Goods Experiments in East Africa. In *Foundations of Human Sociality: Economic Experiments and Ethnographic Evidence from Fifteen Small-Scale Societies,* ed. J. Henrich, R. Boyd, S. Bowles, C. Camerer, E. Fehr, and H. Gintis. Oxford: Oxford University Press.

Ensminger, J., and J. Knight. 1997. Changing Social Norms: Common Property, Bridewealth, and Clan Exogamy. *Current Anthropology* 38 (1): 1–24.

Ensminger, J., and A. Rutten. 1991. The Political Economy of Changing Property Rights: Dismantling a Pastoral Commons. *American Ethnologist* 18 (1): 683–99.

Escobar, A. 1995. *Encountering Development: The Making and Unmaking of the Third World.* Princeton: Princeton University Press.

Evans-Pritchard, E. E. 1950. *The Nuer: A Description of the Modes of Livelihood and Political Institutions of a Nilotic People.* Oxford: Clarendon Press.

Fehr, E., and U. Fischbacher. 2004. Third Party Punishment and Social Norms. *Evolution and Human Behavior* 25:63–87.

Fehr, E., and S. Gachter. 2000. Fairness and Retaliation: The Economics of Reciprocity. *Journal of Economic Perspectives* 14 (3): 159–81.

Fehr, E., and S. Gachter. 2002. Altruistic Punishment in Humans. *Nature* 415: 137–40.

Fleuret, A. 1988. Some Consequences of Tenure and Agrarian Reform in Taita, Kenya. In *Land and Society in Contemporary Africa,* ed. R. E. Downs and S. P. Reyna. Hanover: University Press of New England.

Fox, R. 1985. *Lions of the Punjab: Culture in the Making.* Berkeley: University of California Press.

Fratkin, E. 1991. *Surviving Drought and Development: Ariaal Pastoralists of Northern Kenya.* Boulder: Westview Press.

Fratkin, E. 1998. *Ariaal Pastoralists of Kenya: Surviving Drought and Development in Africa's Arid Lands.* Boston: Allyn and Bacon.

Fratkin, E. 1999. When Nomads Settle: The Effects of Commoditization, Nutritional

Change, and Formal Education on Ariaal and Rendille Pastoralists. *Current Anthropology* 40 (5): 729–35.

Fratkin, E., K. A. Galvin, and E. Roth, eds. 1994. *African Pastoralist Systems: An Integrated Approach.* Boulder: Lynne Rienner.

Fratkin, E., and E. Roth, eds. 2005. As Pastoralists Settle: Social, Health, and Economic Consequences of Pastoral Sedentarization in Marsabit District, Kenya. New York and London: Kluwer Academic.

Fumagalli, C. 1977. A Diachronic Study of Socio-Cultural Change Processes among the Samburu of Northern Kenya. PhD dissertation, SUNY Buffalo.

Galaty, J. G. 1992. The Land Is Yours: Social and Economic Factors in the Privatization, Sub-Division and Sale of Maasai Ranches. *Nomadic Peoples* 30:26–40.

Galaty, J. G. 1993. The Eye that Wants a Person, Where Can It Not See? Inclusion, Exclusion, and Boundary Shifters in Maasai Identity. In *Being Maasai: Ethnicity and Identity in East Africa,* ed. T. Spear and D. Waller. London: James Currey.

Galaty, J. G. 1994. Ha(l)ving Land in Common: The Subdivision of Maasai Group Ranches in Kenya. *Nomadic Peoples* 34–35:109–22.

Galaty, J. G. 1997. Grounds for Appeal: Maasai Customary Claims and Conflicts. *Anthropologica* 39:113–18.

Galvin, K. A., P. K. Thornton, J. Roque de Pinho, J. Sunderland, and R. B. Boone. 2006. Integrated Modeling and Its Potential for Resolving Conflicts between Conservation and People in the Rangelands of East Africa. *Human Ecology* 34 (2): 155–83.

Grandin, B. E. 1981. *Group Ranches in Kaputiei: The Impact of the Kenya Livestock Development Project, Phase 1.* Programme Document No. 62. ILCA/Kenya.

Hardin, G. 1968. The Tragedy of the Commons. *Science* 162:1243–48.

Hardin, R. 1995. *One for All: The Logic of Group Conflict.* Princeton: Princeton University Press.

Harris, M. 1999. *Theories of Culture in Postmodern Times.* London: Sage.

Hedlund, H. 1979. Contradictions in the Peripheralization of a Pastoral Society: The Maasai. *Review of African Political Economy* 15–16:15–34.

Henrich, J. 2001. Cultural Transmission and the Diffusion of Innovations: Adoption Dynamics Indicate that Biased Cultural Transmission Is the Predominate Force in Behavioral Change. *American Anthropologist* 103 (4): 992–1013.

Henrich, J., R. Boyd, S. Bowles, C. Camerer, E. Fehr, and H. Gintis, eds. 2004. *Foundations of Human Sociality: Economic Experiments and Ethnographic Evidence from Fifteen Small-Scale Societies.* Oxford: Oxford University Press.

Henrich, J., R. Boyd, S. Bowles, H. Gintis, and E. Fehr. 2001. In Search of Homo Economicus: Behavioral Experiments in Fifteen Small-Scale Societies. *AEA Papers and Proceedings* 91 (2): 73–78.

Henrich, J., and R. McElreath. 2002. Are Peasants Risk-Averse Decision Makers? *Current Anthropology* 43 (1): 172–81.

Henrich, J., R. McElreath, A. Barr, J. Ensminger, C. Barrett, A. Bolyanatz, J. C. Cardenas, M. Gurven, E. Gwako, N. Henrich, C. Lesorogol, F. Marlowe, D. Tracer, and J. Ziker. 2006. Costly Punishment across Human Societies. *Science* 312:1767–70.

Hodgson, D. L. 2001. *Once Intrepid Warriors: Gender, Ethnicity, and the Cultural Politics of Maasai Development.* Bloomington: Indiana University Press.

Holtzman, J. 1996. The Transformation of Samburu Domestic Economy. PhD dissertation, University of Michigan.

Holtzman, J. 2001. The Food of Elders, the "Ration" of Women: Brewing, Gender, and Domestic Processes among the Samburu of Northern Kenya. *American Anthropologist* 103 (4): 1041–58.

ILCA (International Livestock Center for Africa). 1981. Introduction to the East African Range Livestock Systems Study, Kenya. Nairobi: ILCA Working Document no. 23.

Jacobs-Huey, L. 2002. The Natives Are Gazing and Talking Back: Reviewing the Problematics of Positionality, Voice, and Accountability among "Native" Anthropologists. *American Anthropologist* 104 (3): 791–804.

Juma, C., and J. B. Ojwang. 1996. *In Land We Trust.* Nairobi: ACTS Press.

Kanazawa, S., and M. Still. 2001. The Emergence of Marriage Norms: An Evolutionary Psychological Perspective. In *Social Norms,* ed. M. Hechter and K. Opp. New York: Russell Sage.

Kennedy, E., and P. Peters. 1992. Household Food Security and Child Nutrition: The Interaction of Income and Gender of Household Head. *World Development* 20 (8): 1077–85.

Kenya Colony. 1943, 1945. Annual Reports Samburu/Laikipia District. Nairobi: Kenya National Archives.

Kimani, K., and J. Pickard. 1998. Recent Trends and Implications of Group Ranch Sub-division and Fragmentation in Kajiado District, Kenya. *Geographical Journal* 164 (2): 202–13.

Kitching, G. 1980. *Class and Economic Change in Kenya.* New Haven: Yale University Press.

Knight, J. 1992. *Institutions and Social Conflict.* Cambridge: Cambridge University Press.

Lamphear, J. 1991. *The Scattering Time: Turkana Responses to the Imposition of Colonial Rule.* Oxford: Oxford University Press.

Lanyasunya, A. R. 1990. The Impact of Land Adjudication on the Nomadic Pastoral Communities of Northern Kenya with Close Reference to the Samburu. B.A. thesis, University of Nairobi.

Larick, R. 1986. Iron Smelting and Interethnic Conflict among Precolonial Maa-Speaking Pastoralists of North-Central Kenya. *African Archaeological Review* 4:165–76.

Lawrance, J. C. D., G. J. Humphries, S. R. Simpson, G. M. Gaitta, C. P. R. Nottidge, and J. D. MacArthur. 1966. *Report of the Mission on Land Consolidation and Registration in Kenya, 1965–1966.* London: Republic of Kenya.

Ledyard, J. O. 1995. Public Goods: A Survey of Experimental Research. In *The Handbook of Experimental Economics,* ed. A. E. Roth. Princeton: Princeton University Press.

Lesorogol, C. 1998. *Life on the Margins: Perspectives on Pastoralism and Development in Kenya.* Nairobi: United States Agency for International Development.

Lesorogol, C. 2000. Community Participation in Rehabilitation of Degraded Rangelands: A Case Study from Samburu District. In *Rangeland Resources in East
Africa: Their Ecology and Development*, ed. D. Herlocker. Eschborn: GTZ.

Lessig, L. 1996. Social Meaning and Social Norms. *University of Pennsylvania Law
Review* 144:2181–89.

Leys, C. 1974. *Underdevelopment in Kenya: The Political Economy of Neo-Colonial-
ism, 1964–1971.* Berkeley: University of California Press.

Leys, C. 1978. Capital Accumulation, Class Formation, and Dependency: The Significance of the Kenyan Case. *Socialist Register* 15: 241–66.

Libecap, G. 1989. *Contracting for Property Rights.* Cambridge: Cambridge University Press.

Little, P. D. 1985. Absentee Herd Owners and Part-time Pastoralists: The Political
Economy of Resource Use in Northern Kenya. *Human Ecology* 13 (2): 131–51.

Little, P. D. 1992. *The Elusive Granary: Herder, Farmer, and State in Northern
Kenya.* Cambridge: Cambridge University Press.

Little, P. D., K. Smith, B. Cellarius, D. L. Coppock, and C. Barrett. 2001. Avoiding
Disaster: Diversification and Risk Management among East African Herders.
Development and Change 32:401–33.

Malinowski, B. 1922. *Argonauts of the Western Pacific: An Account of Native Enter-
prise and Adventure in the Archipelago of Melanesian New Guinea.* New York:
E. P. Dutton.

Marcus, G. E. 1998. *Ethnography through Thick and Thin.* Princeton: Princeton
University Press.

McAdams, R. 1997. The Origin, Development, and Regulation of Norms. *Michigan
Law Review* 96 (2): 338–433.

McCabe, T. 1990. Turkana Pastoralism: A Case Against the Tragedy of the Commons. *Human Ecology* 18 (1): 81–103.

McCabe, T. 2003. Sustainability and Livelihood Diversification among the Maasai of
Northern Tanzania. *Human Organization* 62:100–111.

McCay, B., and J. Acheson, eds. 1987. *The Question of the Commons: The Culture
and Ecology of Communal Resources.* Tucson: University of Arizona Press.

McPeak, J. 2006. Confronting the Risk of Asset Loss: What Role Do Livestock Transfers in Northern Kenya Play? *Journal of Development Economics* 81:415–37.

Mwangi, E. 2005. The Transformation of Property Rights in Kenya's Maasailand:
Triggers and Motivations. *CAPRi Working Paper 35.* Washington, DC: International Food Policy Research Institute.

Nadasdy, P. 2002. "Property" and Aboriginal Land Claims in the Canadian Subarctic:
Some Theoretical Considerations. *American Anthropologist* 104 (1): 247–61.

North, D. 1981. *Structure and Change in Economic History.* New York: W. W. Nor-
ton.

North, D. 1990. *Institutions, Institutional Change, and Economic Performance.*
Cambridge: Cambridge University Press.

Norton-Griffiths, M. 2000. Wildlife Losses in Kenya: An Analysis of Conservation
Policy. *Natural Resource Modelling* 13 (1): 1–16.

Okoth-Ogendo, H. W. O. 2000. Legislative Approaches to Customary Tenure and

Tenure Reform in East Africa. In *Evolving Land Rights, Policy, and Tenure in Africa,* ed. C. Toulmin and J. Quan. London: DFID/IIED/NRI.

Olson, M. 1965. *The Logic of Collective Action: Public Goods and the Theory of Groups.* Cambridge: Harvard University Press.

Ortner, S. 1984. Theory in Anthropology since the Sixties. *Comparative Studies in Society and History* 26 (1): 126–66.

Ostrom, E. 1990. *Governing the Commons: The Evolution of Institutions for Collective Action.* Cambridge: Cambridge University Press.

Ostrom, E., J. Walker, and R. Gardner. 1993. Covenants With and Without a Sword: Self-Governance Is Possible. In *The Political Economy of Customs and Culture: Informal Solutions to the Commons Problem,* ed. T. Anderson and R. Simmons. Lanham, MD: Rowman and Littlefield.

Parsons, T. 1999. *The African Rank and File: Social Implications of Colonial Military Service in the King's African Rifles, 1902–1964.* Portsmouth, NH: Heinemann.

Peters, P. 1994. *Dividing the Commons: Politics, Policy, and Culture in Botswana.* Charlottesville: University Press of Virginia.

Posner, E. A. 2000. *Law and Social Norms.* Cambridge: Harvard University Press.

Putnam, R. D. 1993. *Making Democracy Work.* Princeton: Princeton University Press.

Republic of Kenya. 1970. *Laws of Kenya, The Land (Group Representatives) Act, Chap. 287.* Nairobi: Government Printer.

Republic of Kenya. 1996. Ministry of Lands, Samburu District, Report on Group Ranch Membership and Acreages.

Republic of Kenya. 1997. *District Development Plan,* Samburu District.

Republic of Kenya. 2001. Ministry of Agriculture and Rural Development, Samburu District, Report on Farm Census.

Rigby, P. 1992. *Cattle, Capitalism, and Class: Ilparakuyo Maasai Transformations.* Philadelphia: Temple University Press.

Rist, G. 1997. *The History of Development: From Western Origins to Global Faith.* London: Zed Books.

Rosaldo, R. 1989. *Culture and Truth: The Remaking of Social Analysis.* Boston: Beacon.

Roth, E. 2000. On Pastoral Egalitarianism: Consequences of Primogeniture among the Rendille. *Current Anthropology* 41:269–71.

Ruttan, L., and M. Borgerhoff Mulder. 1999. Are East African Pastoralists Truly Conservationists? *Current Anthropology* 40 (5): 621–52.

Rutten, M. M. 1992. *Selling Wealth to Buy Poverty: The Process of the Individualization of Landownership among the Maasai Pastoralists of Kajiado District, Kenya, 1890–1990.* Nijmegen Studies in Development and Cultural Change 10. Saarbrucken: Verlag Breitenback.

Salzmann, P. C. 1999. Is Inequality Universal? *Current Anthropology* 40 (1): 31–61.

Salzmann, P. C. 2001. Toward a Balanced Approach to the Study of Equality. *Current Anthropology* 42 (2): 281–84.

Salzmann, P. C. 2002. On Reflexivity. *American Anthropologist* 104 (3): 805–13.

Sandford, S. 1983. *Management of Pastoral Development in the Third World.* New York: Wiley.

Schneider, H. K. 1979. *Livestock and Equality in East Africa: The Economic Basis for Social Structure.* Bloomington: Indiana University Press.

Scoones, I., ed. 1994. *Living with Uncertainty.* London: Intermediate Technology.

Scott, J. 1976. *The Moral Economy of the Peasant: Rebellion and Subsistence in Southeast Asia.* New Haven: Yale University Press.

Scott, J. 1985. *Weapons of the Weak: Everyday Forms of Peasant Resistance.* New Haven: Yale University Press.

Scott, R. E. 2000. The Limits of Behavioral Theories of Law and Social Norms. *Virginia Law Review* 86:1603–47.

Shipton, P. 1988. The Kenyan Land Tenure Reform: Misunderstandings in the Public Creation of Private Property. In *Land and Society in Contemporary Africa,* ed. R. E. Downs and S. P. Reyna. Hanover: University Press of New England.

Sobania, N. 1991. Feasts, Famines, and Friends: Nineteenth-Century Exchange and Ethnicity in the Eastern Lake Turkana Regional System. In *Herders, Warriors, and Traders,* ed. P. Bonte and J. G. Galaty. Boulder: Westview Press.

Spear, T., and R. Waller, eds. 1993. *Being Maasai: Ethnicity and Identity in East Africa.* London: James Currey.

Spencer, P. 1965. *The Samburu: A Study of Gerontocracy in a Nomadic Tribe.* London: Routledge and Kegan Paul.

Spencer, P. 1973. *Nomads in Alliance.* London: Oxford University Press.

Straight, B. 1997. Altered Landscapes, Shifting Strategies: The Politics of Location in the Constitution of Gender, Belief, and Identity among the Samburu of Northern Kenya. PhD dissertation, University of Michigan, Ann Arbor.

Sunstein, C. R. 1996. Social Norms and Social Roles. *Columbia Law Review* 96:903–55.

Swainson, N. 1980. *The Development of Corporate Capitalism in Kenya, 1918–1977.* Berkeley: University of California Press.

Taylor, M. 1982. *Community, Anarchy, and Liberty.* Cambridge: Cambridge University Press.

Tracer, D. 2003. Selfishness and Fairness in Economic and Evolutionary Perspective: An Experimental Economic Study in Papua New Guinea. *Current Anthropology* 44 (3): 432–38.

Tversky, A., and D. Kahneman. 1987. Rational Choice and the Framing of Decisions. In *Rational Choice: The Contrast between Economics and Psychology,* ed. R. M. Hogarth and Melvin W. Reder, 67–94. Chicago: University of Chicago Press.

Ullmann-Margalit, E. 1977. *The Emergence of Norms.* Oxford: Clarendon Press.

USAID. 2002. *A Better Way of Working: Creating Synergies in the Pastoral Zones of the GHA.* Summary Report and Recommendations, Regional USAID Pastoral Coordination Workshop, Nairobi, Kenya.

Voss, T. 2001. Game-Theoretical Perspectives on the Emergence of Social Norms. In *Social Norms,* ed. M. Hechter and K. Opp. New York: Russell Sage.

Waller, R. 1999. Pastoral Poverty in Historical Perspective. In *The Poor Are Not Us:*

Poverty and Pastoralism in Eastern Africa, ed. D. Anderson and V. Broch-Due. Oxford: James Currey.

Western, D., S. Russell, and K. Mutu. 2006. The Status of Wildlife in Kenya's Protected and Non-protected Areas. Paper commissioned by Kenya's Wildlife Policy Review Team presented at the first Stakeholders symposium of the Wildlife Policy and Legislation Review.

Wrong, D. 1994. *The Problem of Order: What Unites and Divides Society.* Cambridge: Harvard University Press.

Young, M. D., and O. T. Solbrig, eds. 1993. *The World's Savannas: Economic Driving Forces, Ecological Constraints, and Policy Options for Sustainable Land Use.* Man and the Biosphere Series, vol. 12. Paris: UNESCO.

Index